3-19-96

D1173813

# Intelligent Behavior in Animals and Robots

**Complex Adaptive Systems**

John H. Holland, Christopher Langton, and Stewart W. Wilson, advisors

*Adaptation in Natural and Artificial Systems: An Introductory Analysis with Applications to Biology, Control, and Artificial Intelligence*
John H. Holland

*Toward a Practice of Autonomous Systems: Proceedings of the First European Conference on Artificial Life*
edited by Francisco J. Varela and Paul Bourgine

*Genetic Programming: On the Programming of Computers by Means of Natural Selection*
John R. Koza

*Intelligent Behavior in Animals and Robots*
David McFarland and Thomas Bösser

# Intelligent Behavior in Animals and Robots

David McFarland
Thomas Bösser

A Bradford Book
The MIT Press
Cambridge, Massachusetts
London, England

Set in Helvetica and Trump.
Printed and bound in the United States of America.

Library of Congress Cataloging-in-Publication Data

McFarland, David.
  Intelligent behavior in animals and robots / David McFarland,
Thomas Bösser.
    p.  cm.—(Complex adaptive systems)
  "A Bradford book."
  Includes bibliographical references and index.
  ISBN 0-262-13293-1
  1. Animal intelligence. I. Bösser, Tom, 1947–. II. Title.
III. Series.
QL785.M46  1993                                    92-40583
156'.3—dc20                                              CIP

# Contents

# Introduction

Historically, the idea of automata—physical devices that are self-governing in a way that we normally associate with living beings—has been tied to the simulation of animal forms (McCorduck 1979). With the development of cybernetics (Wiener 1948), negative feedback was the main control principle used in early robots, such as Walter's (1953) "tortoise."

In an influential paper, Rosenblueth et al. (1943) defined purposeful behavior in terms of negative feedback systems. The behavior of such a system is controlled by the difference between the present state of the system and the "desired" state, or goal. Miller et al. (1960) developed this idea, and proposed that action can be understood in terms of Test-Operate-Test-Exit (TOTE) units. According to this model, the actions that an animal or a person performs are continually guided by the outcomes of various tests. The "image" of a goal supplies the criteria that must be met before the test is passed. Comparison of test outcomes continues until the incongruity between test outcome and criterion is zero. TOTE units can be arranged hierarchically into larger TOTE units. This basic principle, which we will call the *goal-directed principle*, has persisted in artificial intelligence and in robotics up to the present day.

Recently, with the development of cognitive science, the simple cybernetic approach has been abandoned, and attempts have been made to simulate human mental activities, such as beliefs, desires, intentions, and plans. The strategy is to interpose mental operations between the environmental stimuli and the response. This strategy is, in our opinion, misguided. The mentalistic constructs employed in this type of cognitive science are ill-founded, being based primarily on "folk psychology" (Dennett 1987) and involving anthropomorphic assumptions about the way cognition works, rather than being tailored to the requirements of the job. Basic behavioral principles have been ignored, and little attention has been paid to the mechanisms used by animals faced with similar problems.

The root of the problem lies with Turing's (1950) claim that the appropriate test of machine intelligence is accountable rationality. A rational person is supposed to be, at least, coherent, responsive, and self-critical. Thus, a person holds beliefs irrationally, if one conflicts with another, if they are not adapted in the face of contrary evidence, or if their assumptions are not open to question. In everyday life, a rational person, to be credible, must be able to muster a good defense of a belief, an argument, or an opinion when the occasion demands. Turing claimed that, if a machine can answer questions in such a way that the person asking the questions cannot tell whether the answers are being given by a machine or by another human, then the machine displays a human-like intelligence. Turing (1950, p. 435) discounted the possibility that the apparently intelligent machine might employ processes that had little resemblance to human thought, holding that success in passing the Turing test was, regardless of the mechanism, evidence for intelligence.

Quite apart from the question of the justifiability of Turing's assertions, the Turing test was unfortunate in focusing attention on human language as the main vehicle for intelligence, despite the evident intelligence of nonlinguistic animals. An early attempt to explore the implications of the Turing test was the development of ELIZA by Joseph Weizenbaum in the 1960s. ELIZA consisted in a family of computer programs designed to carry out "conversations" with humans through the medium of the teletype. Notwithstanding the apparent success of ELIZA in convincing people that another human was responsible for its contributions to the conversation, Weizenbaum (1983, p. 23) denied that the programs were intelligent, describing them as "a mere collection of procedures."

The apparent success of ELIZA has been attributed to the tendency of people to find sense in actions and messages that they assume to be purposeful or meaningful. Indeed, there is now considerable evidence that people readily attribute to other people, to animals, and even to machines mental processes that they imagine to be responsible for much of their own behavior (Weizenbaum 1983; Suchman 1987; Morris, 1989). It has been suggested that this tendency is part and parcel of our primate heritage. The political lives of primates are complex and require continual assessment of the "intentions" of other members of the group (de Waal 1982). Thus, people are predisposed to attribute intention and purpose to other people, and to some animals. Mc-

Farland (1989a) suggests that our evolutionary inheritance predisposes us to interpret the world in terms of meanings and purposes, as if the rivalries of our political life were relevant to the inanimate world. The result is that we attribute purpose where there is no purpose, and seek for meaning where there is no meaning.

This general attidude is also prevalent in the study of problem solving. The planning approach to cognitive science, largely due to Newell and Simon (1972), regards a plan as a representation of a sequence of actions designed to accomplish some preconceived end. Planning is a form of problem solving, the actor's problem being to find a path from some initial state to a desired goal state. Much AI effort has gone into such problem-solving systems, but the results seem rather disappointing.

The concept of planning was first introduced to artificial intelligence by the programmers of the General Problem Solver (GPS) (Newell and Simon 1963). The planning strategy used in GPS was "means-end analysis," a method that has been widely used since. Means-end analysis is a hierarchical planning strategy that works backward from a clear idea of the goal to be achieved. It employs comparison procedures to identify differences between the goal representation and the current state.

An early attempt using this approach was the robot "Shakey," developed at the Standford Research Institute in the mid 1960s. The aim was to build a robot that could move autonomously from one room to another, avoid obstacles, and shift specified objects from one place to another. Shakey was controlled by a problem-solving program, called STRIPS (STanford Research Institute Problem Solver), that employed means-end analysis to determine the robot's path (Fikes and Nilsson 1971). The STRIPS program examines the stated goal and then determines the subset of activities (or operations) that are both necessary to reach the goal and available to the robot. The preconditions for these operations, in turn, identify particular sub-goal states, which are examined in the same way. Thus, STRIPS works back from the desired goal state until a plan is defined that can guide the robot from the initial state to the goal state.

In addition to the problems inherent in constructing plans, notably the problem of search through possible solution paths (Sacerdoti 1977), artificial intelligence researchers have to address the problems of "failure and surprise" (Nilsson 1973) that result from the practical exigencies of performing activities in an unpredictable environment. In the case of Shakey, the execution of the plan generated by STRIPS is monitored by programs such as PLANEX and NOAH. PLANEX compares the planned and actual movement of Shakey; when the cumulative error reaches a certain threshold, it initiates corrective action, updating the plan. Thus PLANEX builds up a "model of the world" and depends upon feedback from sensing the actual location of the robot to update the model.

NOAH (Nets Of Action Hierarchies) was designed by Sacerdoti (1977) to cope with changes in the location of objects in Shakey's environment. NOAH generates a "procedural net," a hierarchy of partially ordered actions, which provides the input to the execution-monitoring portion of the system. NOAH has a number of general-purpose CRITICS that continually oversee the plan as a whole while it is being elaborated. (For further details see Boden 1987.) Like PLANEX, NOAH builds up a representation of the robot's environment (with respect to movable objects) and compares this with feedback gained from sensing the actual environment. When this comparison reveals a sufficiently large disparity between the two, corrective action is initiated. Thus NOAH tracks and assesses the robot's behavior in response to the instructions generated.

It is noteworthy that, even with the introduction of sophisticated "cognitive" models, the goal-directed principle has been retained throughout modern developments in AI and robotics. Basically, a goal-directed system, as opposed to a goal-attaining and a goal-seeking system (McFarland 1989b), is any system in which behavior is determined as a result of a comparison between a representation of the goal to be achieved and the actual (usually current) state of affairs. Thus, servomechanisms, TOTE systems, STRIPS, NOAH, and any system based on means-end analysis all employ the goal-directed principle in one form or another.

It is understandable that the goal-directed approach is popular. It is easy to comprehend. It conforms with what we think we normally do, and hence it is intuitively appealing. It can produce results, provided the requirements are modest. In our view this approach is naive, is full of methodological pitfalls, and violates some fundamental behavioral principles.

Our point of departure from the traditional AI approach to problem solving and decision making comes from a consideration of multi-tasking. In optimized (well-designed) single-task systems there is no formal (mathematical) difference between the goal-directed principle and a maximization principle. Both are designed to achieve equivalent performance criteria. In optimized multi-task systems, however, there is necessarily some tradeoff among the decision variables, and this requirement is incompatible with the goal-directed principle. Moreover, this discord occurs in any system capable of more than one activity (where activities are defined as mutualy exclusive outputs), even though the different activities may seem to be designed to fulfill the same task.

In this book we advocate an approach to artificial intelligence and robotics that is very different from the traditional approaches. It is based on the belief that a successful robot must be situated in its environment, and may not be an entirely new idea (Suchman 1987). But what is the environment of a robot? At present the most common robot environment is the laboratory, but soon robots will enter the more competitive world of the marketplace. Here they will experience competitive forces very similar to those faced by animals. Like animals, they will have to be cost-efficient and time-efficient. Like animals, they will develop survival strategies and strategies for pleasing the customer.

In this book we try to see robots as if they were animals. Indeed, animals can themselves be seen as cost-based robots (McFarland 1992). We develop a view of robots, and of robot intelligence, that is niche-based and closely related to robot ecology.

# Intelligent Behavior in Animals and Robots

# 1  Intelligent Behavior

In this chapter we attempt to arrive at a view of intelligent behavior that is radically different from the view current in classical artificial intelligence. Our reasoning is derived partly from current thinking in biology and partly from a distaste for anthropomorphism (the tendency to assume that our minds work the way we think they work and to attribute such workings to other agents, both animate and inanimate). In some respects anthropomorphism is an incurable disease, because we are probably incapable—for good evolutionary reasons—of resisting the temptation to interpret the behavior of other agents in terms of our own subjective experience. Nevertheless, as scientists we should recognize that our introspection is probably not a good guide to reality, and we should make some attempt to break the spell. Making robots forces us to address issues that we might otherwise overlook or avoid, and it provides some acid tests for models and theories of behavior.

## 1.1  Assessing Intelligent Behavior

How are we to assess intelligent behavior? Much of the book will be devoted to this question, but we can state some basic principles right away.

First, behavior requires a body. Disembodied behavior is not possible. Both animals and robots have bodies that are capable of intelligent behavior, and can influence the world around them. An intelligent computer that has no body, and that cannot influence its environment, is not capable of intelligent behavior.

The second principle is that only the *consequences* of behavior can be called intelligent. Behavior is intelligent only by virtue of its effect on the environment. The consequences of behavior are due to both the behavior itself and the environment that it influences. Intelligent behavior is behavior the consequences of which are judged to be intelligent.

The third principle is that intelligent behavior requires judgement. The consequences of the behavior have to be judged in relation to some criteria of intelligence. Whether the judgement is conducted by nature, by market forces, or by man is a question that we will discuss in this book. To specify behavior as intelligent, we must have established criteria for judgement.

So far so good, but we seem to have departed from what people normally mean by intelligence. To understand why we have made this departure, consider a little history. The term *intelligence* is derived from the distinction, in ancient Greek philosophy, between intellectual and emotional faculties of mind. In our view, this dichotomy is more apparent than real, because it is based on introspection. Another distinction, equally anthropomorphic, is that between the learning and reasoning abilities of humans and the instinctive behavior of animals. Much human behavior is highly instinctive and genetically influenced, while much animal behavior is based on learning. Thus, the early notions of intelligence were based on assumptions about the nature of animals and humans that are simply incorrect.

Among scientists, the traditional way to approach intelligent control of the body is to consider input, control, and output as separate functions. This approach originated with Descartes' notion of the soul as the ultimate arbiter and the autocratic controller of behavior. It entered psychology through medical physiology, and through psychology it influenced the early thinking in artificial intelligence and robotics.

The alternative approach has its origins in zoology, where it is recognized that, although primitive animals have no central nervous system, they do have quite complex behavior, and they are well adapted to their environment. Recently it has been realized that robots, which are still at a very primitive stage of their evolution, might better be designed along the zoological lines of primitive animals than along the traditional lines of autocratic central control. For example, Brooks (1986) distinguishes between the traditional decomposition by function and the alternative decomposition by activity. The former involves division into many subsystems, each of which is essential for even the simplest behavior. The essential subsystems are those providing perception, memory, planning, decision-making, effector control, and so on. This decomposition results in a serial input-output architecture, as illustrated in figure 1.1. The alternative, "distributed" architecture, involves a number of task-accomplishing procedures acting in parallel, as shown in figure 1.2. Such systems already exist in the animal kingdom, as the following example shows.

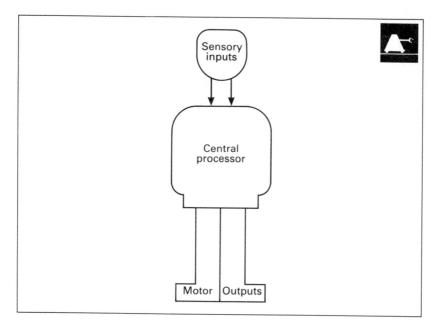

**Figure 1.1**   Vertical architecture for robots.

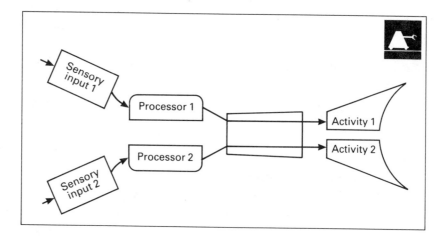

**Figure 1.2**   Horizontal architecture for robots.

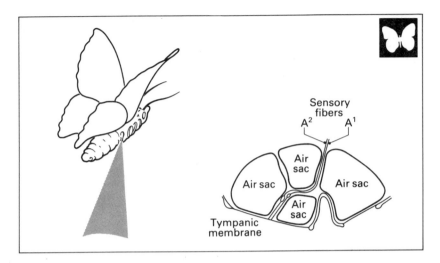

**Figure 1.3**  The ear of a noctuid moth. Vibrations of the tympanic membrane are detected by the $A^2$ and $A^1$ neurones. (After Roeder 1970.)

Noctuid moths are preyed up on by bats as they fly about at night. The moths have a very simple auditory system. There are two ears, each composed simply of a tympanic membrane on the side of the thorax and two receptor cells embedded in a strand of connective tissue, as illustrated in figure 1.3. These remarkably simple ears enable the moths to hear the ultrasonic cries of hunting bats. By means of an elegant series of experiments, Kenneth Roeder (1963, 1970) showed how this is achieved. One receptor, called the $A_1$ cell, is sensitive to low-intensity sounds and responds to cries from bats that are about 30 meters away—too far for the bat to detect the moth. The frequency of impulses from the $A_1$ cell is proportional to the loudness of the sound, so the moth can tell whether or not the bat is approaching. By comparing the time of arrival and the intensity of the stimulus at the two ears, the moth can determine the direction of approach. The difference occurs because the moth's body shields the sound more from one ear than from the other. The relative altitude of the bat also can be determined. When the bat is higher than the moth, the sound reaching the moth's ears will be interrupted intermittently by the beating of the moth's wings; this will not happen when the bat is below the moth. The $A_1$ cells give the moth early warning of an approaching bat and may enable it to fly away from the bat before it is detected. By heading directly away from the bat, the moth presents itself as the smallest possible target, because its wings are edge-on rather than broadside-on relative to the bat. The moth can do this simply by turning so as to equalize the sound reaching the bat's two ears. If, however, the bat detects the moth, the moth cannot escape simply by outflying the bat, because the bat is a much faster flier. Instead, the moth employs evasive action when the bat comes within 2 or 3 meters. The $A_2$ cell produces nerve impulses only when the sound is loud. It starts responding when the bat is near-by, and its impulses probably disrupt the moth's flight-control mechanisms. The moth consequently flies erratically and drops toward the ground. By means of such evasive action, moths have been observed to escape just as the bats come within striking distance.

This example illustrates both intelligent design and distributed architecture. By relatively simple means, the moth is able to detect the distance and the direction of an approaching bat. To compute this information in the conventional manner would involve a much larger brain, bringing with it the need for increased weight and a greater energy supply. The problem is solved, intelligently, by having two simple ears, strategically placed on the body. We are claiming, not that the moth has great intelligence, but that it is capable of intelligent behavior. It does what any intelligent being would do under the circumstances: When the bat is far away it flies away from it, and when the bat is near it takes evasive action. The intelligent behavior of the moth comes about as a result of its physical and neural design. The two are inseparable in achieving a solution to the problem of predation by bats.

The auditory system of the moth is tuned specifically to detect the bat's echo-locating cries. The ears have no other function. The $A_1$ and $A_2$ cells provide simple behavioral remedies to specific environmental situations. They have no other function. In other words, the bat-evasion system of the moth is an autonomous sub-system that acts in parallel with other systems, such as the olfactory-based mate-finding system. This is a prototypical example of distributed architecture.

Intelligent behavior in animals stems from the costs and benefits that accrue to different aspects of behavior. The forces of evolution by natural selection tend toward the behavioral strategy and tactics that will best enable the animal to adapt to the current circumstances. It does not much matter how the optimal strategy is achieved. What matters is the behavioral outcome, and this is judged (by evolution) in relation to the particular circumstances pertaining to each species. Intelligent behavior is the behavior that comes up with the right answer, irrespective of how the answer is arrived at. If we think otherwise we may find ourselves in the ridiculous position of judging a poorer solution to a problem to be more intelligent (because it involves reasoning) than a better solution that does not involve reasoning.

Thus, in pointing to a particular intelligent behavior in a particular species, we are not saying that other species are stupid in comparison. The other species may have solved the problem in a way that does not involve much intelligent behavior. For example, many marine animals are sessile filter feeders. They do not have any sophisticated foraging behavior, and they do not show much intelligent behavior in connection with feeding. What they do have is an efficient, intelligently designed filtering and pumping system, which enables them to draw in water and extract the food particles from it. Such animals are well adapted to their environment, largely by virtue of their morphological design. Similarly, in comparing pigeons and bats, we can see that pigeons are much better at navigation, whereas bats are much better at foraging at night. It makes no sense to try to compare the general intelligence of these two animals, but it does make sense to ask to what extent their special abilities depend on intelligent behavior rather than on morphology.

## 1.2 Design

Many animals and plants appear to be perfectly designed to fulfil their roles or purposes. Darwin realized that such apparently perfect adaptations can be accounted for in terms of natural selection. Most biologists now agree that the theory of natural selection can adequately account for even the most intricate adaptations (Cain 1964; Dawkins 1986).

In recent years the notion of design has become an important part of biological thinking. We now realize that natural selection is a designing agent. Modern evolutionary theory implies that animals tend to assume characteristics that ensure that, within a specified stable environment, they have no selective disadvantage with respect to the other animals with which they compete. In other words, over a sufficiently long period in a stable environment, animals tend to assume characteristics that are optimal with respect to the prevailing circumstances. This does not mean that every animal is perfectly adapted; all individuals differ genetically, and many are displaced from the habitats to which they would best be suited by competing species.

In this book we will argue that the principles applying to the design of robots are similar to those involved in the design of living organisms. Moreover, we cannot consider intelligent behavior in isolation from the design of the robot or the animal. Suppose we wish to design a robot to lay bricks. If the robot were an animal, the design criteria would be supplied by the selective pressures of the natural environment. In the case of a robot, the design criteria are provided by man. Let us suppose, for the time being, that our prime criterion is that the brick-laying robot should be able to compete with a human bricklayer for jobs, just as an animal must compete with its rivals in the natural world.

To be able to compete with the human bricklayer, the robot must satisfy various criteria, such as cost, quantity of work, quality of work, and safety. The employer has to decide whether the capital cost and the running costs are worthwhile in relation to the work done. In designing the robot, we have also to consider various criteria of mechanical design and relate these to the robot's behavior. Our main task here is to produce a design that is capable of intelligent behavior.

Consider a simple problem. Figure 1.4a shows a prototype for a brick-laying robot. When this robot picks up a brick, it falls over because of the brick's weight. A possible solution that does not involve intelligent behavior is shown in figure 1.4b. Altering the shape of the robot so as to broaden its base alters the center of gravity, so that the robot no longer falls over when it picks up a brick. This is not a good solution, because the altered shape implies decreased height and possible increased weight—both undesirable traits because they constrain the robot's reach and increase its fuel requirements. Figure 1.4c shows an alternative solution. The robot is equipped with a counterweight (either a special limb or another arm capable of holding another brick), which can be raised at the appropriate time to keep the robot from falling over when it lifts a brick.

It may be objected that the intelligence (or lack of it) applied to this problem is a property of the designer rather than of the robot. We have to be careful here. It is intelligent behavior of the robot in figure 1.4c to raise the counterbalance when it picks up a brick. Whether the robot thinks up this solution itself or whether it per-

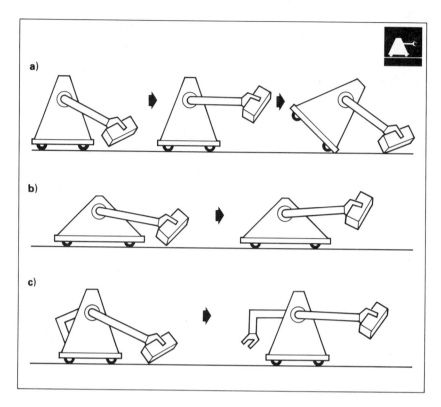

**Figure 1.4**  Design problems associated with a brick-laying robot. (a) The robot is unstable once a brick is grasped. (b) Stability is achieved by altering the body shape at the expense of reduced height and increased weight. (c) Stability is achieved by the intelligent behavior of using the free arm as a counterweight.

forms the solution automatically is not really relevant. The robot in figure 1.4a, which has no counterbalance, cannot perform this intelligent behavior no matter how much thinking power it has. Similarly, the robot in figure 1.4b, however big its on-board computer, cannot overcome the fact that it is overweight. So intelligent behavior is not simply a matter of cognition; rather, it is a product of the behavioral capacity and the environmental circumstances.

Mechanical design is not the only design factor affecting intelligent behavior. Although disembodied behavior is not possible, it is possible to imagine disembodied intelligence. Suppose we imagine a computer that contains a special program, called WIZARD, which predicts future share prices with a high degree of accuracy. We would normally consider this a capability requiring high intelligence. The computer is not capable of intelligent behavior on its own. However, when the computer is used by a human operator (who may be ignorant of investment techniques), the human-computer system produces intelligent behavior at the stock exchange. The relationship between the computer and the human operator is the same in principle as that between an animal and its environment. (Remember, its environment contains other animals.) One manipulates the other.

## 1.3 Intelligence in Animals

Charles Darwin believed in the evolutionary continuity of mental capabilities, and he opposed the widely held view that animals are merely automata, far inferior to humans. In his book *The Descent of Man* (1871) Darwin argued that "animals possess some power of reasoning" and that "the difference in mind between man and higher animals, great as it is, certainly is one of degree and not kind."

The intelligence of animals was exaggerated by Darwin's disciple George Romanes, whose book *Animal Intelligence* (1882) was the first attempt at a scientific analysis of it. Romanes defined intelligence as the capacity to adjust behavior in accordance with changing conditions. His uncritical assessment of the abilities of animals, often based on anecdotal evidence, provoked a revolt by those who wanted to turn animal psychology into a respectable science.

Conway Lloyd Morgan and the subsequent behaviorists attempted to pin down animal intelligence in terms of specific abilities. In *An Introduction to Comparative Psychology* (1894), Lloyd Morgan suggested that higher faculties evolved from lower ones, and he proposed a psychological scale of mental abilities. Lloyd Morgan's view persists today in elementary psychology textbooks, in the minds of the educated general public, and (unfortunately) in the minds of many of those working in artificial intelligence. This view is unacceptable for four basic reasons:

1. Although the idea of a ladder-like evolutionary scale of abilities has had a considerable influence upon animal psychology, it is not an acceptable view today. Studies of brain structure (e.g., Hodos 1982) and of the abilities of various species (e.g., Macphail 1982) make it abundantly clear that different species in different ecological circumstances exhibit a wide variety of types of intelligence. This makes intelligence difficult to define. Indeed, Macphail (1985,

pp. 38–39) goes so far as to claim that, if we exclude man, "remarkably few specific proposals have been made concerning the differences in intellect between vertebrate groups; second, none of the proposals applicable to vertebrates . . . appears to enjoy convincing support."

We should appreciate the importance of studying animal intelligence from an evolutionary viewpoint, as well as investigating the mechanisms involved, and we should be prepared to entertain what Macphail (1982, p. 15) calls the null hypothesis—"the possibility that there are, excluding humans, neither qualitative nor quantitative differences in intellectual capacity amongst the various groups of vertebrates." This viewpoint is now beginning to be taken seriously by both scientists and philosophers (see, e.g., Wilkes 1991).

There are two main ways of assessing the intelligence of animals: to make a behavioral assessment and to study the brain. In the past, both approaches have been dominated by the idea that there is a linear progression from lower, unintelligent animals with simple brains to higher, intelligent animals with complex brains. A survey of the animal kingdom as a whole tends to confirm this impression, but when we look closely at specific cases we find many apparent anomalies. These are not exceptions to an overall rule; rather, they are due to the fact that evolution does not progress in a linear manner. It diverges among a multiplicity of routes, each involving adaptation to a different set of circumstances. This means that animals may exhibit considerable complexity in some respects but not others, and that different species may reach equivalent degrees of complexity along different evolutionary routes.

2. Intelligence has often been linked to brain size, but many traditional ideas about the evolution of the vertebrate brain have recently been challenged. Thus, it has been claimed that, contrary to popular belief, there is no progressive increase in relative brain size in the sequence fish, reptile, bird, mammal or in the relative size of the forebrain in the sequence lamprey, shark, bony fish, amphibian, reptile, bird, mammal (Jerison 1973). Indeed, some sharks have forebrains equivalent to those of mammals in relative size (Northcutt 1981). It was long thought that the telencephalons of sharks and bony fishes are dominated by the olfactory sense, but it is now claimed that the representation of the olfactory sense in this region is no greater in nonmammalian vertebrates than in mammals (Hodos 1982). The idea that an undifferentiated forebrain

is characteristic of lower vertebrates has also been challenged (Hodos 1982).

In reviewing our understanding of animal intelligence in the light of modern knowledge of neuroanatomy, Hodos (1982, pp. 52–53) comes to the following conclusion: "If we are to find signs of intelligence in the animal kingdom and relate them to developments in neural structures, we must abandon the unilinear, hierarchial models that have dominated both searches. We must accept a more general definition of intelligence than one closely tied to human needs and values. We must accept the fact that divergence and nonlinearities characterize evolutionary history, and we must not expect to find smooth progression from one major taxon to another. Finally, we must not allow ourselves to be biased by our knowledge of the mammalian central nervous system in our search for neural correlates of intelligence in other vertebrate classes. Without such changes in our thinking, we would appear to have little hope of progressing any further than we have in our attempt to understand the relationships between the human mind and the animal mind and their respective neural substrates."

The logical conclusion from this view is that we cannot rely upon the anatomy of an animal, or of its brain, in assessing intelligence. Can we, then, test for animal intelligence behaviorally?

3. Until recently, attempts to assess animal intelligence concentrated on abilities that normally would be taken as signs of intelligence in humans. A modern IQ test includes various subtests designed to assess a person's memory, arithmetic and reasoning power, language ability, and ability to form concepts. Now, pigeons appear to have a prodigious ability to form concepts such as 'water', 'tree', and 'human being' (Herrnstein et al. 1976). They can make discriminations even though the relevant cues are presented in a variety of ways. Thus, a pigeon can recognize water in the form of droplets, a turbulent river, or a placid lake, and can discriminate humans from nonhumans, whether clothed or naked and whether alone or in a crowd. Are we to take these abilities as signs of great intelligence?

In comparing the intelligences of different species, it is difficult to devise a test that is not biased in one way or another. Many of the early tests of animals' problem-solving abilities were unreliable (Warren 1973). Sometimes the same test, with the same species, gave different results according to the type of apparatus employed. Macphail (1982) gives many examples, and comes to the conclu-

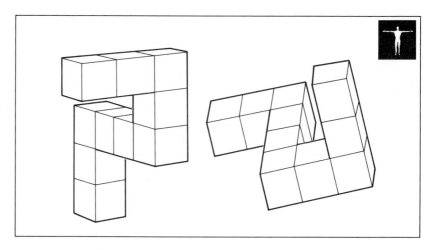

**Figure 1.5**  Identical shapes differing by 80° rotation. (After Shepard and Metzler 1971.)

sions outlined above. In some cases it has been possible to compare the abilities of man and animal directly. The results may be surprising, as the following example shows.

Mental chronometry is a technique that uses the time required to solve a spatial problem as an index of the processes involved (Posner 1978). In a classic study, Shepard and Metzler (1971) required human subjects to view pairs of drawings of three-dimensional objects. On each trial the subject had to indicate whether two objects were the same in shape or were mirror images. As well as being different in shape, the objects could differ in orientation, as shown in figure 1.5. In this type of experiment it is usually found that the time required to indicate whether or not the two objects are the same shape increases, in a regular manner, with the angular difference between the pairs of drawings presented to the subject (see figure 1.6). The usual conclusion is that the subjects mentally rotate an internal representation of one object, to make it line up with the other, before comparing the shapes of the two representations. Although the precise nature of the representation used in this type of task is a matter of controversy (Cooper 1982; Kosslyn 1981), the most straightforward interpretation is that some form of mental imagery is involved and that the processes of rotation and comparison are carried out in series. The fact that reaction time is a function of presentation angle is taken to show that mental rotation takes time (about 30 milliseconds for every 20 degrees) (Cooper and Shepard 1973).

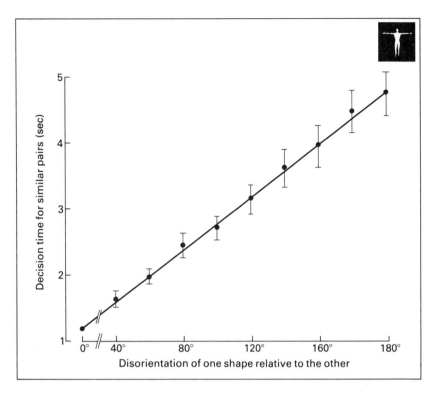

**Figure 1.6** Time taken to decide whether pairs of similar shapes are the same, plotted as a function of the orientation of one shape relative to the other. (After Shepard and Metzler 1971.)

Proficiency in the visual recognition of objects, regardless of their relative spatial orientation, has been assessed by several intelligence and aptitude tests (Petrusic et al. 1978), and subjects with higher IQs are generally less affected by the angle of rotation in experiments of this type. On this basis, it would be a reasonable expectation that animals would perform less well than humans on tasks of this type.

Hollard and Delius (1983) trained pigeons in a Skinner box to discriminate between shapes and their mirror images presented in various orientations, as shown in figure 1.7. They then measured the pigeon's reaction times in tests for rotational invariance. When this part of the study was complete, the chamber was disassembled, and the test panel, containing the lights and keys, was presented to human subjects in a series of similar tests. In this way a direct comparison of the performance of pigeons and humans could be made on the basis of the same stimulus patterns. The results showed that pigeons and humans were capable of similar accuracy,

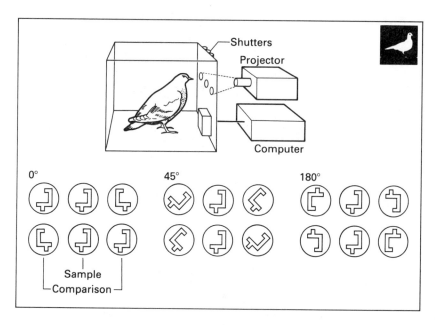

**Figure 1.7** Experimental apparatus (above) used to display symbols (below) to pigeons. The birds were trained to indicate which of the two comparison symbols most resembled the sample symbol. The comparison symbols were presented at 0°, 45°, and 180° rotation. (After Hollard and Delius 1983.)

as judged by the errors made. However, whereas the humans' reaction times increased with the angular disparity between the sample and comparison forms, as shown by previous studies, the pigeons' reaction times remained unaffected by the angular rotation (figure 1.8). It appears that pigeons are able to solve problems of this type more efficiently than humans, presumably through some parallel form of processing. This result not only has implications for the assessment of intelligence in animals but also raises questions about the validity of studies of mental representations. Furthermore, this example highlights an important point about intelligent behavior. What matters is the behavioral outcome, not the nature of the mechanism by which the outcome is achieved. We do not know what mechanisms are used by pigeons or humans. It has been assumed that humans make use of some cognitive ability that involves mental imagery; however, if pigeons can solve such problems without using mental images, can we be sure that mental images are used by humans, or is it merely that we find it easier to account for the results in terms of mental representation? (See also Dennett 1978, pp. 167–169.)

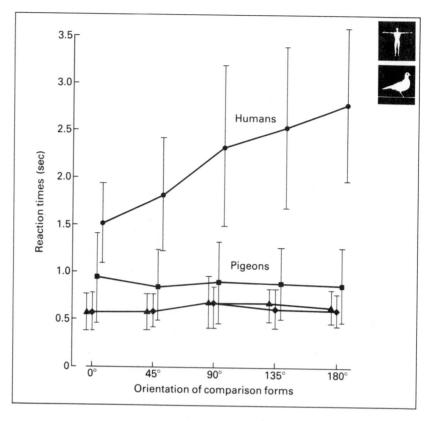

**Figure 1.8** Mean reaction times as a function of the rotation of the comparison symbols. Data from 9 pigeons and 22 humans. Note that the human reaction time increases with the angle of rotation (as in figure 1.6), but the pigeon reaction time does not. (After Hollard and Delius 1983.)

4. Intelligent behavior and cognitive ability are often linked. This is a very anthropocentric view. We are animals that are capable of cognition. When we think about cognition in other animals, we tend to think of abilities that are similar to our own cognitive abilities. Such anthropomorphism is not good scientific practice, and is not tolerated by psychologists dealing with animal perception, motivation, or learning. When it comes to animal cognition, many seem prepared to abandon the dispassionate view.

Some (see, e.g., Griffin 1981) argue, on the grounds of evolutionary continuity, that some animals are likely to have cognitive abilities similar to those of humans. The danger with this type of argument is that evolution is a double-edged sword. On the one hand, we can argue that man is an animal, and we should not assume that he is all that different from other animals. "Must we reject evolutionary continuity in order to preserve our gut feeling of human superiority . . . ?" (Griffin 1981, p. 112). On the other hand, an evolutionary argument would lead us to suppose that each species has to solve the problems appropriate to its niche. Just as the sensory world of bats is very different from our own, so may be their mental experiences and cognitive abilities (Nagel 1974). Thus, as a justification for supposing that animals have mental experiences similar to our own, the evolutionary argument cuts both ways.

Our general point is that it is unsatisfactory to pin the label 'intelligent' on certain mechanisms and not others. Our theories about the mechanisms controlling behavior are bound to change from time to time, whereas our description of the behavior and its suitability to the environmental circumstances is likely to be much more stable. This view is in tune with recent evolutionary thinking. For example, toward the end of his historical analysis of the changing views on the nature of intelligence, Tuddenham (1963, p. 517) comes to the conclusion that "intelligence is not an entity, nor even a dimension in a person, but rather an evaluation of a behavior sequence (or the average of many such), from the point of view of its adaptive adequacy. What constitutes intelligence depends upon what the situation demands. . . ." This view is endorsed by Hodos (1982), who promotes the idea of animal intelligence as an abstract characterization of the individual's behavioral responses to pressures from the environment. Hodos points out that animal intelligence should not be judged by comparison with human intelligence, because human intelligence is special as a result of "language and related cognitive skills, which permit us to communicate not only with each other, but with past and future generations" (p. 37). Moreover, animals have special capabilities which suit them to their respective ways of life. (See also Corning et al. 1976, pp. 216–217.)

In summary: (1) There is no ladder-like evolutionary scale of intelligence in animals. (2) There is no good evidence that intelligence is correlated with brain size in animals. (3) It is not possible to compare the intelligence of animals of different species by means of psychological tests. (4) Intelligent behavior is not necessarily the result of cognition. In view of these conclusions, it seems reasonable to abandon the quest for general intelligence and to focus instead on intelligent behavior.

### 1.4 Animal Cognition

In assessing the role of cognition in intelligent behavior, we should ask what advantage an animal or a robot would gain from a cognitive solution to a problem. If the environment never changed, animals would gain no benefit from learning or cognition. A set of simple rules designed to produce appropriate behavior could be established by natural selection and incorporated as a permanent feature of the animal's behavior-control mechanisms. There are some features of the environment that do not change, and we usually find that animals respond to these in a stereotyped manner. For example, gravity is a universal feature of the environment, and anti-gravity reflexes tend to be stereotyped and consistent (Mittelstaedt 1964; Delius and Vollrath 1973).

Some features of the environment change on a cyclic basis, engendering circadian, circalunar, or circannual rhythms of physiology and behavior. There is no real necessity for animals to learn to adapt to such environmental changes, because the necessary responses can be preprogrammed on the basis of an endogenous biological clock, as has been well documented (McFarland and Houston 1981). Thus, in general, environmental changes that are predictable over long periods of time can be handled by preprogrammed changes in the animal's makeup. Similar consideration should apply to robot design.

Unpredictable environmental changes that occur within an individual's lifetime cannot be anticipated by preprogrammed forms of learning or maturation. The individual must rely on its own ability and experience in adapting to such changes. There are various simple forms of learning, such as habituation and stimulus substitution, that would seem to provide a limited means of adjustment, but the ability to modify behavior appropriately in response to unexpected environmental change calls for some form of cognition.

It used to be thought that learning by association (classical conditioning) and learning through the consequences of behavior (instrumental learning) were fairly automatic processes, requiring no cognition. This view is now disputed, and it is claimed (see, e.g., Dickinson 1980 and Mackintosh 1983) that some form of cognition is required for associative learning. Be that as it may (for the time being), we should be clear that in talking about cognition we are talking about a form of phenotypic adaptation (i.e., we are talking about the way in which the individual adapts to environmental changes, remembering that such adaptations are not passed on genetically to the next generation). This may seem obvious; however, we have to be careful here, because the apparatus responsible for cognition is a product of genotypic adaptation. In taking an evolutionary perspective, we need to define cognition in a way that is both free from anthropomorphic overtones and distinct from other forms of phenotypic adaptation. It is here that problems arise.

The fact that some species do have sophisticated hard-wired mechanisms for dealing intelligently with certain well-specified situations suggests that the alternative (cognitive) approach is either more expensive or less efficient in some way. It might be that a cognitive mechanism requires more brain than a hard-wired solution, or it might be that the cognitive approach is more fallible. To be able to tackle this kind of problem, we need to have some idea of the nature and the limitations of cognition (McFarland 1991).

Cognition involves learning and thinking processes that are not directly observable, but for which there often seems to be indirect evidence. Evidence for what, precisely? In asking this question we discover that cognitive processes in animals are very difficult to pin down. For Toates (1986, p. 14) it seems sufficient that "information may be stored in a form not directly tied to behavior. Such information may be exploited in different ways according to context." This seems to us to be more like a definition of memory, but Toates goes on to endorse the definition of Menzel and Wyers (1981): "Our principal definition boils down to a negative one: cognitive mechanisms may be assumed to be necessary when all other alternatives may reasonably be rejected—that is, when description in terms of Newtonian or sequential stimulus-response, input-output relations falls short and the animal seems to be filling in certain information gaps for itself or going beyond the information or stimuli that are immediately available in the external environment."

There are a number of problems here. Unless we are to take the stimulus-response notion literally, we suspect that it will always be possible for the ingenious computer programmer to come up with an "input-output" model that does the job. Like Dennett (1983), we see the behaviorist and cognitive explanations as possible and plausible alternatives. The question is partly one of which is correct in a particular case (a problem solved cognitively by one animal might be solved noncognitively by another) and partly one of which type of explanation is to be preferred.

In assessing stimuli, animals often go beyond the information that is immediately available in a way that suggests that cognitive processes are at work. We have to be careful here, because there may be a more simple explanation. For example, navigating bees can sense the direction of the sun even when it is obscured by clouds. They are able to make use of the pattern of polarization of daylight, but the information they obtain can be ambiguous. When there are two patches that look the same, positioned symmetrically with respect to the sun, the bees overcome the problem by acting as if the patch they see is the one to the right of the sun (Gould 1980). Thus, the bees go beyond the immediately available information by adopting a convention. They pass this information to other bees, which also have the same convention and which therefore can follow the instructions without ambiguity. This need not imply cognition, since it could be the result of a simple hardwired rule. Moreover, animals do not react solely on the basis of external stimuli; they are also influenced by internal factors, such as their endogenous clock and their memory of past situations. Thus, they inevitably "interpret" external stimuli in terms of their internal state, but again there is no compelling reason to regard this as a form of cognition.

If there are some aspects of cognitive mechanisms that set them apart from other mechanisms of learning and adaptation, they are likely to be discovered by inquiry into the functional role of cognitive processes. There are a number of possibilities here. First, if cognition provides a way of coping with unpredictable aspects of the environment (see above), we might expect the individual's perceptual evaluation of the situation to be flexible. The stimulus situation would not be automatically categorized into sign stimuli, or associated with a set of conditioned reflexes. It must be evaluated in some way that poses a problem for the animal; otherwise there is no call for a cognitive solution. (In other works, cognition involves declarative knowledge. See chapter 6.) Second, the animal's response to the situation must be novel, in the sense that the individual has not hitherto typically given the same response to the same situation. Third, the animal's evaluation of the consequences of its own behavior must somehow deal with the fact that an unusual situation has been responded to, or a novel response made. The problems posed by unusualness and novelty do not arise in the cases of preprogrammed learning, maturation, or physiological adaptation; however, if the animal is to adapt in an unpredictable environment, then its responses must in some sense be constructive.

An animal that interferes with its environment without knowing the consequences is conducting an experiment, except in cases of preprogrammed behavior (discussed above) where the consequences are evolutionarily predictable and the individual does not have to monitor them. The idea that some animals may form hypotheses about the consequences of their own behavior has long been a theme in the psychological literature (see, e.g., Krechevsky 1932). We are concerned here, not with the evidence for such a view, but rather with the scope and the limitations of such a process. To what extent is cognition that is based on monitoring the consequences of one's own behavior a desirable design feature of an animal or a robot? In this book we will attempt to answer this question.

## 1.5 Human Intelligence as a Basis for Artificial Intelligence

Classical AI is founded upon notions about human intelligence. Since intelligence tests for humans were introduced (by Albert Binet, in 1905), considerable progress has been made in improving and refining them. This has been possible largely because it is possible to evaluate different tests by checking on the subsequent educational progress of individuals. Modern IQ tests are reasonably accurate in predicting how well a person will progress in intellectual achievement. However, difficulties remain, especially in attempting to compare the general intelligence of persons from differing cultural backgrounds.

Intelligence is notoriously difficult to define. In 1921 the *Journal of Educational Psychology* sought the views of experts in the field, and from the fourteen replies there seemed to be almost as many definitions of intelligence as there were experts. In general, intelligence was regarded as having something to do with adaptation to changes in the environment. In more recent times, Neisser (1979, p. 185) observed that "there are no definitive criteria of intelligence, just as there are none for chairness; it is a fuzzy-edged concept to which many features are relevant. Two people may both be quite intelligent and yet have very few traits in common."

Heim (1987, p. 379) observed that "definitions of 'intelligence' vary with the theoretical position (and also the political persuasion) of the definer. The biologist tends to stress concepts such as healthy adaptation, capacity for adjustment to the environment, and learning to learn. The more philosophically minded intellectual is liable to emphasize the element of abstraction . . . the capacity for abstract thought." The computer engineer, interested in artificially intelligent machines, may focus on capabilities of the machine that make its performance difficult to distinguish from human performance (Turing 1950).

In humans, it seems (from introspection) that cognition involves symbolic reasoning. Some forms of symbolic reasoning, such as algebra and geometry, can be performed by computers. To produce intelligent behavior, however, the reasoning must be connected to meaning. It is often thought that language, a distinctly human attribute, provides the necessary link between symbolic reasoning and meaning. Since only humans have language, it is argued, only humans are capable of true cognition. In looking for the precursors of cognition in animals, therefore, we should regard as evidence of cognition anything remotely akin to human cognition. As we have already argued, this is unacceptable, if only because this diagnosis of human cognition may be incorrect.

Another difficulty with the above argument is that the distinctive attributes of language are not entirely clear. A number of the characteristic features of human language can be found in other species. For example, the signals employed in human language are arbitrary in that they do not physically resemble the features of the world they represent. This abstract quality is found also in the communicative behavior of honeybees. When a foraging honeybee returns to the hive, it may communicate the whereabouts of food by means of a dance, as illustrated in figure 1.9. The dance is symbolic in a number of respects. The rate of the waggle indicates the distance of the food source from the hive, the precise relationship between the rate of dancing and the distance being a matter of local convention. Different geographic races seem to have different dialects; one waggle indicates about 5 meters to an Egyptian honeybee, about 25 meters to an Italian bee, and 75 meters to a German bee. If all the bees in a colony agree on the convention, it does not matter what precise value is used.

The honeybee's dance refers to features remote from the communicating animal—a feature widely considered to be an impor-

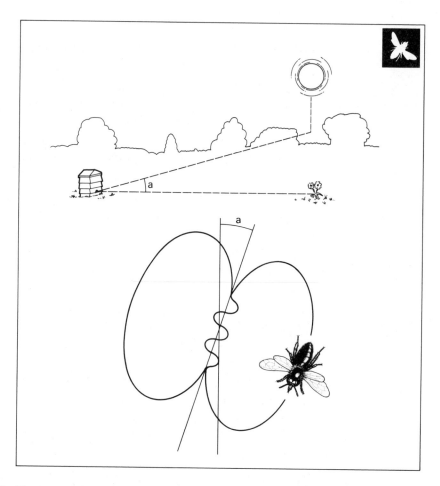

**Figure 1.9**  The waggle dance of the honeybee. The angle between the axis of the dance and the vertical is the same as the angle between the food source and the sun.

tant property of human language. The dance refers not only to food sources remote in space (up to 10 kilometers), but also to those that may have been visited some hours earlier. During the intervening period, the forager keeps a mental track of the sun's movements and corrects the dance accordingly. Another feature of human language is that it is an open system into which new messages can be incorporated. The bee's dance can refer to new sources of food; it can also be used to direct other bees to water, to propolis (a type of tree sap used to caulk the hive), and to possible new hive sites at swarming time. All in all, it is difficult not to agree with Gould (1981, p. 332) that "language is considered by many to be a purely human attribute. The possibility that other animals may have language has driven some linguists, philosophers, and other students of language to take refuge in definition, the last sanctuary of a threatened idea. Lists of the features required of language are drawn up and constantly amended, specifically to exclude interloper species. However, each year scientists are uncovering new and ever more astonishing abilities of animals, abilities which we certainly never suspected, and many of which we ourselves lack."

One problem with using human intelligence as a basis for AI is the tendency to confuse intelligence and cognition. As is true of animal behavior, many aspects of human behavior do not involve cognition. For example, the system that controls spatial orientation in humans is a highly sophisticated, prewired adaptive control system (Howard 1982), and the behavior it controls would seem extremely intelligent if performed by a robot. The control of spatial orientation requires no cognition (as far as we know), but the behavioral outcome appears to be intelligent. We must distinguish between cognition (a possible means to an end) and intelligence (an assessment of performance on the basis of some functional criteria).

Because it is so difficult to attain agreement as to what human intelligence involves, it might be more profitable to consider the nature of intelligent behavior than to try and define intelligence. This approach also might enable us to compare the intelligent behavior of humans, animals, and machines.

### Points to Remember

- Three basic principles of intelligent behavior are that behavior requires a body, that behavior is intelligent only by virtue of its effect on the environment, and that intelligent behavior requires judgement. The consequences of the behavior have to be judged in relation to some criteria of intelligence.

- We distinguish between the traditional decomposition by function and the alternative decomposition by activity. The former involves a serial input-output architecture; the latter involves a number of task-accomplishing procedures acting in parallel.

- In defining intelligent behavior, what matters is the behavioral outcome, not the nature of the mechanism by which the outcome is achieved.

- The principles that apply to the design of robots are similar to those that apply to the design of living organisms by natural selection.

- The idea of a ladder-like evolutionary scale of abilities is not acceptable today. Studies of brain structure and of the abilities of various species show that different species in different ecological circumstances exhibit a wide variety of types of intelligence.

- In assessing the role of cognition in intelligent behavior, we should ask what advantage an animal or a robot would gain from a cognitive solution to a problem. Cognition provides a way of coping with unpredictable aspects of the environment, and an animal's evaluation of the consequences of its own behavior must somehow deal with the fact that an unusual situation has been responded to, or a novel response made.

- We must distinguish between cognition (a possible means to an end) and intelligence (an assessment of performance in terms of some functional criteria).

*Current thinking about computers and their impact on society has been shaped by a rationalistic tradition that needs to be reexamined and challenged as a source of understanding.*
—Winograd and Flores (1986, p. 14)

Rationality, the use of reason, has long been thought to be an exclusively human attribute. Plato maintained that human behavior was the result of voluntary and rational processes, man's will being free to choose whatever course of action his reason dictates. He did recognize certain "forced" movements, which he argued were due to "animal passion," or emotion; however, he thought of these as disruptive and not as normal and natural aspects of human behavior. This view became incorporated into Christian doctrine—largely through the writings of Thomas Aquinas (1224– 1274), who held that "man has sensuous desire, and rational desire or will. He is not absolutely determined in his desires and actions by sense impressions as is the brute, but possesses a faculty of self determination, whereby he is able to act or not to act. . . . The will is determined by what intelligence conceives to be the good, by a rational purpose. . . . Man is free because he is rational, because he is not driven into action by an external cause without his consent, and because he can choose between the means of realising the good or purpose which his reason conceives." (*Summa Theologica*)

René Descartes, in *Passions of the Soul* (1649), maintained that all physical phenomena could be adequately explained mechanically, and that animals were merely automata. In the case of man, reasoning intervened to guide an individual's behavior in accordance with his knowledge and wishes. Descartes thus proposed that human conduct was under the dual influence of mind and body, with the mind subject to certain agitations (passions) emanating from the body and also from mental processes. The passions "dispose the soul to desire those things which nature tells us are of use, and to persist in this desire, and also to bring about that same agitation of spirits which customarily causes them to dispose the body to the movement which serves for the carrying into effect of these things" (ibid., article 52). This dualism has persisted, though today it is not very influential among scientists. In more recent times it has become usual to distinguish between rational thought and rational action.

Rational thought must, at least, be coherent, responsive, and self-critical. Thus, a person holds beliefs irrationally if one conflicts with another, if they are not adapted in the face of contrary evidence, or if their assumptions are not open to question. In everyday life a rational person does not have to subject each and every belief to constant or conscious deliberation; he or she may hold beliefs intuitively, through habit, or on some authority. However, a rational person must be able to muster a good defense of a belief when the occasion demands.

Rational thought is difficult to formalize. It may be based on rules of logic, probability, and statistics, but these fields have a long and unfinished history. It should be based on the concepts of deductive and inductive reasoning, but even these are open to dispute. Rational thought does not necessarily guarantee rational behavior. Indeed, as we shall see, the behavior of animals may be more easily seen as rational than that of humans.

Rational action can, for the purposes of the social sciences, be defined rigorously. An ideally rational agent is capable of performing a number of actions, knows the consequences of each, and has a complete and consistent order of preferences among them. The agent acts rationally if there is no other feasible action the consequences of which are preferable. Thus, the agent is a maximizer of its own utility. In the simplest case the agent knows the consequences with certainty, but decision theory can also provide for risk and uncertainty. The most common approach is to discount the utility of an outcome by the likelihood of achieving it, thus making the rational agent a maximizer of expected utility. Other technical aspects of decision theory include discounts associated with the time and information costs involved in decisions. The theory of games studies choices in social situations, where the benefit to each agent depends on what others choose. Often the rational choice of each agent conflicts with the common good. For example, in a period of drought, each individual gardener may be rational in his use of water even though all would be better off if each gardener used less water. For a recent review of this type of approach, see Baron 1988, Brand 1984, or Rachlin 1989.

## 2.1 Experiments on Transitive Inference

If rational action is determined by rational thought, then we might expect to find that individuals incapable of rational thought would generally be incapable of rational action.

Suppose we tell a subject that A is bigger than B and that B is bigger than C, and then ask if C is smaller than A. We would expect a normal adult human to be able to infer that C is smaller than A from the information provided. Such a problem is called a *transitive inference* problem. If a person was unable to deal with such a problem, or was inconsistent in answering such questions, we would say that the person was not being rational.

Psychologists are divided in their explanations of the mental processes that occur during transitive inference. For some (see, e.g., Clark 1969) the solutions to such problems are to be understood in terms of a linguistic deep-structural account in which the premises and the questions are decoded into their underlying base strings. Thus, when given the premises "A is better than B" and "B is better than C," the subject will decode these into the form "A is good +; B is good; C is good −." When asked "Who is best?," the subject can translate this as "Who is most good?" and can find the answer from the string. However, if asked "Who is worst?" the subject must translate this as "Who is least good?"

Other psychologists believe that adults often form spatial images when solving transitive inference problems. Typically, the subject "arranges the items described in the first premise, starting at the top or left of his imaginary space. . . . After constructing an array from the first premise," the subject "uses the second premise to add the third item to his construction" (Huttenlocher 1968, p. 558). A protocol from a study by Chalmers and McGonigle (1983) illustrates the use of a similar mental device by 9-year-old children: "I see a picture in my head and names are written underneath them. . . . If you say Gill is bigger than Linda, Gill comes in and then Linda comes in. . . . [After some practice,] if you say Eve is bigger than Polly and Marion is bigger than Eve, I put Marion at the beginning, Eve in the middle and Polly at the end—left to right, biggest, middle, smallest. That was how I was doing it today. In the beginning I was doing it in my head: they were all different sizes but they all looked the same . . . all just girls and they stood the way you say them. Now when you said them all I turned them round . . . left to right." (McGonigle and Chalmers 1986, p. 144)

McGonigle and Chalmers (1986) have doubts about this approach. They point to two main problems which emerge from the analysis of protocol reports. The first, called *representational incongruity*, has to do with the direction of encoding: "People learn an evaluative ordering more readily from better to worse than from worse to better." (de Soto et al. 1965, p. 515) A major implication of this (McGonigle and Chalmers 1986, p. 145) is that "only some statements of relation can be mapped directly onto a model of the state of affairs implied by the premises; in the case of non-congruent statements, conversion and translation will be required. For some statements, therefore, an extra cost is incurred in their decoding. This cost should be registered in terms of extra processing time. Compelling as this notion is, there exists little evidence in its favor (see, e.g., Foos 1980; Potts and Scholz 1975). One reason is that the locus of congruity is unclear within the logical paradigm as it is used conventionally. This is due to a difficulty endemic to the conventional transitive inference paradigm insofar as the experimenter is required to provide information to the subject before asking any questions of him. Thus the experimenter must decide which form and direction to use in the premises and the question. In these tasks, therefore, the possible sources of congruity lie between the language of the premises, the language of the question and the underlying representation."

The second characteristic is the use of a spatial paralogical device in which the order of premises and objects is important. A major psychological implication of this feature is mental distance. This concept implies that the more remote the items to be compared "in the mind's eye," the faster inferential decisions are made, because they are less confusable. Such results have been well established by Trabasso and Riley (1975); however, as McGonigle and Chalmers (1986) point out, it is not clear what these phenomena imply for the nature of mental representation. In particular, they suggest, the spatial paralogical phenomena may be due to prelogical structures, in which case they may be present in subjects that are incapable of using conventional logical procedures.

In order to investigate the problems inherent in representational congruity and spatial paralogical phenomena, McGonigle and Chalmers (1986) suggest two types of experimental strategy. First, to deal with the congruity issue, they suggest an alternative paradigm known as "internal psychophysics" (Moyer 1973). This requires subjects to decide the serial relationships between objects as rapidly as they can from memory alone. For example, subjects might be presented with a the names of two animals and asked to denote which animal is larger by pressing a switch below a panel bearing a printed name, or a picture scaled to a standard size. "As the knowledge representation is assumed to be established prior to the task, the problem of congruity endemic to the logical task can be eliminated. Now there is no basis for ambiguity. The degree of mapping achieved has to be between the question and the representation, and not between the question, the informing statement and the representation. Second, we investigated the causal role of the spatial paralogical device using younger subjects, whose failures in logical tasks have been documented (e.g. Inhelder and Piaget 1964) and monkeys (not well-known for their logical skills)." (McGonigle and Chalmers 1986, p. 146)

McGonigle and Chalmers (1984) carried out experiments in which 6- and 9-year-old children were required to compare the sizes of familiar animals, presented either as written names (lexical mode) or as pictures (pictorial mode) of a standard size, as described above. They measured the time taken to compare symbols, and they also required the children to verify statements of size relationship in the conventional manner (e.g., is a cow smaller than a cat?). Their results with the conventional methods show the "symbolic distance effect" obtained by Trabasso and Riley (1975). That is, the time taken to compare stimuli varies inversely with the distance between the stimuli along the dimension being judged. Along the size dimension, therefore, the time taken to compare the relative sizes of a cat and a whale is less than the time taken for a cat versus a fox. This is the type of result usually obtained with adults (Moyer 1973; Paivio 1975).

Similar results were obtained when 6-year-old children were presented with pictures scaled to equal size, as illustrated in figure 2.1. Overall, McGonigle and Chalmers (1984) found that children as young as 6 show a significant symbolic distance effect in both pictorial and lexical modes when the simple comparative question (bigger or smaller?) was used in the test. They also found marked categorical asymmetry, particularly in the lexical mode. Not only was less time taken to judge an item big than that to judge one

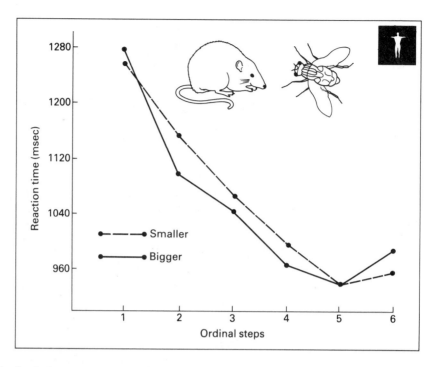

**Figure 2.1** Symbolic distance effect produced by 6-year-old children comparing sizes of an insect and a mouse. (After McGonigle and Chalmers 1986.)

small, but even for items judged small it took less time to deny that they were big than to affirm that they were small.

McGonigle and Chalmers (1986) report a series of experiments designed to test the abilities of squirrel monkeys on transitive inference problems. In one experiment five monkeys were required to learn a series on conditional size discriminations such that within a series of size objects (ABCDE) they had to choose the larger or largest one of a pair or triad if, say, the objects were black; if white, they had to choose the smaller or smallest one (McGonigle and Chalmers 1980). They found that there was a significant and consistent effect of direction of processing: decisions following the "instruction" to find the bigger were made faster than those following the signal to find the smaller. Through practice, the animals became progressively faster, yet the absolute difference between the "instruction" conditions remained invariant. Figure 2.2 summarizes some of the results of this experiment and compares them with the results of similar experiments on children.

In another experiment, based on a modification of a five-term series problem given to very young children by Bryant and Trabas-

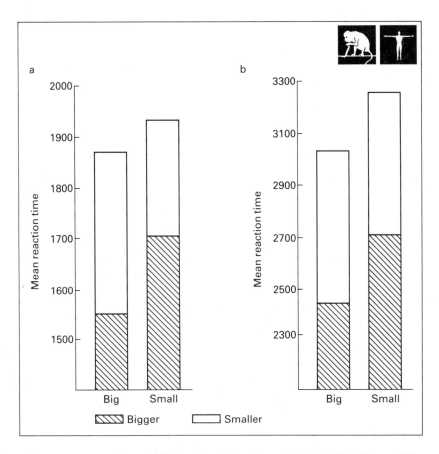

**Figure 2.2** Categorical and contrastive effects produced by (a) monkeys and (b) children. (After McGonigle and Chalmers 1986.)

so (1971), McGonigle and Chalmers tested monkeys on transitive inference tasks in which the animals were trained to solve a series of four discrimination problems. Each monkey was confronted with a pair of differently colored containers that varied in weight (A > B). When B was chosen reliably over A, the monkey moved to the next problem (B > C, where C must be chosen), and so on until the entire series was performed correctly. Only two weight values were used throughout the series, so no specific weights could be uniquely identified with the stimuli B, C, and D. When the monkeys had learned to achieve a high level of performance on all four training pairs, regardless of presentation order, transitivity tests were given in which novel pairings were presented, representing all ten possibilities from the five-term series. The results showed impeccable transitivity, indistinguishable from the results obtained with 6-year-old children by Bryant and Trabasso (1971). Analysis of

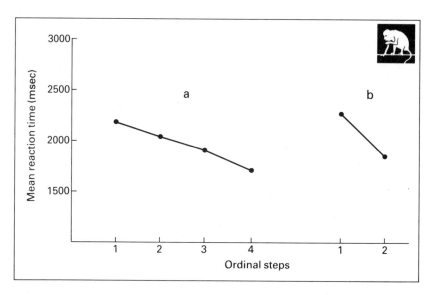

**Figure 2.3** Symbolic distance effect in monkeys: (a) all comparisons, (b) non-end-anchored comparision. (After McGonigle and Chalmers 1986.)

decision times revealed a significant distance effect: the decision times for nonadjacent comparisons were significantly shorter than those for solving the training pairs (figure 2.3).

On all major points of comparison, McGonigle and Chalmers (1986) found that the monkeys were identical in performance to young humans. Similarly, profiles in 6-year-old children, using both nonverbal and verbal forms of the same task, have also been reported (McGonigle and Chalmers 1984). So neither the nature of the task within a species nor a comparison of performance between species seems to affect the conclusion that the symbolic distance effect (taken as evidence of a spatial paralogical device in human adults and older children) and asymmetry in the direction of encoding (a characteristic feature of human transitive inference) occur in subjects unable to perform formal logical tasks. McGonigle and Chalmers (1986) come to the reasonable conclusion that the ability to order items transitively is a prelogical phenomenon.

It seems that young children, squirrel monkeys (McGonigle and Chalmers 1986), and even pigeons (Terrace 1987) can, with training, solve transitive inference problems. They evidently do not achieve this by way of syllogistic reasoning. It seems more likely that they have some basic, noncognitive, seat-of-the-pants ability to order things transitively, which can be tapped by well-designed experiments. It appears that we should be skeptical about the widely held view that rational thought is a necessary precursor of rational action.

## 2.2 Defining Rational Behavior

Theories of rational behavior are commonly used in the disciplines of economics, statistics, and cognitive science. These theories have nothing to say about the psychological processes that generate rational action; they merely state what would be rational under certain circumstances.

There are four basic requirements for rational behavior:

*Incompatibility.* There are certain activities which (by definition) an animal, a person, or a robot cannot perform simultaneously. In the case of robots, we must distinguish between *logical incompatibility* (e.g., a robot cannot move backwards and forwards simultaneously) and *engineered incompatibility* (as when a robot cannot perform two tasks simultaneously). A certain amount of incompatibility is inevitable. This is just another way of saying that the robot has more than one activity in its repertoire. (In McFarland and Sibly 1975, activities are defined as incompatible units of behavior; we may as well stick with this definition.) In animals, incompatibility is engineered at a fairly basic neurological level. When one postural reflex uses the same muscles as another, the reflexes are mechanically incompatible in that both cannot occur simultaneously. Such pairs of reflexes are also neurologically incompatible in that stimulation of one reflex inhibits performance of the other. The inhibition is usually reciprocal, each inhibiting the other. This type of reciprocal inhibition is typical of walking and other types of locomotion.

*Common currency.* If a robot cannot simultaneously perform two activities, it must choose between them on the basis of some index of their potential for performance. In the behavioral final common path—i.e., after all other considerations have been taken into account—there must be a common currency in terms of which the different potential activities can be compared. If the potential for cleaning floors is measured in terms of chalk, and that for washing up is measured in terms of cheese, then in choosing between chalk and cheese there must be a known exchange rate—a common currency in terms of which the merits of chalk and cheese are measured. For disparate potential activities to compete for behavioral expression (note that the behaviors themselves cannot compete), it must be possible for the robot (or part of it) to compare them (i.e., the candidates of McFarland and Sibly 1975) in terms of some common currency. Moreover, the comparison must be made among calibrated candidates, designed to reflect the "merits" of each potential activity (Houston and McFarland 1976). In other words, the robot must be able to decide whether it is better to perform activity A, B, or C, given that it can perform only one at a time. In a simple competition model, the robot simply performs the activity with the greatest strength of candidature, or potential.

*Consistency.* If a person, an animal, or a robot makes a particular choice when in a particular state, then it will make the same choice when it is in the same state again. This follows from the assumption that the set of incompatible activities of which a robot (or person or animal) is capable is uniquely determined by its state. (See McFarland and Sibly 1975, p. 268.) In Chapter 4 we will define the state more precisely.

*Transitivity.* A robot chooses among potential activities on the basis of some common currency. If the robot chooses potential activity A over potential activity B (A > B), and potential activity B over C (B > C), how will it choose between A and C? This question is important because it underlies the concept of rationality. The series A > B > C is said to be *transitive*. If the robot chose A > B, B > C, and C > A, then its choices would be *intransitive*.

As was mentioned above, rational action may be defined as follows: An ideally rational agent is capable of performing a number of actions, knows the consequences of each, and has a complete and consistent order of preferences among them. The agent acts rationally if there is no other feasible action the consequences of which are preferable (Weber 1968). In other words, the rational agent maximizes some entity, usually called *utility*. The rational agent maximizes its own utility, but the concept of utility is not independently defined. Indeed, it could be argued that the above definition of rational action is not sufficiently rigorous. The rational agent is capable of performing a number of actions, but presumably not simultaneously. The rational agent knows the consequences of each action, but what does this mean precisely?

Suppose we say that a rational agent is one that consistently makes the same choice when in the same state and when given the same set of (incompatible) options. (That is, when given one set of options it consistently makes one choice, and when given another set it consistently makes another choice.) This implies that the options can be ordered with respect to one another, that the ordering will be transitive, and that the first option in the ranking will always be the one chosen. It follows that the choices are made according to some maximization principle (always choose the top option in the ranking). Thus, the rational decision-maker maximizes a quantity, usually called *utility*.

So far we have identified the rational agent as one that consistently makes the same choice, when faced with the same options, when in the same state. This may hold for some states, but will it hold for every state? Maybe there are some states of the decision-maker in which it behaves irrationally. If this were the case, then the decision-maker would not be maximizing utility overall, but only when it was in certain states. We would not wish to call such an entity a rational decision-maker, because it would sometimes behave irrationally.

One problem here is the notion of choice. Most economists and psychologists seem to assume that the choosing agent is autonomous, i.e., free to choose among options. We believe that this notion of choice is not really necessary in defining rational behavior. In other words, we do not believe that knowing the likely consequences of one's actions, and then using this knowledge as a basis for choice, is a necessary condition for rational behavior. This is a possible but not necessary, or even universal, scenario. We should define the completely rational decision-maker, not in terms of the choices it makes, but in terms of the behavior it performs when in any particular state—a rational decision-maker being one that always behaves consistently and transitively. As we have seen, such a formulation implies that some entity will be maximized by the behavior of the agent.

In defining a rational decision-maker in this way, we have virtually defined an automaton (see McFarland 1991b). The behavior of an automaton is state-determined, on the basis of certain rules. There is no explicit representation of utility, nor is there any representation of the consequences of behavior. Nevertheless, it remains correct to say that some entity is maximized as the result of the rational behavior of an automaton. An automaton is a machine, subject to the laws of physics. It behavior, therefore, is in accordance with certain extremal principles. These principles necessarily involve the maximization (or minimization) of some entity, such as Hamilton's action S (see McFarland 1993). Thus, the behavior of machines and automata can be regarded as rational, in the sense that the physical processes involved are themselves rational in the sense of the above definition. McFarland (1993) calls this *rationality of process*, in contradistinction to the rationality of (mental) content that may or may not be shown by an agent capable of cognition. In short, any agent that exhibits rational behavior, even a simple machine, shows rationality of process. Some agents also show rationality of content. We will discuss this distinction further in chapter 6.

### 2.3  Evidence for Rational Behavior

Evidence for rational behavior comes from three main sources: (1) studies of transitive inference, which we have discussed above, (2) attempts to determine by direct experiment whether humans behave rationally in the real world, and (3) studies of the microeconomic behavior of humans and animals.

Many of the early experiments were specifically designed to test directly for transitivity of choice. Papandreou (1957) carried out elaborate experiments designed to discover the extent of choice-transitivity in imagined-choice situations. He claimed, at least for his specific experimental conditions, that transitivity does exist. May (1954) required a classroom group to make pairwise choices among three marriage partners who were identified only in terms of wealth, intelligence, and good looks. The results showed that 27 percent of the subjects gave intransitive triads of choices, but this may have been due to the fact that May did not allow judgements of indifference. If subjects are indifferent among all three elements of a triad, and choose between pairs by chance, then they will choose intransitively one-fourth of the time (Edwards 1954). Many such experiments on transitivity of choice were poorly designed, and many were not realistic. Moreover, experimentally testing for transitivity of choice was an impossible task.

Consider the following passage from Edwards 1954:

*In one sense, transitivity can never be violated. A minimum of three choices is required to demonstrate intransitivity. Since these choices will necessarily be made in sequence, it can always be argued that the person may have changed his tastes between the first choice and the third. However, unless the assumption of con-*

*stancy of tastes over the period of experimentation is made, no experiments on choice can ever be meaningful, and the whole theory of choice becomes empty. . . . So this quibble can be rejected at once.*

It appears from this passage that Edwards is willing to accept an invalid assumption simply for the sake of protecting a body of theory. The fact remains that it is not possible to prove by direct experiment that the choices of humans (or those of animals) are always transitive. To attempt this would involve repeated choice experiments with the same subject, under identical circumstances. In reality the circumstances could never be the same twice, if only because the memory of having made one choice changes the circumstances for the next. So the ideal experiment is impossible, at least with a subject that has memory. In other words, we cannot necessarily expect a rational decision-maker to behave consistently in a series of choice tests, because it is not always in the same state, even though the external circumstances may be the same in every test. In a later review, Edwards (1961) recognizes this:

*Two kinds of empirical findings, both of which were quite clear in 1954, underlie and motivate the development of stochastic models. One is the finding that a subject, required to make a choice from the same set of courses of action under the same conditions as a previous choice, may not repeat the previous choice; this is called inconsistency. The other is that sets of choices are often intransitive—that is, a subject may prefer A to B, B to C, and C to A. Non-stochastic models formally exclude both of these empirical facts, and so usually are accompanied by some vague theory about errors. Stochastic models permit both, but put stringent restrictions on them; these restrictions provide the most important empirical tests of the various stochastic models."*

Many of the stochastic approaches model the choice behavior of humans in situations in which they are bound to show inconsistency and intransitivity. In some ways this is a more realistic approach, but it does not really tackle the question of whether the decision-making of individual humans and animals is fundamentally rational in the sense defined above.

There are other reasons for supposing that animals behave rationally. As we have seen, there is evidence that some animals can make transitive inferences when a problem is presented to them in an appropriate manner. Moreover, the evidence suggests that this ability is evolutionarily and developmentally prior to the ability to reason logically.

A further line of evidence, which will be discussed in some detail in the next chapter, suggests that animals do appear to obey microeconomic laws that are logically derived from rationality assumptions. This amounts to strong indirect evidence of rationality, in the sense that an agent that follows microeconomic laws must be basically rational (i.e., show rationality of process). By "basically rational" we mean that the agent is organized in such a way that its behavior is governed by rational processes (McFarland 1993). The nature of these processes in animals is now under investigation. Popular suggestions are that psychological reinforcement mechanisms (Allison 1983; Rachlin 1989) and built-in rules of thumb (Stephens and Krebs 1986) are responsible for the economic behavior of animals. We will discuss this in later chapters.

### Points to Remember

- Rational thought must be coherent, responsive, and self-critical. Thus, a person holds beliefs irrationally if one conflicts with another, if they are not adapted in the face of contrary evidence, or if their assumptions are not open to question.
- Rational thought does not necessarily guarantee rational behavior, and in some respects the behavior of animals may be more easily seen as rational than that of humans.
- A rational person is capable of performing a number of actions, knows the consequences of each, has a complete and consistent order of preferences among them, and can solve transitive inference problems. If a person is unable to deal with such problems, we would say that the person is not being rational.
- Experiments on transitive inference tasks encounter the problem of representational incongruity (which has to do with the direction of encoding) and the spatial paralogical device (which has to do with the mental distance between ordered items). These may be due to prelogical structures, in which case such structures may be present in subjects that are incapable of using conventional logical procedures.
- Experiments designed to test for the transitive inference found that, on all major points of comparison, some animals were identical in performance to young humans. Thus, the ability to order items transitively appears to be a prelogical phenomenon.

- The evidence suggests that young children, squirrel monkeys, and even pigeons can, with training, solve transitive inference problems. They evidently do not achieve this by way of syllogistic reasoning. It seems more likely that they have some basic, noncognitive, seat-of-the-pants ability to order things transitively, which can be tapped by well-designed experiments.
- Theories of rational action are commonly used in the disciplines of economics, statistics, and cognitive science. These theories have nothing to say about the psychological processes that generate rational action. They merely state what would be rational under certain circumstances.
- There are four basic requirements for rational behavior: incompatibility, common currency, consistency, and transitivity. The first three are basically axiomatic. Thus, there are certain activities that (by definition) an animal or a robot cannot perform simultaneously, so a certain amount of incompatibility is inevitable. The agent must choose among them on the basis of some index of their potentiality for performance, and there must be a common currency in terms of which the various potential activities can be compared. If the agent makes a particular choice when in a particular state, then it will make the same choice when it is in the same state again. This follows from the assumption that the activity chosen is uniquely determined by the state of the robot.
- In other words, a rational decision-maker is one that consistently makes the same choice when in the same state and when given the same set of options. This implies that the options can be ordered with respect to one another, that the first option in the ranking is always the one chosen, and that choice is transitive.
- Early experiments were specifically designed to test directly for transitivity of choice, but the task was an impossible one. To attempt it involves repeated choice experiments with the same subject under identical circumstances. This is not possible, because the subject's memory of a previous experiment makes its state different from that in the previous experiment. Thus, we should not expect a rational decision-maker, necessarily, to behave consistently in a series of choice tests.
- Animals behave rationally in the sense that their behavior is transitive and obeys microeconomic laws. Their behavior shows rationality of process and may, in some cases, include rationality of content.

We have seen that the concept of rational behavior implies that some quantity is maximized during the decision-making process. This quantity is called *utility* by economists and some psychologists. Utility is a notional measure of the psychological value of goods, leisure, etc. It is a notional measure because we do not how it influences choice behavior. We only assume that people behave as if utility is maximized. Thus, I may obtain a certain amount of utility from buying china for my collection, a certain amount from sport, and a certain amount from reading books. In spending my time and money on these things, I choose in a way that maximizes the amount of satisfaction or utility that I obtain in return. I am not aware of maximizing utility, but (if I am rational) I appear to behave in a way that is consistent with maximizing utility.

A precursor of utility appears to have been envisaged by Thomas Hobbes in *Leviathan* (1651). Hobbes was a materialist, believing that the explanations of all things were to be found in their physical motions. He distinguished between "vital motion" (responsible for physiological processes in the body) and "animal motion" (responsible for behavior). Pleasure and pain he attributed to physiological processes, which gave rise to emotions and influenced behavior. Hobbes believed that we behave in such a way as to achieve pleasure and avoid pain, and that, whatever we think, these are the only causes of our behavior. Thus, Hobbes stripped the concepts of pleasure and pain of all ethical implications, making them purely motivational. He recognized that when one is deliberating on the next course of action many ideas may come to mind. These ideas have separate endeavors (incipient actions) associated with them, and the one that arouses the greatest pleasure determines the action. Thus, Hobbes had a purely materialistic view of thinking, and he suggested a mechanism for the phenomenon of anticipation: The goal of an action influences the act only through its endeavor, which evokes the degree of pleasure that one associates with the outcome of the action on the basis of one's previous experience. The anticipated pleasure or pain determines the behavior, but we think of this in retrospect as our own volition. Thus, for Hobbes, the will is just an idea that man has about himself.

The hedonistic view—that all actions are directed toward the pursuit of pleasure and the avoidance of pain, in one form or another—was prominent in the work of the utilitarians of the eighteenth and nineteenth centuries. Jeremy Bentham argued that "nature has placed mankind under the governance of two sovereign masters, pain and pleasure. It is for them alone to determine what we ought to do as well as what we shall do." (*Introduction to the Principles of Moral Legislation*, 1789) For Bentham the utility of an act could be calculated by measuring the amount of pleasure it produced. Thus, pleasure was a purely quantitative notion. John Stuart Mill, on the other hand, distinguished between higher and lower pleasures, claiming that pleasures derived from the intellect are superior to others irrespective of the actual amount of pleasure produced (*Utilitarianism*, 1861). This may appear to be a departure from true hedonism, because it implies that the value of an activity is not solely a function of the amount of pleasure involved. It should be evident, however, that, in exercising their influence on behavior, qualitatively different pleasures must be compared in terms of some common currency (called *utility*), as was explained in the previous chapter.

## 3.1 Utility in Economics

The modern concept of utility seems to have originated with Daniel Bernoulli, who in 1738 criticized the previously widely held principle of mathematical expectation. That principle held (approximately) that utility is proportional to wealth. Bernoulli pointed out that the cash value of a person's wealth is not the same as its moral worth to him. Thus, a shilling does not have the same value to a millionaire as to a pauper. Bernoulli argued that a fixed increment of cash wealth typically results in an ever-smaller increment of moral worth as the basic cash wealth to which the increment applies is increased. In modern economic terminology, this is known as the law of *diminishing marginal utility*. In mathematical terms, the law says that utility as a function of money is a concave function. Bernoulli went further and proposed that the slope of utility as a function of wealth is inversely proportional to the cash value of the wealth. "To this day, no other function has been suggested as a better prototype for Everyman's utility function," notes Savage (1954, pp. 91–104).

Bernoulli's idea of moral worth as a measure of a person's psychological well-being or utility was accepted by economists for a long time. The principle of diminishing marginal utility was seen as reflecting many aspects of everyday life. Why else does a poor man walk in the rain while a rich man takes a cab (Marshall 1890, pp. 19 and 95)? The principle was also extended from money to other commodities, and the theory of choice among consequences was expressed by the idea that, among the available consequences, a person prefers those that have the highest utility for him (Savage 1954).

Early economists (including Alfred Marshall, whose great *Principles of Economics* was published in 1890), assumed that the utilities of different commodities can be combined into a total utility by simple addition. This implies that the utilities of different goods are independent. Edgeworth (1881) began the gradual destruction of classical utility theory by pointing out that total utility was not necessarily an additive function of the utilities attached to separate consequences of behavior. He introduced the notion of *indifference curves* (or *iso-utility curves*).

If you are buying fruit, and you derive the same utility from two apples and eight oranges as from eight apples and two oranges, then you will be indifferent between these two alternative selections of fruit. It is unlikely that the utility you attach to oranges will be independent of that you attach to apples, because both are fruits and because they play similar roles in your diet. It is unlikely, therefore, that your total utility will be proportional to the sum of the apples and the oranges you purchase. A more likely alternative is that it will be proportional to the product of the oranges and the apples. If this were so, then you would also be indifferent to four apples and four oranges. This is illustrated by figure 3.1, a type of graph called an *indifference map*.

Edgeworth thought of utility as measurable along an interval scale (i.e., a scale with a common and constant unit of measurement). Pareto (1906) thought that, while people could tell whether they preferred to be in state A or state B, they could not always tell by how much they preferred A to B. He suggested that utility was measurable only on an ordinal scale (i.e., one capable of ranking alternatives, but not capable of sustaining a common unit of

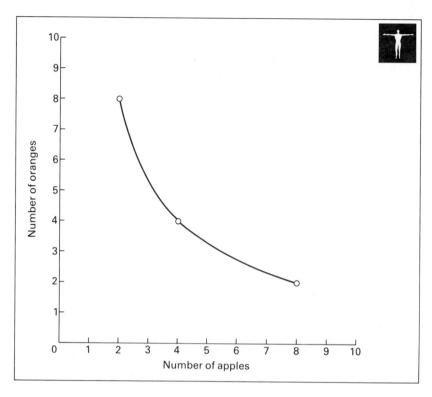

**Figure 3.1**  Indifference curve between oranges and apples. The consumer is indifferent in choosing between those combinations of oranges and apples that are represented by points on the curve.

measurement). Economists now distinguish between *cardinal utility* (measurable on an interval scale) and *ordinal utility* (measurable on an ordinal scale). It is meaningless to speak of the slope, or marginal utility, of an ordinal utility function, because such a function cannot be differentiated. Nevertheless, it is possible to find indifference curves for ordinal utility. Pareto showed that it is possible to draw an indifference map simply by finding the combinations of states among which the person is indifferent. This formulation assumes that higher indifference curves have higher utility, but does not specify how much greater that utility is.

It is possible to deduce from indifference curves all the theorems that were originally deduced from cardinal utility measures (Johnson 1913; Slutsky 1915). Hicks and Allen (1934) attempted to purge the theory of choice of its last introspective elements. Starting from the conventional economic view of indifference curves as derived from an imaginary questionnaire, they derived the usual conclusions about consumer demand without referring to notions of utility. This behaviorist approach was developed further by Samuelson (1938), who showed that indifference curves, and the entire theory of consumer choice, can be derived simply from the observation of choices among the possible purchases available to a consumer. Each choice defines a point and a slope in a commodity space. A whole family of such slopes can be combined mathematically into an indifference hyperplane. A family of such hyperplanes forms an indifference map. This is called the *revealed preference approach* (Samuelson 1948).

While these developments heralded theoretical advances, culminating in the realization that the different versions are mathematically equivalent (Wold 1952), little empirical progress was made. Indeed, Edwards (1954) concluded that "there seems to be little prospect of using large-scale economic data to fill in the empirical content of the theory of individual decision making." Classical utility theory retains its position in consumer economics because it involves a simple set of assumptions that seem intuitively satisfying. Empirical attempts to verify the theory have not been successful, but this may be the result of failure to identify the nature of the psychological processes involved. Most empirical studies are based on the assumption that human choice is a purely cognitive process. We will suggest reasons for doubting this.

## 3.2 Human and Animal Economics

Economics is usually regarded as the study of activities that involve exchange transactions among humans. Prominent among these activities is choosing how to allocate scarce resources among a variety of alternative uses. Economics is normally considered a human activity, but many of its attributes also occur in other species. Perhaps we should reserve judgement about the definition of economics until we have compared human economic behavior with that of other species.

Economists usually distinguish between macroeconomics and microeconomics. The former can be defined as the aggregate performance of all the parts of the economy, including the aggregates of income, employment, and prices. Microeconomics is the study of the particular incomes and prices that make up the aggregates; it is especially concerned with the choices made by individuals between work and leisure and among various economic goods. The biological counterparts of macroeconomics are ecology and evolu-

tionary theory; those of microeconomics are ethology and behavioral ecology (McFarland and Houston 1981).

A global economy should be organized in such a way that the
maximum possible value is attained. This usually requires the
allocation of scarce resources, such as food, time, and money,
among competing ends. However, different opinions as to what is
of maximum value will usually mean that different competing
ends are considered to be of prime importance.

The concept of value itself is often a matter of political ideology.
To socialists, maximum value may be the equilavent of the
greatest happiness for the greatest number; to free-enterprise capi-
talists, it may be the greatest freedom of choice; to fascists, it may
be the greatest good for the state. In some economies, therefore,
the resources will be allocated among individual people; in others
they will be allocated among commercial companies or govern-
ment agencies.

Economic principles apply not only to humans but to all animal
species. All animals have to allocate scarce means among competing ends. The scarce means may be energy, nutrients, or time. The
competing ends may be growth and reproduction (as in a life-
history study), or one activity versus another (as in a study of
everyday decision-making).

At the global level, where economists think in terms of value,
biologists account for behavior in terms of fitness. Just as some
aspects of human economic structure or behavior may be said to
have greater social value than others, so some aspects of animal
physiology or behavior have greater fitness than others. Thus, there
is a parallel between the basic concepts of economics and biology,
as illustrated in figure 3.2.

At the microeconomic level (the level of individual decision-
making), money is spent in such a way that utility is maximized.
As we have seen, utility is a notional measure of the psychological
value of goods, leisure, and so on. Many biologists believe that
animals behave in such a way as to maximize (or to minimize)
some entity, sometimes called the *cost*. This is a notional measure
of the contribution to fitness of the state of the animal and of its
behavior. Note that we say *notional* measure. The animal has no
information as to the real cost. It only has a preprogrammed notion
of the cost. We do not mean by this that the notion is cognitive,
but merely that the information is somehow built into the animal.
As figure 3.2 shows, there is a fairly obvious parallel between cost

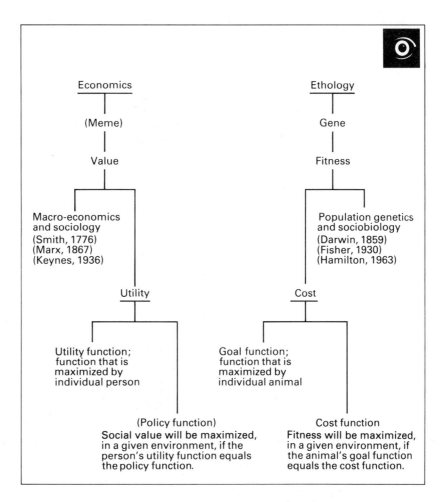

**Figure 3.2** Parallel concepts in economics and ethology. The names in parentheses are those of the most important contributors (with the dates of their major works) to microeconomics and population biology. (After McFarland and Houston 1981.)

and utility. The function that is maximized by rational economic man is generally called the *utility function*. The equivalent function in animal behavior is the *goal function*.

We must distinguish between the function that the animal actually maximizes (the objective function) and the function that it should maximize if it is perfectly adapted to the environment. The latter function, called the *cost function*, is essentially a property of the environment rather than of the individual. If an animal were perfectly adapted to its environment, then the objective function and the cost function would be identical. In reality, animals are rarely perfectly adapted, owing to evolutionary lag, genetic variation between individuals, and competition between individuals (McFarland and Houston 1981).

In economics it appears that the term *utility function* is used to denote both the function maximized by the individual and the function that the individual should maximize to attain maximum social value in a given environment. The latter may be more usefully called a *policy function*. In everyday life we are continually under pressure to change our utility functions so as to make them conform with some currently fashionable policy function. As children we may be pressed by our parents to give up socially undesirable habits. As adults we are pressed by governments to reduce the utility of smoking, or other activities considered to be contrary to current public health policy.

In likening an animal to an economic consumer, we should distinguish between the common currency of decision-making (which is utility or cost) and the price or energy cost of behavior (McFarland and Houston 1981). The energy cost is sometimes, but not always, a common factor in the alternative possible activities open to an animal. It is a mistake, therefore, to regard energy as a common currency for decision-making, even though it may be a common factor in particular cases. Energy will be a factor common to all activities only if its availability acts as a constraint in the circumstances being considered. An everyday economic example may help to make this distinction clear: Suppose a person enters a supermarket to purchase a variety of goods. Associated with each possible item of purchase will be a utility function, the utilities of particular goods depending on the shopper's preferences and experience. The concept of utility makes it possible to envisage how very different items are compared. A person may obtain the same utility from a packet of soap as from a bottle of soy sauce. Utility is thus the currency by which different items are evaluated. However, another currency common to all items is money. If the shopper has a limited amount of money to spend, then money acts as a constraint on the amount of goods that can be purchased. However, money is not always the relevant constraint. A shopper in a hurry may carry more money than can be spent in the time available, and it may turn out that this shopper's choice when he or she is pressed for time is different from that of a shopper with limited cash. (For an example in terms of animal behavior, see Winterhalder 1983.)

There are many constraints that may impinge on an animal's choice behavior, and these may vary with circumstances. But only the constraint that bites at the time is important. For this reason, time and energy should not be confused with utility or cost. In the analogy between an animal and an economic consumer, cost is equivalent to utility, energy is equivalent to money, and time plays the same role in both systems.

An animal can earn energy by foraging, just as a person can earn money by working. The energy or money may be spent on various other activities. Over and above the basic continuous level of metabolic expenditure (or subsistence expenditure, in the human case), an animal can save energy by depositing fat and hoarding food, and a person can save money by banking it or putting it in a sock. Alternatively, an animal can spend energy on various activities, including foraging, and a person can spend money on goods or activities, including working. It is also possible to consider some humans as energy-spending animals (Winterhalder 1981; McFarland 1989b).

A human worker divides the time available into time spent working and time spent at leisure. On a plot of daily hours of work against total income, we can represent wage rates as lines fanning out from the origin, as in figure 3.3. The higher the wage rate, the greater the slope of the line. Usually the wage rate is shown in monetary terms, but it is also possible to think of income as the energy that is gained from work such as foraging (Allison 1983; McFa.'and 1989b). Assuming that a worker is free to choose the amount of work he does each day, we can expect that a tradeoff between work and leisure will occur and will result in a set of indifference curves tangential to the wage-rate lines. All points on a particular indifference curve have equal utility to the worker. The optimum number of working hours, at a particular wage rate, is

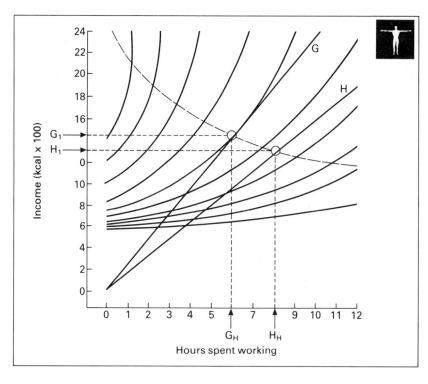

**Figure 3.3** A simple economic model for foraging among the !Kung San. G is the wage rate for gathering, H that for hunting. The dashed curve is the labor-supply function; the solid curves are the iso-utility functions. (After McFarland 1989b.)

given by the point on the line that attains the greatest utility: the point at which the highest possible indifference curve is reached. By joining the optimum points on all of the wage rates, we get the labor-supply curve of economic theory.

The point here is that the analogies between money and energy and between cost and utility enable us to look at animals and humans in the same (economic) terms. If the same economic principles apply to both animals and humans, then we can draw conclusions that apply to both.

The same type of argument can be applied to machines. Most often a machine arises from a design concept, which is shaped by consideration of market forces into a particular design evaluation. In the consideration of the design concept for a mobile robot, for example, the design evaluation would depend on the nature of the potential customers (whether they are likely to favor a stolid and reliable robot to a cheap and cheerful one, for example), on the nature of the competition from other manufacturers, and so on. As

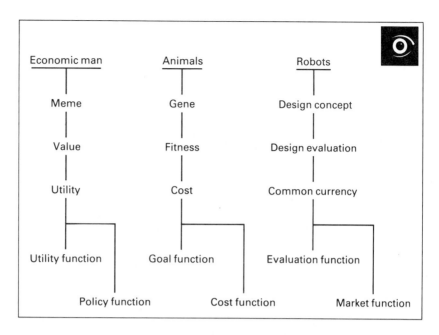

**Figure 3.4** Parallel concepts in economics, ethology, and robotics.

we have seen, a robot capable of more than one activity must, in effect, make decisions on the basis of some common currency, equivalent to utility in economics and cost in biology. (See figure 3.4.) Based upon this common currency, there will be some intrinsic maximand, equivalent to the utility function and the goal function. We have called this the *evaluation function*. Similarly, there will be some extrinsic maximand, equivalent to the policy function and the cost function. To illustrate these analogies, it might be helpful to consider, as an example, a robot as an economic consumer.

### 3.3 A Robot as an Economic Consumer

Consider a robot designed to do kitchen chores. As a human shopper in a supermarket has money to spend, the robot has energy to spend. Whereas the shopper derives utility from the goods purchased, the robot derives utility from fulfilling its kitchen duties with respect to certain criteria. Thus, the robot gains utility from the cleanliness of the floor, as shown in figure 3.5. This curve is an example of an evaluation function. The equivalent utility function for our shopper might be buying wooden spoons. Beyond a certain

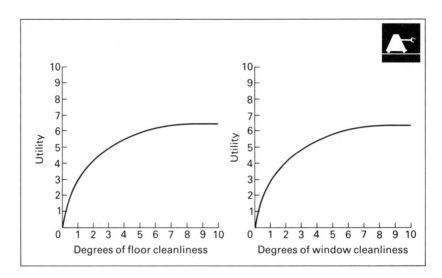

**Figure 3.5** Two hypothetical utility functions for a housekeeping robot.

degree of cleanliness the robot gains no further utility, and beyond a certain number of wooden spoons the shopper gains no further utility. The amount of utility gained by floor-cleaning, or by purchasing another wooden spoon, depends upon the current state of the floor, or the current number of spoons owned.

Suppose the prime considerations for the robot, on a particular day, are floor cleaning and window cleaning, and those for the shopper are wooden spoons and chocolates. There will be evaluation functions for window cleanliness and utility functions for chocolates, similar to those illustrated in figure 3.5. The evaluation functions for floor and window cleanliness can be combined into a single diagram, giving a set of iso-utility curves, as shown in figure 3.6. These iso-utility curves join all points of equal utility, and figure 3.6 shows that the robot may obtain the same utility from a large degree of floor cleanliness combined with a small amount of window cleanliness as from a small degree of floor cleanliness combined with a large degree of window cleanliness. The shapes of the iso-utility curves are determined by the shapes of the corresponding evaluation functions. In terms of the shopping analogy, I might derive the same total utility from purchasing three wooden spoons and one box of chocolates as from one spoon and two boxes of chocolates. In other words, choosing between the two possibilities would be a matter of indifference to me. For this reason, iso-utility curves are often called *indifference curves* by economists.

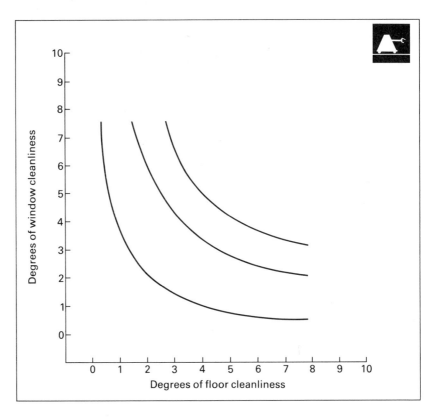

**Figure 3.6** Iso-utility functions derived from figure 3.5.

A shopper usually enters a supermarket with a certain amount of money to spend. This acts as a constraint on the amounts of goods that can be purchased. The equivalent constraint for the robot is the amount of energy that it has available to spend on cleaning, polishing, etc. For the robot there will be an energy "price" associated with each activity. Cleaning the floor may be expensive in energy; cleaning windows may be cheap. What matters to the robot is not the energy spent per minute of cleaning activity, but the amount spent per unit of cleanliness gained. Utility is connected with a change in the state of the robot (in this case, the degree of improvement it perceives). It is the energy spent per change of state that is the important factor. This is easier to see in the case of the shopper. The purchase of goods changes the shopper's state (the amounts of goods owned), so the prices of the goods indicate the money cost of changing the state.

Suppose the robot has 20 units of energy to spend. If it spends all this energy on cleaning the floor, it gains 4 degrees of improve-

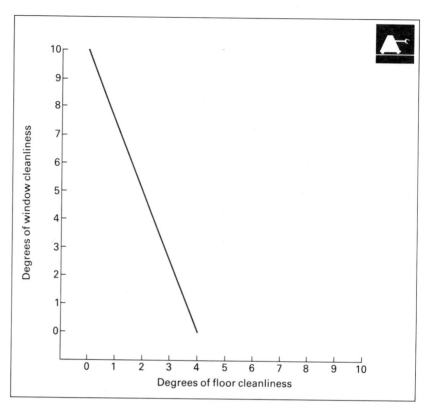

**Figure 3.7**  Budget constraint for the housekeeping robot.

ment; if it spends all the energy on cleaning windows, it gains 10 degrees of improvement. Thus, the energy price of cleaning floors is 5 units per degree of improvement, while that of cleaning windows is 2 units per degree. If the robot were to spend some energy on each activity, the energy budget would be partitioned accordingly. This possibility is indicated by the budget line in figure 3.7. Since any point on the budget line represents all the available energy, the robot's behavior is constrained to lie on or below this line.

We can superimpose figure 3.6 and 3.7 (since the axes are the same) and see which way of partitioning energy between cleaning the floor and cleaning the windows yields the greatest amount of utility. Figure 3.8 shows that the maximum amount of utility is gained by spending 12 units of energy to obtain 6 degrees of window cleanliness and 8 units on 1.6 degrees of floor cleanliness.

Two factors affect the combination that yields the highest utility: the shapes of the iso-utility curves and the slope of the budget line. The shape of an iso-utility curve is determined by the evalua-

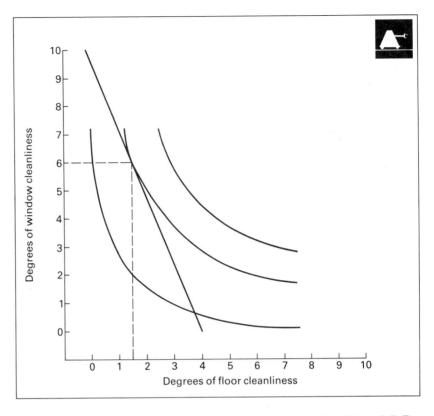

**Figure 3.8** Iso-utility functions from figure 3.6 superimposed on the budget line of figure 3.7. The optimal combination of floor and window cleanliness is indicated by the dashed lines.

tion functions (see figure 3.6), and the slope of the budget line is determined by the relative prices of the two commodities.

In consumer economics, a person who has less money to spend can purchase a lesser amount of goods, and there is a parallel shift in the budget line. Similarly, if our robot has less energy to spend, then the budget constraint will be more severe; however, there will be no change in robot's choice behavior, because the relative prices of the alternatives remain unaltered. However, if the price of a particular activity is altered, then there is a shift in the relative prices of the alternatives. Thus, if the energy price of a particular activity is lowered, then more can be undertaken for the same amount of energy, and this has the effect of making the budget triangle larger. (See figure 3.9.) Thus, a price change for a single item alters the slope of the budget line and changes the corresponding choice behavior.

As the price of the consequences of an activity is progressively increased, less and less of the activity is undertaken. (See figure

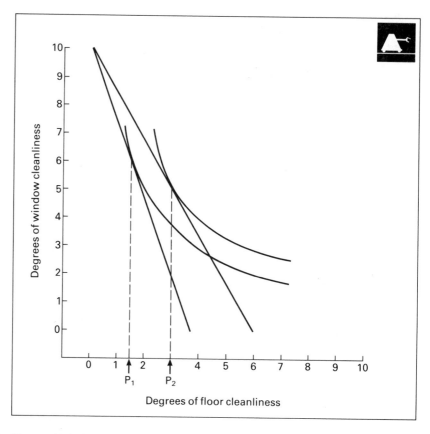

**Figure 3.9** Changes in the budget line due to changes in the price of floor cleanliness.

3.10.) In other words, the demand for the consequences of an activity falls off as the price increases. As in human and animal consumer economics, the laws of demand and substitution are inevitable consequences of maximizing utility or its equivalent. If a robot is designed so as to always make transitive choices (i.e., to be completely rational), then it will inevitably behave so as to maximize some quantity (called utility), and it will inevitably obey the demand laws of consumer economics.

Demand functions are used by economists to express the relationship between the price and the consumption of a commodity. Normally, the amount purchased by a shopper depends partly on the price. For example, when the price of coffee is increased, people continue to buy about the same amount as before, or perhaps a little less. As the price of fruit is increased, however, the demand for fruit falls off. When the price of fresh fish is increased, the demand falls markedly. Presumably, people are willing to pay more to

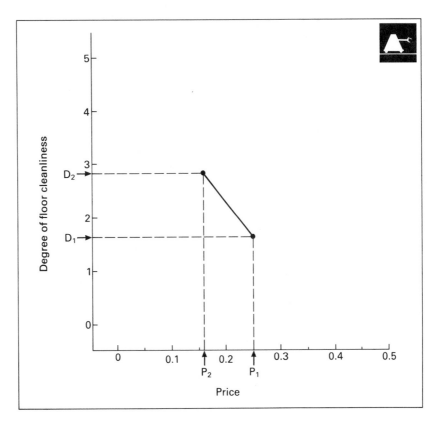

**Figure 3.10** Demand function for floor cleanliness.

maintain their coffee-drinking habits. The demand for coffee is said to be *inelastic*. If the price of fresh fish increases, however, people tend to buy less of it and to switch to substitute foods, such as meat or canned fish. The demand for fish is said to be *elastic*. The demand laws of consumer economics can be derived mathematically from the assumption that the consumer makes purchases in a way that maximizes utility.

Exactly analogous phenomena occur in animal behavior. If an animal expends a particular amount of energy on a particular activity, it usually does less of that activity if the energy requirement is increased. Numerous studies have shown that the demand functions for animals follow the same general pattern as those for humans (Allison 1983; Rachlin 1989; Stephens and Krebs 1986). The examples cover a wide variety of animals, from humans to protozoa, performing many different kinds of responses as behavioral payments for a wide variety of commodities, including food, water, sucrose, saccharin, heat, cigarettes, alcohol, and various drugs

(Allison 1983). Figure 3.11 shows some examples. As we mentioned in the previous chapter, the implication of these findings is that the behavior of many animals obeys the microeconomic laws, thus providing strong indirect evidence that animal behavior is rational.

When a commodity (or an activity) increases in price, the income of a consumer (or an animal) is effectively reduced. A consumer may buy less of the commodity for the same money (a case of elastic demand), or may pay more for the same amount of the commodity (a case of inelastic demand). In the latter case, the consumer will often have less money to spend on other goods. Thus, an increase in the price of a commodity can be thought of as a decrease in the consumer's income under conditions of constant prices. This is known as the *income effect*. Another result of one commodity's becoming more expensive is that other commodities become relatively cheaper. If the demand for the commodity whose price has risen is elastic, then the consumer buys less of that commodity and has more to spend on other commodities. This is known as the *substitution effect*. The demand for a commodity whose price has risen is usually elastic when there are good substitutes available (Allison 1983; Rachlin 1989).

In addition to minute-to-minute considerations, we should take a more global account of the time and energy budgets of humans, animals, and robots. Animals vary considerably in the time that they devote to various activities in the long term. Some aspects of behavior are essential for survival, but others (such as thermoregulatory behavior) may be important only when physiological mechanisms cannot cope. Thus, drinking is a daily necessity for some species, but other species can manage without drinking at all.

In animals, each activity has value in terms of fitness, and animals are designed to allocate priorities to activities in a general way as well as from minute to minute. Houston and McFarland (1980) approached this problem by considering a measure of the cost to an animal of abstaining from each activity in its natural repertoire. If an animal did no feeding, for instance, the cost would be high, but if it abstained from grooming the cost might be relatively low. An animal that had a high motivational tendency toward both feeding and grooming but did not have time to do both would sacrifice less, in terms of fitness, if it devoted its available time to feeding.

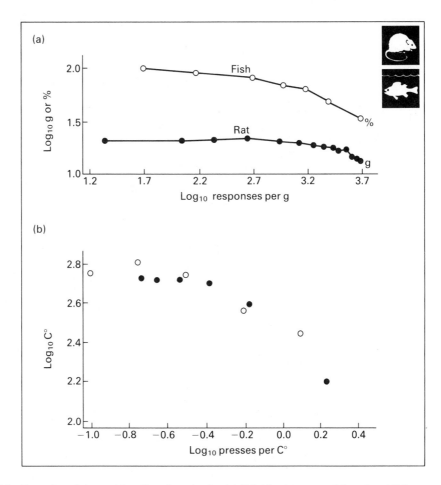

**Figure 3.11** Examples of demand functions in animals. (a) Total food consumed by rat and fish as function of behavioral price of food. (b) Heat consumption by rat as function of behavioral price of heat. (After Allison 1983.)

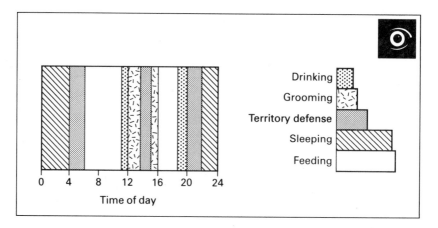

**Figure 3.12** How an animal might spend its time throughout the day. (After McFarland 1985.)

Suppose an animal fills its typical day with useful activities (figure 3.12). If the environment is much the same from day to day, the animal will adjust its activities to the time available. Suppose, however, there is a change in the environment such that it now takes much longer to obtain the normal amount of food (figure 3.13). The animal can respond to the changed circumstances by spending the same amount of time feeding as before and settling for less food. Alternatively, it can insist on the same amount of food as usual, or it can compromise between the two extremes. If the animal spent a long time obtaining the usual amount of food, it would have less time for all the other activities in its repertoire. These would have to be squashed into the remaining time. Houston and McFarland (1980) found that the extent to which an activity resists squashing can be represented by a single parameter, which they called *resilience*. In the case where the animal feeds for the normal amount of time and ends up with a reduced food intake, the resilience of feeding is relatively low, because feeding has not compressed the other activities even though the animal's hunger has increased. In the case where the animal insists on the normal amount of food, the resilience of feeding is relatively high, because feeding has ousted the other activities from the time available without itself being curtailed in any way.

*Behavioral resilience* is a measure of the extent to which the time devoted to each activity can be squashed by other activities in the animal's repertoire. It also reflects the importance of an activity in a long-term sense. During periods when time is a budget constraint, activities with low resilience will tend to be ignored.

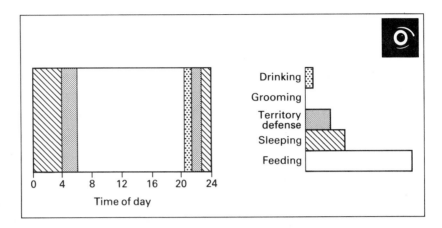

**Figure 3.13** How the animal of figure 3.12 might adjust its daily routine when required to spend much more time to obtain the same amount of food. (After McFarland 1985.)

Indeed, if an activity disappears completely from an animal's repertoire when time is rationed, we might call it a luxury or leisure activity.

Behavioral resilience is difficult to measure directly, but it can be measured indirectly by means of demand functions. The elasticities of the demand functions indicate the relative importances of the commodities (or activities) on which the person (or animal) spend money (or energy). There is a close relationship between elasticity of demand and resilience (Houston and McFarland 1980). Thus, demand functions can be used as indirect measures of resilience. If activity A has higher resilience than activity B, then A will tend to show a relatively inelastic demand function and B will show an elastic one (McFarland and Houston 1981). An example of this approach can be found in Dawkins 1983.

## 3.4 Decision-Making under Uncertainty

In the context of riskless choice, human agents are assumed to rank the alternatives according to their utilities, and to choose that with the highest utility. It is assumed that the human decision-maker "knows" for certain what utility will be gained as a consequence of the chosen behavior. If the decision-maker does not know for certain what the outcome will be, the choice is either risky or uncertain. If some probability can be associated with the future consequences of an activity (e.g., calling "heads" at the flip of a coin), the choice of that activity is risky. If no probability can be associated with the consequences (as in the case of betting that miniskirts will be in fashion in the year 2000), the choice is simply uncertain. Most models of risky choice are based on the maximization of some form of expectation. The expected value of a bet, for example, is found by multiplying the value of each possible outcome by its probability of occurrence and summing these products across all possible outcomes. Unfortunately, human (and animal) decision-makers do not always pick the option with the highest expected value.

Consideration of problems in the field of insurance led Bernoulli (1738) to suggest that humans act so as to maximize expected utility, not expected value. However, it was a long time before a satisfactory theory was developed. The modern period of the study of risky decisions was heralded by John von Neumann and Oscar Morgenstern's monumental work *The Theory of Games and Economic Behavior* (1944), in which they showed how a lottery (a situation in which the outcome is determined in a probabilistic manner) could be included in a ranking of deterministic choices. The gambler's perceptions of value are related to monetary rewards via a utility function. The expected utility hypothesis claims that even complicated sets of preferences (including lotteries) can be related to a utility function. To take a simple example, suppose a person is indifferent between a certainty of $7 and a 50 percent chance of gaining $10 or nothing. Assume that the person attaches the same utility to each of these two possibilities. Define the utility of $0 as 0 utiles (the name of a unit of utility), and that of $10 as 10 utiles (these arbitrary definitions simply scale the utility function). The utility of $7 can be calculated as follows:

$$U(\$7) = 0.5U(\$10) + 0.5U(\$0) = 0.5(10) + 0.5(0) = 5 \text{ utiles.}$$

By varying the probabilities and making use of the utilities already obtained, it is possible to discover the utility of any other amount of money.

Bunn (1982) gives a more complicated example. He imagines a small newsagent who pays 3 cents for each paper and sells them for 5 cents. Those unsold have no value. If $n$ is the number ordered and $x$ is the number demanded, then the payoff is given by

$$0.5x - 0.3n \quad \text{if } x \le n,$$

$$0.5n - 0.3n \quad \text{if } x \ge n.$$

| A \ θ | \multicolumn{9}{c}{Number of papers demanded} |
|---|---|---|---|---|---|---|---|---|---|
| | 16 | 17 | 18 | 19 | 20 | 21 | 22 | 23 | 24 |
| 16 | 3·2 | 3·2 | 3·2 | 3·2 | 3·2 | 3·2 | 3·2 | 3·2 | 3·2 |
| 17 | 2·9 | 3·4 | 3·4 | 3·4 | 3·4 | 3·4 | 3·4 | 3·4 | 3·4 |
| 18 | 2·6 | 3·1 | 3·6 | 3·6 | 3·6 | 3·6 | 3·6 | 3·6 | 3·6 |
| 19 | 2·3 | 2·8 | 3·3 | 3·8 | 3·8 | 3·8 | 3·8 | 3·8 | 3·8 |
| 20 | 2·0 | 2·5 | 3·0 | 3·5 | 4·0 | 4·0 | 4·0 | 4·0 | 4·0 |
| 21 | 1·7 | 2·2 | 2·7 | 3·2 | 3·7 | 4·2 | 4·2 | 4·2 | 4·2 |
| 22 | 1·4 | 1·9 | 2·4 | 2·9 | 3·4 | 3·9 | 4·4 | 4·4 | 4·4 |
| 23 | 1·1 | 1·6 | 2·1 | 2·6 | 3·1 | 3·6 | 4·1 | 4·6 | 4·6 |
| 24 | 0·8 | 1·3 | 1·8 | 2·3 | 2·8 | 3·3 | 3·8 | 4·3 | 4·8 |

(Row label: Number of papers ordered)

**Figure 3.14** Payoff matrix for newspaper dealer. (After Bunn 1982.)

A payoff matrix for this example is shown in figure 3.14. If the newsagent stocks 18 newspapers and the demand is only 16, then the payoff is $2.60. If he buys 18 and sells them all, the payoff is $3.60. If he stocked 24 and sold them all, the payoff would be $4.80, but there would be a risk that he would sell only 16, with a payoff of only 80 cents. This risk may be too much to bear, relative to the certain return of $3.20 if only 16 are ordered. Thus, the newsagent is in a dilemma of choosing between a safe low return and a risky high return.

There are various decision criteria which the newsagent might employ here. Some are reviewed by Bunn (1982). An example is the expected-value criterion, which suggests that a human agent takes the action that has the maximum expected payoff value. The problem is that the criteria are somewhat arbitrary, but the decision-maker has to choose between them. Bunn shows that the problem of selecting a decision criterion can be reduced to computing appropriate certainty equivalents.

Suppose a person had an opportunity to receive $100 with a probability of 0.5, or $0 with a probability of 0.5. By the expected-value criterion, this would be as good as receiving $50 with certainty. In other words, the certainty equivalent for this opportunity would be

$$CE = \$(100 \times 0.5) + \$(0 \times 0.5) = \$50.$$

If the person did indeed have no preference between a certainty of $50 and either $100 or $0 based upon the toss of a coin, then the expected value would be an appropriate criterion for this type of decision. On the other hand, the person may be averse to the risk of gaining nothing, especially if a fee has to be paid for the opportunity. A wealthy person may be prepared to pay a greater fee for the chance of gaining $100 than a poor person. Moreover, a wealthy person may be prefer the risk of a large profit to the certainty of a small profit when the fee is $300 but may prefer the certainty of a small profit to the risk of a large profit (with the same odds) when the fee is $300,000. Thus, the certainty equivalent, and therefore the decision criterion for uncertain prospects, is a matter of the decision-maker's attitude toward risk.

In the general decision problem, under uncertainty the consequences of a possible activity are associated with a probability distribution over the elements of the consequences (as in a payoff matrix). For any given set of consequences, we can define a value function, which refers to comparisons without uncertainty (Bunn 1982, p. 77). Such a value function is known as a *utility function* if the consequences involve at least one lottery. Von Neumann and Morgenstern (1944) showed that the utility of a lottery can be derived as the expected utility of the set of consequences. The decision-maker chooses the activity for which the expected utility is maximized.

In the newsagent example, the best and worst outcomes (see figure 3.14) are $4.80 and $0.80. By definition, these are given the end-point utilities 1 and 0. Thus,

$$U(0.8) = 0$$

and

$$U(4.8) = 1.$$

The certainty equivalent giving $0.80 with probability 0.5 or $4.80 with probability 0.5 is found; it has an expected utility of 0.5. Suppose that the newsagent gave $2 as the certainty equivalent for that prospect. We would then have

$$U(2) = 0.5u(0.8) + 0.5u(4.8).$$

We now have another point on the utility-function curve:

$$U(2) = 0.5.$$

The certainty equivalent for $2 with probability 0.5 and $4.8 with probability 0.5 then gives us the value on the curve for an expected utility of 0.75. Let us suppose that the newsagent gives $3.30, so that

$$U(3.3) = 0.75.$$

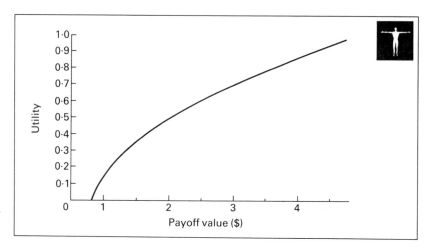

**Figure 3.15**  The newspaper dealer's utility function. (After Bunn 1982.)

Similarly, if the newsagent said that he would have no preference between a certain outcome of $1.20 and the uncertain prospect of $0.80 with probability 0.5 and $2 with probability 0.5, we would have U(1.2) = 0.25, giving a total of five points on the utility function. Further points could be obtained by continuing the process of finding certainty equivalents for equally probable outcomes of known utilities. These points give the utility function shown in figure 3.15.

It is now possible to map all the payoff values plotted in monetary terms in figure 3.14 into utility values, using the utility function of figure 3.15. This results in figure 3.16. It is also possible to estimate the subjective expected probabilities for each action. The advantage of this approach is that it allows us to replace complex decision problems (from the point of view of the decision-maker) with a few contrived choices whose implications are fairly obvious. Thus, the basic attitude of the decision-maker—in particular, his risk-averse, risk-neutral, or risk-prone attitude—can easily be identified.

In relation to attitudes to risk, consider a hypothetical choice between a certain payoff and a lottery with the same mean value. A decision-maker who is indifferent between the two is said to be *risk-neutral*. A decision-maker who prefers the certain outcome to the lottery is *risk-averse*, and one who prefers the lottery is *risk-prone*. Different utility functions are associated with these three attitudes toward risk, as shown in figure 3.17. Suppose a decision-maker is offered an even bet, and the probability of gaining the

| A \ θ | Number of papers demanded | | | | | | | | |
|---|---|---|---|---|---|---|---|---|---|
| | 16 | 17 | 18 | 19 | 20 | 21 | 22 | 23 | 24 |
| 16 | 0·73 | 0·73 | 0·73 | 0·73 | 0·73 | 0·73 | 0·73 | 0·73 | 0·73 |
| 17 | 0·68 | 0·77 | 0·77 | 0·77 | 0·77 | 0·77 | 0·77 | 0·77 | 0·77 |
| 18 | 0·62 | 0·71 | 0·8 | 0·8 | 0·8 | 0·8 | 0·8 | 0·8 | 0·8 |
| 19 | 0·56 | 0·66 | 0·75 | 0·84 | 0·84 | 0·84 | 0·84 | 0·84 | 0·84 |
| 20 | 0·5 | 0·6 | 0·69 | 0·78 | 0·88 | 0·88 | 0·88 | 0·88 | 0·88 |
| 21 | 0·42 | 0·54 | 0·64 | 0·73 | 0·82 | 0·9 | 0·9 | 0·9 | 0·9 |
| 22 | 0·33 | 0·48 | 0·58 | 0·68 | 0·77 | 0·86 | 0·94 | 0·94 | 0·94 |
| 23 | 0.25 | 0·39 | 0·52 | 0·62 | 0·71 | 0·8 | 0·89 | 0·97 | 0·97 |
| 24 | 0 | 0·28 | 0·45 | 0.56 | 0·66 | 0·75 | 0·84 | 0·1 | 0·1 |

Number of papers ordered (row label A)

**Figure 3.16**  The newspaper dealer's utility matrix. (After Bunn 1982.)

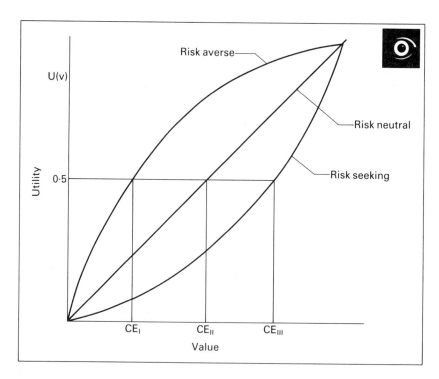

**Figure 3.17**  Typical utility curves for three risk attitudes, where v is the value of the gamble and U(v) is utility as a function of the value. The CEs are the certainty equivalents for the three attitudes toward risk. (After Bunn 1982.)

reward is the same as that of losing it (i.e., 0.5). If the decision-maker's utility function is concave-down, the utility gained from winning is smaller than that lost from losing, and the decision-maker should be risk-averse. If the utility function is concave-up, the utility gained from winning is larger than that lost from losing the bet, and the decision-maker should be risk-prone, as illustrated in figure 3.18.

In consumer economics, utility functions are usually assumed to obey the law of decreasing marginal utility. We have seen that a decision-maker with this type of utility function should be risk-averse. However, the degree of sensitivity to risk will depend on the shape of the function, as indicated in figure 3.19. The two decision-makers portrayed in this example (A and B) have different certainty equivalents (CE = 8 in the case of A, and CE = 4 in the case of B). B is more risk-averse than A, because there is a greater difference between B's certainty equivalent and the mean of the probability distribution than is the case for A. This difference (between the CE and the mean) is a measure of risk sensitivity called the *risk premium*.

If a decision-maker is faced with consequences (x) and the equivalent asset level (the relevant state variable) is $X$, then the risk premium, RP(x, X), is equal to

EV(x) − CE(x),

where EV(x) is the expected value and CE(x) is the certainty equivalent. When RP(x, X) is positive, the decision-maker is risk-averse, and the size of the risk premium for a particular value of x will depend upon $X$. Usually the risk premium decreases with $X$, reflecting a decrease in risk aversion as the assets become greater. Intuitively, the risk premium represents the maximum amount that the decision-maker is prepared to forgo to avoid the risk associated with a particular behavioral consequence.

To summarize: If outcomes are transformed through the utility function, then the operation of the expected-utility criterion will identify that activity with the highest certainty equivalent that is coherent with the preference attitude of the decision-maker as revealed in the derivation of the utility function (Bunn 1982). The maximum amount that the decision-maker is prepared to forgo to avoid the risk associated with a particular behavioral consequence can be expressed as a risk premium.

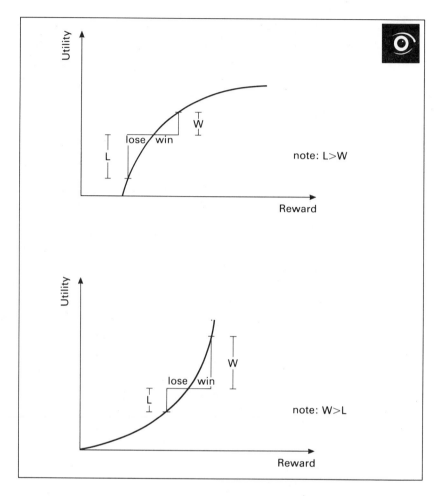

**Figure 3.18**  An illustration of the roles of concave-down (upper curve) and concave-up (lower curve) utility functions. In both cases there is a fair lottery in which the same amounts may be lost or won. Winning and losing have equal probability. In the concave-up case the consumer might win more utility than it might lose, so it prefers to take the gamble. In the concave-down case it might lose more than it might win, so it prefers not to gamble. (After Stephens and Krebs 1986.)

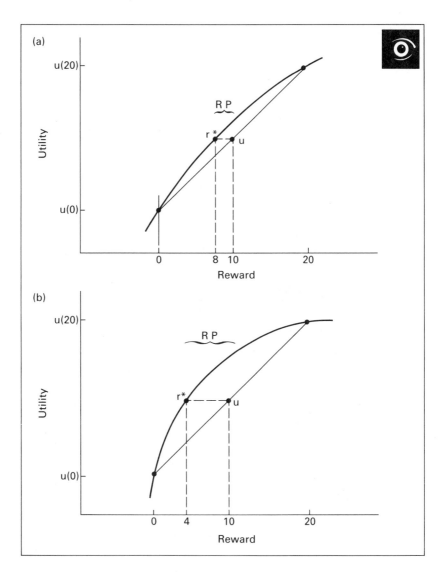

**Figure 3.19** A comparison of (a) less and (b) more risk-averse utility functions. The expected utility of a gamble can be found by connecting the points u(0) and u(20) with a straight line. The expected utility is the point u on this line corresponding to the mean reward (10 units). The certainty equivalent can be found by constructing a horizontal line from point u. The reward that specifies the point (r*) of intersection with the utility function is the certainty equivalent. In (a) the certainty equivalent is 8 reward units and the risk premium (RP) is 2 units. In (b) the certainty equivalent is 4 units and the risk premium is 6 units. (After Stephens and Krebs 1986.)

### 3.5 Utility and Intelligent Behavior

In chapter 1 we argued that, in defining intelligent behavior, what matters is the behavioral outcome, not the nature of the mechanism by which the outcome is achieved. Behavior is intelligent only by virtue of its effect on the surrounding environment. Intelligent behavior requires judgement, and the consequences of the behavior must be judged in relation to some criteria of intelligence.

The criteria of intelligence for animals relate to natural selection, whereas those for robots relate to market forces. Cooper (1987) maintains that the theory of rational choice under uncertainty can be mathematically reduced to a basis of evolutionary theory. In other words, it is of evolutionary advantage for animals to be rational. We should note, however, that the entity (e.g., expected utility) maximized by a rational agent is a property of the individual, and will vary from one individual to another. For an agent to exhibit intelligent behavior, it is not sufficient for its behavior to be rational. In addition, the criteria that determine the utility functions must be the right criteria in relation to the environment in which the agent has to operate. In other words, although intelligent behavior is a form of adaptive behavior, in order for an agent to be adaptive its behavior must not merely be flexible; it must also change in an advantageous manner (McFarland 1991). We will discuss this topic further in the next chapter.

### Points to Remember

- Utility is a notional measure of the psychological value of goods, leisure, etc. It is a notional measure because we do not how it influences choice behavior, although we can assume that utility is maximized by a rational decision-maker.
- Total utility is not necessarily an additive function of the utilities attached to separate consequences of behavior. To assess total utility requires the notion of indifference (iso-utility) curves.
- Economic principles apply not only to humans but to all animal species, because all animals have to allocate scarce means among competing ends.
- Animals behave in such a way as to minimize notional cost (or maximize utility). Cost is a notional measure of the contribution to fitness of the state of the animal and of its behavior. We say *notional* measure because the animal has no information as to the real cost; it has only a (given) notion of the cost.

- We must distinguish between the notional cost that the animal minimizes and the real cost. Functions of the latter, called *cost functions*, are essentially a property of the environment rather than the individual.
- In likening an animal to an economic consumer, we should distinguish between the common currency of decision-making, which is utility or cost, and the price or energy cost of behavior. The energy cost is sometimes, but not always, a common factor in the alternative possible activities open to an animal. It is a mistake, therefore, to regard energy as a common currency for decision-making, even though it may be a common factor in particular cases. Energy will be a factor common to all activities only if energy availability acts as a constraint in the circumstances being considered.
- There are many constraints that may impinge on an animal's choice behavior. These may vary with the circumstances. Only the constraint that bites at the time is important. For this reason, time and energy should not be confused with utility or cost. In the analogy between an animal and an economic consumer, cost is equivalent to utility, energy is equivalent to money, and time plays the same role in both systems.
- Economists use demand functions to express the relationship between the price and the consumption of a commodity. The demand laws of consumer economics can be derived mathematically from the assumption that the consumer makes purchases in a way that maximizes utility. Exactly analogous phenomena occur in animal behavior. If an animal expends a particular amount of energy on a particular activity, then it usually does less of that activity if the energy requirement is increased. Numerous studies have shown that the demand functions of animals follow the same general pattern as those of humans. The same principles can be applied to machines.
- If the decision-maker does not know for certain what the outcome will be, the choice is either risky or uncertain. If some probability can be associated with the future consequences of an activity, the choice of that activity is risky. If no probability can be associated with the consequences), the choice is simply uncertain.
- Most models of risky choice are based on the maximization of some form of expectation. The expected value is found by multiplying the value of each possible outcome by its probability of occurrence and summing these products across all possible out-

comes. The most widely accepted model maintains that the decision-maker chooses the activity for which the expected utility (not the expected value) is maximized.

- If outcomes are transformed through a utility function, the operation of the expected-utility criterion will identify that activity with the highest certainty equivalent that is coherent with the preference attitude of the decision-maker as revealed in the derivation of the utility function.

- A decision-maker who is indifferent between a certain payoff and a lottery with the same mean value is said to be risk-neutral. A decision-maker who prefers the certain outcome to the lottery is risk-averse, and one who prefers the lottery is risk-prone. Different utility functions are associated with these three attitudes toward risk.

- The risk premium represents the maximum amount that the decision-maker is prepared to forgo to avoid the risk associated with a particular behavioral consequence.

# 4 State and Cost

In this chapter we introduce two concepts that will be important in our subsequent discussions of intelligent behavior: state and cost. By *state* we mean physical state, in the normal scientific sense. The state is specified by the values of the essential state variables, which correspond (ideally) to the degrees of freedom of the system. By *cost* we mean a decrement in the fitness of an animal or a decrement in the market value of a machine.

## 4.1 Changes of State in Animals

At any particular time, an animal is in a specific physiological state, which is monitored by the brain. The animal's observed behavior is determined by the animal's brain in accordance with this monitored state and with the animal's perception of environmental stimuli. The combined physiological and perceptual state, as represented in the brain, is called the *motivational state* of the animal. It includes factors relevant to incipient activities, as well as factors relevant to the animal's current behavior.

The motivational state of an animal at any particular time depends on the animal's physiological state, on the cue state arising from its perception of the external world, and on the consequences of its current behavior. The relationship among these factors has been discussed at some length elsewhere (McFarland and Sibly 1972; Sibly and McFarland 1974; McFarland and Houston 1981). For nontechnical accounts see Huntingford 1984; Halliday and Slater 1983; McFarland 1985). Here we will merely outline the situation.

An animal's physiological state can be represented as a point in a physiological space (see figure 4.1). The axes of the space are the important physiological variables, such as temperature. The space is bounded by the tolerance limits for these variables. As the state approaches the lethal boundary, increasingly desperate physiological and behavioral mechanisms come into play. Many of these mechanisms will be very stereotyped and specific, like the panting

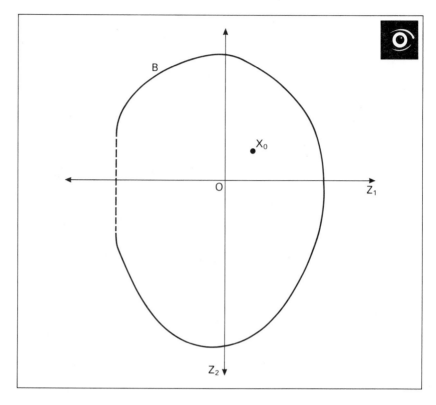

**Figure 4.1**  A two-dimensional physiological space. $O$ = origin, B = lethal boundary, $X_0$ = current state, $Z_1$ = axis of a quantity-limited variable, $Z_2$ = axis of an unconstrained variable. (After Sibly and McFarland 1974.)

that occurs when a bird's brain temperature reaches a threshold. The region of the state space within which such emergency mechanisms come into play (see figure 4.2) has been called *purgatory* (McFarland, 1989). If these automatic restorative mechanisms break down, or if they fail to stop the drift in state, then the animal will die.

The origin of the physiological state space is characterized by biochemical optima (McFarland and Houston 1981). In this region the animal has no physiological imbalances. It does not need to regulate its temperature, to feed, to drink, or to perform any other homeostatic behavior. It therefore has more time for other types of behavior. One would expect, from an evolutionary point of view, that the animal would be designed to be motivated toward reproduction, hibernation, or migration when its state entered this region. In other words: When food is plentiful, time and energy are available for those activities that more directly promote reproduc-

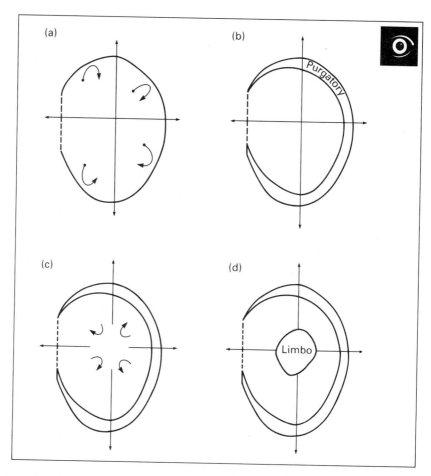

**Figure 4.2** Architecture of the physiological space in animals. (a) Trajectories in the state space are repelled from the lethal boundary by physiological emergency mechanisms. This leads to a region, called *purgatory* (b), in which the animal is under physiological strain. (c) Trajectories in the state space turn back from the origin by physiological mechanisms designed to take advantage of the favorable situation, creating a region, called *limbo* (d), which is not usually penetrated under natural conditions. (After McFarland 1989b.)

tive success, or that ensure survival in anticipated hard conditions. As soon as the animal indulges in one of these activities, the consequent time and energy expenditures ensure that the trajectory moves away from the origin. Thus, it is probable that the origin is never reached under natural conditions. This region of the state space has been called *limbo*. It has been suggested that animals may enter this state when, as in captivity, they have plentiful material resources but are unable to carry out their normal sexual and political activities (McFarland 1989b).

The animal's motivational state can be represented by a point in a motivational space. The axes of this space are the important motivational stimuli, such as the degree of thirst or the strength of some external stimulus. Strictly, the motivational space is a subset of the physiological space, though the relationship between the two is not straightforward (Sibly and McFarland 1974).

Animals' sensory abilities, like those of humans, may be described in terms of the physical attributes of the stimuli. But this does not tell us about the animal's subjective assessment of the stimulus. In motivational studies, we may wish to know what importance an animal attaches to the various aspects of a stimulus situation. The most successful attempts to determine this have been those in which the animal is persuaded, experimentally, to reveal its internal standards of comparison among stimuli.

A study of this type was conducted by Baerends and Kruijt (1973) on egg recognition in herring gulls. These birds lay three eggs in a shallow nest on the ground, and they retrieve eggs that have rolled out of the nest—including dummy eggs, provided they resemble real eggs in certain respects. Baerends and Kruijt set out to discover the features by which herring gulls recognize an egg in this type of situation. By systematically removing eggs from the nest and placing dummy eggs on the rim of the nest, they were able to construct a quantitative model of the main features of egg recognition. This model is illustrated in figure 4.3.

Four types of dummy eggs—green-speckled, plain green, plain brown, and cylindrical brown-speckled—are compared with a standard-size series of dummy eggs having the same brown-speckled coloration as real eggs. Apparently, the gulls prefer a green background to the normal brown background. They also prefer eggs with speckles to eggs without speckles. More important, however, is the finding that the differences among eggs of different sizes remain the same when other features, such as coloration, are

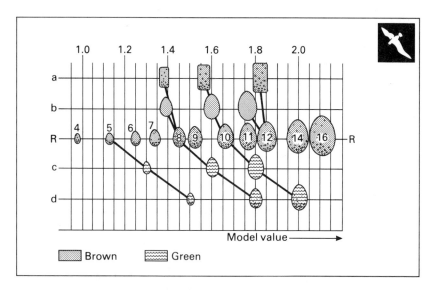

**Figure 4.3**  Results of egg-preference tests in herring gulls. The average values for various egg dummies are shown in relation to the standard-size series R. The dummies used were (a) brown, speckled, block-shaped, (b) brown, unspeckled, egg-shaped, (c) green, unspeckled, egg-shaped, and (d) green, speckled, egg-shaped. The numbers 4 through 16 indicate egg size. Equal distances between points on the model value scale imply equal preference. (After Baerends and Kruijt 1973.)

changed. This means that each feature adds a specific contribution that is independent of the contribution of other features. In other words, the size, the shape, and the coloration of the eggs are additive in their effects on the animal's behavior. Such a state of affairs had been proposed long ago (Seitz 1940) and called the *law of heterogeneous summation*. This law states that the independent and heterogeneous features of a stimulus situation are additive in their effects on behavior. Studies of other species have come to similar conclusions (Leong 1969; Heiligenberg et al. 1972), although the various aspects of a complex stimulus are not always additive (Curio 1975; Heiligenberg 1976).

Where stimulus summation operates within a relatively restricted range of features, such as those pertaining to egg recognition, the additive components can be combined into a single index called the *cue strength* (McFarland and Houston 1981). Thus, all the additive cues involved in egg recognition can be combined into a single cue strength for egg-recognition features and represented along a single dimension, as shown in figure 4.4. Other independent features of the egg-retrieval situation, such as the distance of the egg from the nest, must be represented along a different dimen-

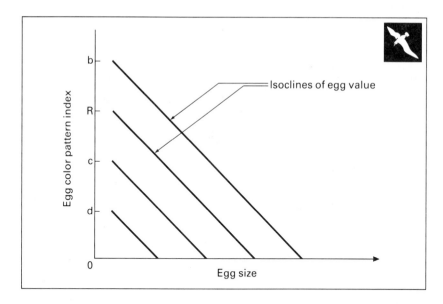

**Figure 4.4** Cue space for egg value. The parallel isoclines indicate that egg color pattern and egg size are additive in their effects and could be represented by a single index of egg value. (After McFarland 1985.)

sion (figure 4.5). Suppose we now measure the gull's tendency to retrieve eggs as a joint function of the stimulus properties of the egg and the distance from the nest. We would find that certain combinations of these two factors would give rise to the same retrieval tendency. The line joining all points giving rise to a certain motivational tendency is called the *motivational isocline*. When independent factors combine multiplicatively, as in the example illustrated in figure 4.5, the motivational isocline is hyperbolic in shape.

Thus, quantitative measures of the motivational effectiveness of external stimuli can be combined into an index called cue strength, and the relationships among different stimuli can be represented by a motivational isocline. For example, the tendency to seek food that arises from a high degree of hunger and a low strength of cues indicating the availability of food could be the same as the tendency due to the combination of a low degree of hunger and a high cue strength for food availability. The points representing these two different motivational states lie on the same motivational isocline, as illustrated in figure 4.6. The shape of a motivational isocline gives an indication of the way in which the various factors combine to produce a given tendency. For example, the internal

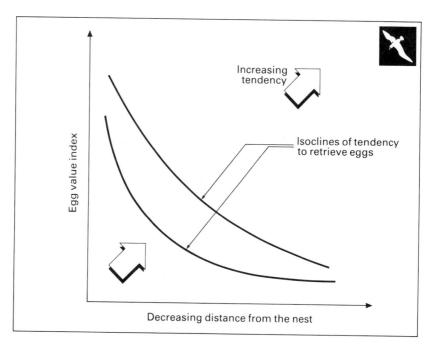

**Figure 4.5** Cue space for egg retrieval into the nest. The hyperbolic shape of the isoclines indicates that the egg value index combines multiplicatively with the distance of the egg from the nest. (After McFarland 1985.)

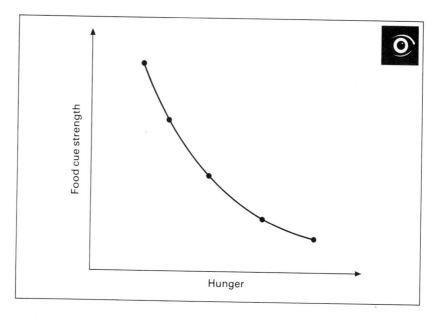

**Figure 4.6** Motivational isocline of tendency to eat, based on hunger state and food cue strength, indicating likely availability of food.

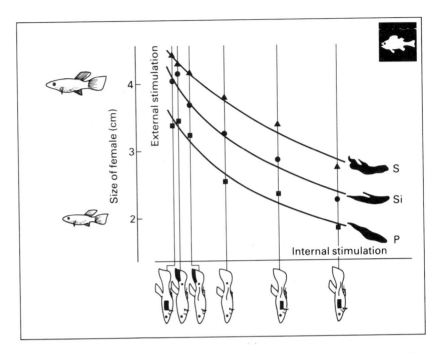

**Figure 4.7** Courtship behavior of male guppies. The strength of external stimulation (measured by the size of the female) and of the male's internal state (measured by the color pattern of the male) jointly determine the strength of the courtship tendency (measured by the typical courtship postures S, Si, and P). Each isocline joins points of equal courtship tendency. The hyperbolic isoclines suggest a multiplicative relationship between internal and external stimulation, but notice that the scaling of the axes appears to be arbitrary. For a full discussion of this problem see Houston and McFarland 1976. (After Baerends et al. 1955.)

and external stimuli controlling the courtship of the male guppy (*Lebistes reticulatus*) seem to combine multiplicatively (see figure 4.7), although we have to be careful about our scales of measurement before coming to any firm conclusion. The problem is that the experimenter is obliged to use an arbitrary scale of measurement without knowing how this corresponds to the subjective evaluation made by the animal. This problem is discussed at some length in Houston and McFarland 1976 and in McFarland and Houston 1981.

Finally, we have to consider the consequences of behavior. The consequences of an animal's behavior are due to interaction between behavior and environment. The consequences of foraging behavior, for instance, depend partly on the foraging strategy used and partly on the availability and accessibility of food. Thus, a bird foraging for insects may search in appropriate or inappropriate places, and insects may be abundant or scarce at the particular time. Similarly, the consequences of courtship activity, in terms of the reaction of the partner, depend partly on the type and intensity of the activity and partly on the motivation and behavior of the other animal.

Thus, the behavior of an animal has consequences which depend on the situation in which the behavior occurs. These consequences influence the animal's motivational state in four main ways: (1) By altering the external stimuli perceived by the animal, and hence altering the cue state. For example, in drinking at a water hole an animal may (typically) encounter other members of its species, the perception of which alters its state. (2) By direct feedback onto the motivational state. For example, the act of drinking may have short-term satiation effects that are independent of water ingestion (3) By altering the animal's physiological state. For example, ingestion of water has many physiological effects, not only on the thirst system but also on the thermoregulatory and hunger systems (McFarland 1985). (4) By preventing the animal from engaging in some other behavior. For example, an animal attentive to drinking may not notice a predator lurking by the water hole; moreover, by visiting the water hole, it has postponed some other activity.

Another important consequence of behavior is energy expenditure. Energy, and other physiological commodities such as water, are expended as a result of all behavior to a degree that depends on the level of activity, the weather, etc. Such expenditure must be taken into account because it influences the animal's state. Thus, every activity has some effect on the state. So does immobility. An immobile animal has reduced its energy expenditure (etc.) by virtue of not engaging in activities. Indeed, in terms of changes of state, the activities the animal is not performing may be as important as those it is performing at a particular time.

The consequences of behavior can be represented in a motivational state space. The motivational state of an animal is portrayed as a point in the space. As a consequence of the animal's behavior, the state changes, and so the point describes a trajectory in the space. On a two-dimensional page it is possible to portray the trajectory in only a single plane of the space, but we can imagine that the changing state describes an equivalent trajectory in a multi-dimensional space. The advantage of this type of representation is that it enables us to portray very complex changes in state in a relatively simple manner. In the case of an animal drinking

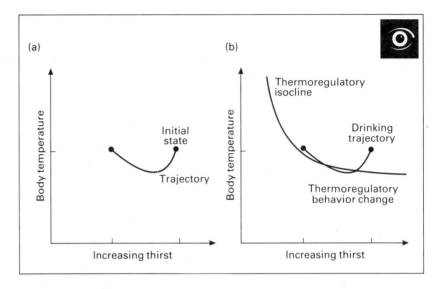

**Figure 4.8**  The consequences of behavior described as a trajectory in a motivational space. (a) The consequences of drinking cold water (a short-term reduction in body temperature and a long-term reduction in thirst). (b) Where the trajectory cuts a motivational isocline, changes in behavior can be expected. (After McFarland 1985.)

cold water, for example, we can see that decisions to change behavior depend partly on the trajectory and partly on the position of the relevant motivational isoclines, as shown in figure 4.8.

Changes in state are of prime importance in the study of motivation. Basically, the state at any particular time determines which behavior occurs. The state changes continually as a result of the animal's behavior, and this can be described as a trajectory in a state space. As the state changes, either as a result of the animal's behavior or as a result of outside influences, we can expect to see changes in behavior. Indeed, it is a cardinal rule that the behavior is uniquely determined by the state (McFarland and Sibly 1975).

## 4.2  Changes of State in Robots

The state of a freely mobile robot, like the state of an animal, is influenced both by environmental conditions and by the robot's own behavior. A robot does not have a physiology as such, but it has some equivalent state variables, such as fuel supply and operating temperature. For example, a robot will be designed to operate within certain upper and lower temperature limits, analogous to the tolerance limits of animals. At any particular time, the robot will

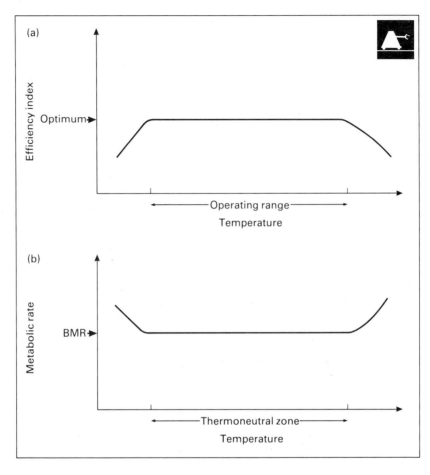

**Figure 4.9** Comparison of robot (a) and mammal (b) body temperature and its behavioral consequences.

be operating at a particular temperature (the *operating temperature*), and it is probable that this will have little effect on its performance over a wide range (the *operating temperature range*). The situation for animals is similar in principle, as is illustrated in figure 4.9.

A robot may or may not be equipped with devices for taking corrective action if the operating temperature comes close to the edge of the operating range. A robot designed to operate within a building might not require any such devices, but we can imagine that some robots are equipped with a fan that cuts in at a certain temperature threshold, or with a heater that comes on if the temperature drops too low. Such robots would be able to operate in a wider range of environments than those without any thermoregulatory devices. Similarly, we can imagine robots that take certain actions when their fuel level becomes low, and even robots that automatically refuel themselves. Thus, we can begin to construct a state space for robots similar to that of animals. A robot designed to carry out a particular task, such as laying bricks, would probably be designed to monitor other state variables pertaining to the task. Thus, a brick-laying robot should keep track of the amounts of bricks and mortar available, and of the number of bricks laid, as shown in figure 4.10. (It is worth noting that one axis of the right graph in figure 4.10 is based on the robot's perception—a cue-state variable—while the other is based on memory.)

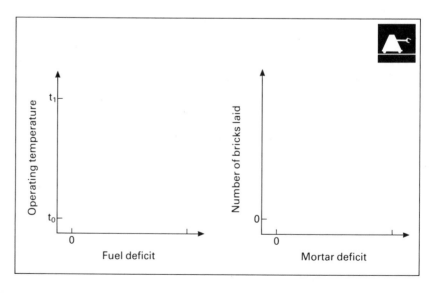

**Figure 4.10** Possible state planes for a brick-laying robot.

**Figure 4.11**  A greylag goose retrieving an egg into its nest.

We can expect that a mobile multi-task robot will be similar to an animal, but many robots are rather different from animals in that they are sessile (fixed in one place) and dedicated to a particular stereotyped task. An example is a car-washing machine. Some of these machines have sensors which can determine when the car is in the correct position. As the car goes forward they signal STOP, and if it is too far forward they may signal REVERSE. When the car is in the correct position the machine begins the car-washing routine. Some machines have the following routine: spray soap—wash-brush front—wash-brush top and sides—wash-brush back—wash-brush top and sides—spray rinse—blow-dry. Although this sequence is stereotyped, some machines can be adjusted to suit the size and shape of the car. Thus, while the overall sequence is stereotyped, the exact movements are adjusted to the circumstances. Similar behaviors occur in animals, and are usually called *fixed-action patterns*. A classic example is the egg-retrieving behavior of the greylag goose, as described by Lorenz and Tinbergen (1938). These birds nest on the ground. When an egg has been displaced a short distance from the nest, the incubating bird attempts to roll it back with its bill, as illustrated in figure 4.11. If the egg rolls slightly to one side during retrieval, the bill is moved sideways to correct for the displacement. In other words, the bird makes small adjustments in its behavior to suit the circumstances. However, if the bill loses contact with the egg, the bird does not immediately seek to reestablish contact, but first completes the retrieval movement. The fixed-action pattern consists in the bird's extending its head to reach the egg and then moving the bill along the ground to a position between its legs, whether or not the bill is still in contact with the egg.

Stereotyped behavior progresses by virtue of changes in state. The behavior is state-determined in the sense that the state of having done one activity leads to another. The car-washing machine does not attempt to dry the car before it has washed it. Therefore, the state-space approach remains relevant to even the most primitive robots.

We now come to the question of how changes of state are translated into behavior. Changes of state do not themselves cause changes in behavior. They can be thought of as analogous to mechanical displacement or electrical charge, requiring some compliance or capacitance mechanisms to exert an effort (force or voltage) on the mechanisms responsible for behavior (McFarland 1971). In the case of animal behavior, the displacements in physiological state have to be monitored by sensors that relay nervous messages to the brain. For example, the osmosity of the blood is monitored by osmoreceptors in the hypothalamus. Robots will presumably have equivalent monitors for fuel deficit, operating temperature, etc. It is important to recognize that there are two stages in this monitoring process, as illustrated in figure 4.12. The

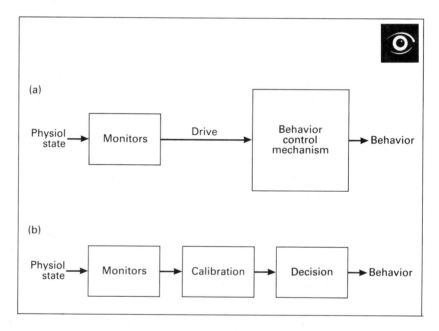

**Figure 4.12**  (a) Conventional representation of the influence of physiological state on behavior. (b) Modification to allow for division of the behavior-control mechanism into calibration and decision subsystems. (After Houston and McFarland 1976.)

first involves monitoring the state variables with appropriate sensors, while the second involves some sort of calibration of the monitored message. Obviously, the same monitored displacement in state will differ in significance for different robots or animals. Moreover, decisions have to be made among various displacements in state, all monitored by different kinds of sensors. Clearly, these parallel messages must all be calibrated in terms of their significance, or importance, to the robot or animal making the decisions. In animal behavior, this topic has been explored fairly extensively (see e.g., Houston and McFarland 1976 and McFarland and Houston 1981) and has been seen to be intimately linked with the question of cost (as we will discuss below).

## 4.3  Finite-State Automata

So far we have envisaged the state of an animal or a robot as being represented by a point in a space, with axes that are continuous variables. Changes is state occur in continuous time, and all regions of the state space are assumed to be reachable. This type of representation may be adequate for some purposes, but it must be recognized that it is a rather elementary, idealized view. In reality, there will be some regions of the state space that are not reachable from a particular state (Sibly and McFarland 1974). Moreover, defining the axes of the state space may pose problems the solutions to which are inevitably somewhat arbitrary. Finally, some systems, such as the car-washing machine described above, are better described in terms of discrete states and discrete time. An alternative form of representation, that obviates some of these problems, is to describe the system as a *finite-state automaton*—a simple mathematical "animal" that can be regarded as a discrete-time system with finite input and output sets (i.e., it responds to only a finite number of different stimuli (the *input set*, or *alphabet*), and it has a finite behavioral repertoire (the *output alphabet*).

Historically, automata theory started with Turing's (1936) computing machines and the neural networks of McCulloch and Pitts (1943). Although the major part of present-day automata theory is applied to mathematics and computer science, it has also been applied to animal behavior (Metz 1981), neurophysiology (Arbib 1973), and neural networks (Arbib 1987). Examples of applications in AI include pattern recognition (Minsky and Papert 1969) and learning machines.

Suppose we present to our animal a finite sequence of input letters (the *input word*) from the input alphabet $X$, and it responds
with letters (the *output word*) from the output alphabet $Y$. The output $y(t)$ that is generated at time $t$ depends deterministically on the
input letter and the state at the previous time step $(t - 1)$. Thus,

$$y(t) = Q(s(t - 1), x(t - 1),$$

where $Q$ is the mapping from state to behavior and where the state
$s$ is an element of a set of possible internal states, called the state
space $S$. We can determine $s(t)$ by specifying an initial state $s(0)$ and
a map $T$:

$$s(t) = T(s(t - 1), x(t - 1).$$

If the state space $S$ is finite, we have a finite automaton.

Let us now look at a simple man-machine system. Suppose we
are devising a secure entry system for a laboratory. Each legitimate
laboratory worker is issued a magnetically coded card and a code
number. To enter the building, it is necessary to have the card read
by the appropriate machine and to enter the code number that corresponds to the card. Suppose we wish to design a system that is
foolproof. One approach is to represent the man-machine system as
a finite-state automaton.

Let us follow a potential user through the system. The user is
initially outside the laboratory, and we designate this state as
OUTSIDE. Not only is the user outside, but the machine is in a
particular state. The state of the machine must be included in
the specification of the state OUTSIDE. In this state there are
three possible activities open to the user: go away $(a_g)$, insert card
$(a_c)$, and press alarm $(a_a)$. In designing the system we assume
that these are the only possible activities, and we use the term
COMMAND STATE for a state in which the possible activities
are finite and specified. In specifying this command state, we have
made provision for the three most likely eventualities: that the
user is carrying a card that can be inserted into the machine; that
the user is not carrying a card, but wishes to enter the building in
an emergency; and that the user is not carrying a card, and there is
no emergency, so the user goes away.

We now have to specify what happens as a result of each activity. If the user goes away, then the system remains in the same
state. If the user inserts a card, then a red light comes on and the
system moves to another command state, called RED LIGHT. If

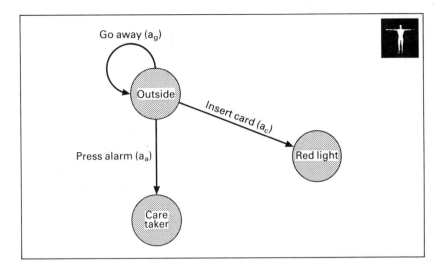

**Figure 4.13**   Finite-state automaton representing three possible state transitions for a person entering a building with a card-key system.

the user presses the alarm button, the caretaker is summoned and the system enters a state called CARETAKER. The three possible state transitions are illustrated in figure 4.13.

Now consider what is to happen when the caretaker arrives. If the user has adequate identification and can explain the emergency, then entry should be permitted. We therefore specify an activity called "identification OK" $(a_d)$, which moves the system to a new state, called GREEN LIGHT. If the user cannot provide adequate identification, then the activity is called "identification not OK" $(a_e)$, the caretaker does not activate the green light, and the system moves back to the OUTSIDE state.

We now move to the more complicated situation of the RED LIGHT command state. There are three possible activities: that the user decides not to enter the building after all and presses the quit button $(a_q)$, that the user enters the correct code $(a_k)$, and that the user enters an incorrect code. If the user quits, the state of the system returns to OUTSIDE. If the user enters the correct code, a green light comes on and the system moves to the GREEN LIGHT state. If the user enters an incorrect code, another attempt should be permitted, so the system stays in the RED LIGHT state. However, we may not want to allow potential users an indefinite numbers of attempts to enter the correct code, so we design the system to allow three attempts. This means that we have to install a counter which operates in the RED LIGHT state, and which changes the consequences of entering an incorrect code when an incorrect code has already been entered three times in succession. (Thus, we split activity a into two activities: $a_3$ = enter incorrect code up to three times and $a_4$ = enter incorrect code for the fourth time). After three attempts, the system moves back to the OUTSIDE STATE.

The green light indicates that the user may enter the building. The door is opened, either automatically or by the caretaker, and the user may enter the building. However, the user may delay entering, or may even walk away. Obviously, we do not want to have a system in which the door is left open indefinitely. Suppose we allow 5 seconds for the user to enter. In designing the system, we suppose that each delay of 1 second is a separate instance of the activity delay (a). (Thus, we distinguish between $a_5$ = delay up to five times and $a_6$ = delay for the sixth time). Delay up to five times results in a return to the GREEN LIGHT state; delay for the sixth time returns the system to the OUTSIDE STATE. The third possible activity is that the user enters the building ($a_1$), in which case the system moves to the LAB STATE.

In the LAB STATE there are two possible activities: stay ($a_5$), which returns the system to the LAB STATE, and exit ($a_x$), which moves the system back to the OUTSIDE STATE. The whole system can now be described in terms of a directed graph, as shown in figure 4.14.

The example above is a design exercise. That is, we have been designing a device that forms part of a man-machine system. In this case the design results from a manual exercise, but computer-aided design is also possible. Bösser (1986, 1989) has developed a formal methodology, called SANE (Skill Acquisition NEtwork), that facilitates the modeling and simulation of procedural knowledge in well-structured domains. Manual modeling of devices is complicated by the author's limited ability to systematically overview a complex system. The principle adopted by the SANE approach is to represent the device as a finite-state machine as a first step in modeling the man-machine task as a whole.

The user, when in a particular command state, has a limited range of alternative activities. Although the designer may think that all possible eventualities are covered, a desirable unspecified alternative is always possible. For example, when in the OUTSIDE STATE the user may wish to perform two activities simultaneously (press alarm + insert card). The user may wish to enter in the normal manner, but also to alert the caretaker to the presence of a

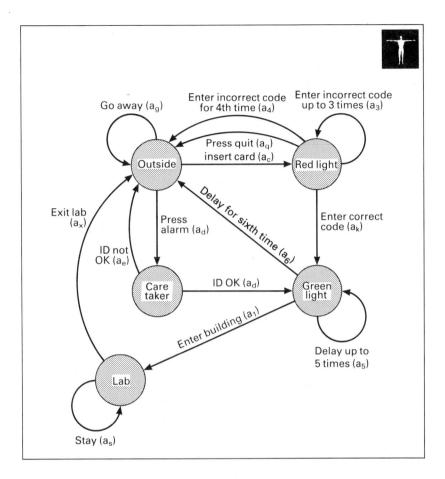

**Figure 4.14** Finite-state-automaton representation of complete card-key system.

(possibly undesirable) stranger prowling around the building. If this possibility is not specified in the design, then it is not open to the user.

Design is not the only way to obtain a finite-state model. It is also possible to arrive at such a model by means of *system identification procedures,* which use observations of the input and the output of a system to determine its internal structure. Arbib (1973) discusses this approach in relation to brain function, and Metz (1981) gives examples of its use in the modeling of animal behavior. An important concept here is that called *Nerode equivalence* (after Nerode 1958). This is an equivalence relation between pairs of input strings (or words). For a pair of strings $x_1$ and $x_2$, consider two identical copies of the system in question, and apply $x_1$ to one version and $x_2$ to the other. If the response to any further input is the same for each version of the system, then $x_1$ and $x_2$ are Nerode-equivalent. The system states are identical with the sets of Nerode-equivalent states, so a state can be thought of as a set of equivalent histories. For any member of a Nerode-equivalent class, the output depends only on the input. In other words, specifying the equivalence class and the subsequent input suffices to determine the future output. This formulation thus agrees with the normal definition of the state of a system.

In practice, we can construct a state-space representation by taking two words (or input strings) $x_a$ and $x_b$, presenting each separately, and noting the output. If the responses to $x_a$ and $x_b$ are the same, we then present various test words in combination with $x_a$ or $x_b$, and if we find no test word that differentiates between the two treatments we say that $x_a$ and $x_b$ are Nerode-equivalent. The two Nerode-equivalent treatments bring the system into the same state, since after the two treatments the system will always show the same behavior. It may appear that a very large number of experiments on the system in its initial state may be required to establish all the equivalence classes. However, Arbib and Zeigler (1969) show that if, at any state, the length of the input strings is increased by one input and no further increase in the number of equivalence classes occurs then all the states have been discovered. Once such a model has been obtained, it may be possible to give the states a topology and to produce a continuous-time model. An elegant example of this is given in Metz 1977, where Nelson's (1965) model of the behavior of the male stickleback is reinterpreted. Other examples involving animal behavior are given in Metz 1981.

## 4.4 Real Costs

We now come to the question of the costs of being in a particular state. In chapter 3 we saw that at the microeconomic level (the level of individual decision-making) money or energy is spent in such a way that utility is maximized. It appears that many animals behave in such a way as to maximize or to minimize some entity, sometimes called the cost. This is a notional measure of the contribution to fitness of the state of the animal and of its behavior. Note that we say *notional* measure. The animal has no information as to the real cost. It only has a preprogrammed notion of the cost. We do not mean by this that the notion is cognitive, but merely that the information is somehow built into the animal. The fairly obvious parallel between notional cost and utility was illustrated in figure 3.2.

As we saw in chapter 3, real cost relates to fitness. We define *cost* as the contribution to fitness of the animal's life history after time $T$, where $T$ is the end of the natural period, $[0, T]$ (McNamara and Houston 1986). (Many biological systems have a natural period, such as a day, a tide cycle, or a season, during which the state of the system describes a nearly closed trajectory (McFarland 1989a). In studying the short-term economic behavior of animals, it is convenient to define the time horizon of the analysis in terms of the natural period.) The contribution to fitness can be defined as the expected future reproductive success after time $T$ (McNamara and Houston 1986). There are various ways of defining fitness (for an elementary introduction see McFarland 1985), but this approach can be applied whenever it is meaningful to work in terms of the contribution to the life history after time $T$.

An animal in a particular state runs a specifiable risk of incurring real costs. Obviously it is more risky to be near a lethal boundary (i.e., in purgatory) than to be far from it, but can we be more precise than this? Let us consider the fuel supply of our bricklaying robot. We assume that the robot has some sort of on board energy store, and that laying bricks is an energy-consuming business. The robot is equipped with a sensor for monitoring the fuel level, but this sensor is not perfectly accurate. In figure 4.15 we assume that $x$ is the state of the fuel reserve at a particular time and that the probability $P$ of the state $x$ moving to a new position along the state axis is given by a normal distribution. As the robot goes about its business, the state $x$ moves toward the boundary $B$ at which the fuel reserve is 0. The area $A$ represents the probability of crossing the boundary $B$ (see McFarland and Houston 1981, appendix 7.1). The area $A$ increases as the square of the distance $Ox$, as shown in figure 4.16. In other words, the risk of crossing the boundary $B$ increases as the square of the fuel deficit.

In animal behavior it seems reasonable to suppose that the risk of death must increase steeply the nearer a variable is to its lethal boundary. Thus, it is obviously dangerous to allow hunger to approach lethal levels if the food supply is not guaranteed. McFarland and Houston (1981) argue that the risk function will generally be quadratic for state variables that have a lethal boundary. In studies of animal behavior, the term *cost* is generally used to signify

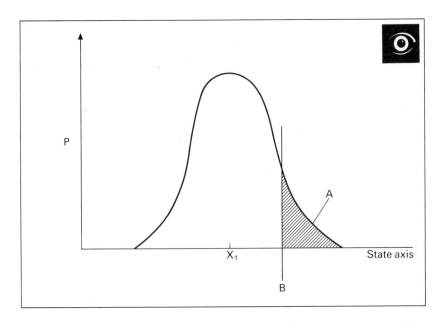

**Figure 4.15** The probability P of the state X moving to a new position along the state axis. Area A is the probability of crossing boundary B. (After McFarland and Houston 1981.)

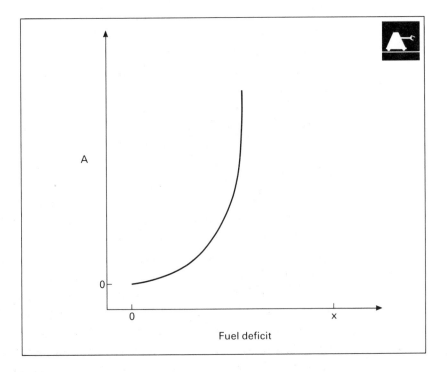

**Figure 4.16** Increase in A (cost of being in state x) as a function of x, derived from figure 4.15.

the risk of death plus other factors that may lead to a decrement in Darwinian fitness. This is a useful term for general discussion, but we have to remember to distinguish between the actual cost (i.e., the cost function mentioned in chapter 3) and the animal's notional cost (i.e., the goal function). For the time being, however, we must distinguish among three aspects of the cost: the cost of *being in a particular state*, the cost of *performing an activity*, and the cost of *changing between activities*.

The cost of being in a particular state is a function of each state variable. Where there are lethal limits to a state variable, we can expect the cost to be quadratic, as we have seen. But this will not always be the case. For our brick-laying robot, for example, the cost of running out of mortar will probably be the square of the mortar deficit, but the cost associated with the number of bricks laid will probably follow a different function. If we look more closely at this aspect, we can suppose that the cost will diminish linearly with the number of bricks laid, but that it will increase with the number of bricks in surplus (because these have to be transported elsewhere). Similarly, we can suppose that the cost will not only increase with the mortar deficit, but will also increase with mortar surplus (because leftover mortar has to be used on another job, before it sets and becomes useless). Thus, we can imagine a situation like that shown in figure 4.17. The total cost is complicated by the fact that the amount of mortar required depends on the number of bricks laid. In other words, these two components of the cost function are not independent.

The components of the total cost vary with the environmental circumstances. Obviously, in a situation where the supply of mortar is reliable, the risk of running out of mortar will differ from that where the supply is variable. To assess the risks involved we have to look at the robot or animal operating in its normal environment. At this point it may be helpful to look at an example of animal behavior.

The female herring gull lays three eggs in a shallow nest on the ground, usually in a large breeding colony. Normally, the female and the male take turns incubating, and they cover the eggs 98 percent of the time during the four-week incubation period (Drent 1970). A sitting bird will not leave the nest until relieved by its partner, unless it is flushed from the nest by a predator. Usually the partner leaves the nest to forage for food for a few hours. Sometimes, however, the partner's return may be delayed as a result of

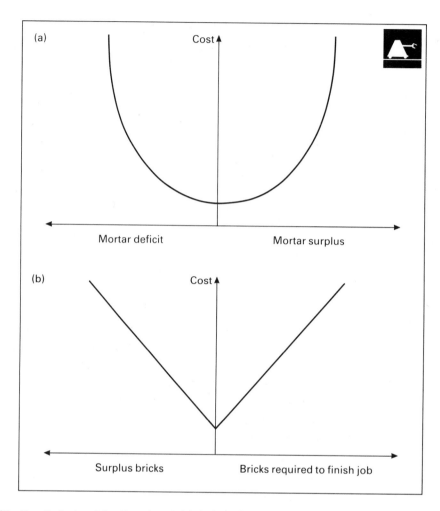

**Figure 4.17**  Hypothetical cost functions for a brick-laying robot.

some mishap. When that happens, what should the sitting bird do? Its partner may return at any time, but on the other hand the sitting bird becomes increasingly hungry as time passes. Eventually the sitting bird should quit the nest and search for food, even though this means that the eggs will almost certainly be lost to predators or marauding neighbors. Herring gulls breed in many successive generations, and it is not in the genetic interests of the individual to endanger its life for a clutch of eggs, which are likely to produce only 0.8 fledglings.

To investigate this question, we need to know (among other things) the cost of not sitting on the eggs. That is, we need to measure, in the field, the risk to the eggs of being left unattended and the risk to the bird of being without food. Drent (1970) measured the risk to the eggs due to exposure to the weather. He found that, in the absence of the parent, the embryo risks death from either overheating or chilling. However, a more important factor is the total amount of heat supplied by the time the hatching date arrives. The rate of development of the embryo depends on its metabolism, which in turn is affected by the temperature inside the egg. During incubation the egg gradually loses weight as a result of water evaporation. This loss of water results in an air space at one end of the egg, necessary for the embryo to breathe during the period shortly before hatching. The embryo must not develop too quickly, or the air space will not be formed properly by the time it is ready to hatch. It must not develop too slowly, or the egg will have lost so much water that the embryo will become dehydrated. Hatching must occur when only a certain amount of water has been lost from the egg, and when the embryo has received enough heat to be ready to hatch. Thus, two parallel processes must reach their critical points simultaneously. These provide two components of the cost function, as illustrated in figure 4.18. It does not matter much if the eggs are allowed to cool for relatively short periods, as long as their temperature does not fall very low. On a hot day, exposed eggs may be in danger of overheating, but the danger of physiological damage is slight if the eggs are exposed for only an hour or two. Thus, the eggs can survive the climatic exposure that occurs when birds are forced to leave the nest by predators. However, if the birds are disturbed repeatedly, the average rate of heat supplied to the eggs may fall short of that required for successful hatching.

A herring gull egg is about twice as likely to be lost through predation as from failure to develop properly. The risk to an egg can be

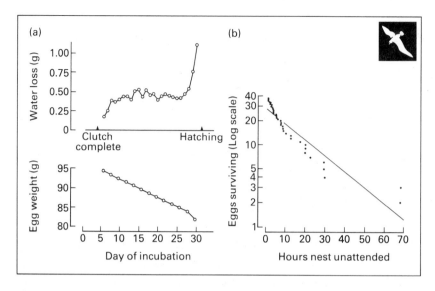

**Figure 4.18** Components of the cost function for herring gull eggs: (a) Those associated with climatic factors; (b) that associated with predation. (After Drent 1970 and Sibly and McCleery 1985.)

estimated by experiments in which the parents are removed from the nest (Sibly and McCleery 1985). The results of one such study show a half-life of about 8 hours (figure 4.18). The risk to a sitting bird of being without food can also be investigated experimentally. For example, the body weight of an incubating bird can be measured by placing a specially designed balance under the nest. The amount of fat a bird is carrying can be calculated from its weight in relation to its skeletal size (measured when the bird is initially caught and marked). The amount of food a herring gull obtains from foraging can be estimated from the change in weight measured on the nest balance before and after foraging trips. The quality of the food can be estimated from analysis of the fecal remains gathered from around the nest and from observations made of the bird while foraging. Herring gulls may fly a number of miles while foraging; thus, to obtain observations on foraging, particular birds are fitted with radio transmitters and tracked by means of a directional radio receiver. Thus, by using a variety of experimental techniques it is sometimes possible to arrive at fairly accurate estimates of the costs and benefits incurred by animals living a normal life in a natural environment (Sibly and McCleery 1985).

There are two general points worth noting about the Sibly-McCleery study. The first is that it is an experimental study designed to investigate the actual risks, costs, and benefits incurred in the working environment. To obtain such information about the various states of a robot, it would be necessary to do a similar study. (Reliability studies of automobiles provide an example of this sort of approach.) The second point is that the herring gull study provides information about various components of the cost function, and there remains the problem of how these components are to be combined into a single cost function. Is the risk of egg death due to dehydration independent of the risk relating to heat input? (It probably is not.) Is the risk of developmental failure independent of the risk of predation? (It probably is.) There is no direct way of finding the answers to these questions experimentally. The best approach is to incorporate the probable answers as assumptions in a model which attempts to account for the behavior of the animal concerned.

We now come to the second of the three tasks mentioned above: estimating the cost of performing an activity. A general rule, suggested by Sibly and McFarland (1976), is that the cost increase is the square of the rate of performing the activity. A general observation that goes part of the way toward justifying this assumption is that animals often do not feed at their maximum possible rate, especially when there is apparent danger from predators. There are two possible reasons for this. One is that faster behavior consumes proportionately more energy; the other is that an increase in feeding rate involves a reduction in the time spent looking around for potential predators. There is a fair amount of direct evidence relating to the latter point (Milinski and Heller 1978; Lendrem 1986), and this assumption has been successfully incorporated into a number of optimization models (see, e.g., Lima et al. 1985).

Robots, of course, do not have predators, and we must ask ourselves afresh how cost is likely to be related to the rate at which an activity is performed. Whenever a robot (or an animal) has a hard-wired preoccupation, its behavior in other respects will be repeatedly interrupted. Thus, if an animal is preoccupied with vigilance with respect to predators, its other behavior will be repeatedly interrupted by scanning for danger. Certain types of robots, while having no predators, are likely to have some hard-wired preoccupations, and these could provide a basis for supposing that their behavior will be frequently punctuated by these preoccupations. In other words, such robots are (by interleaving) performing

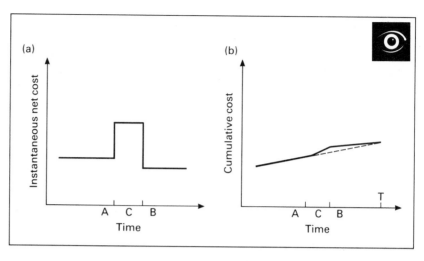

**Figure 4.19** (a) The instantaneous cost of changing, C, from activity A to activity B is generally higher than the cost of A or B. (b) The cumulative cost of changing: The changeover becomes worthwhile at T, when the cumulative cost is overtaken by the cost (dashed line) of staying with activity A. (After Larkin and McFarland 1978.)

two activities concurrently. The tradeoff between concurrent inter-leaved activities is likely to result in quadratic costs.

Our third and final task concerns the cost of changing from one activity to another. When an animal changes from one activity to another, it often has to pay for the change in energy or in time. Thus, a feeding animal may have to travel to find water to drink, an incubating bird has to travel away from its nest to find food, and so on. Moreover, the activity of changing may incur risks from predation. Thus, an antelope en route to a water hole is vulnerable to waiting predators, and a bird that quits its hidden nest may thereby reveal the location of the nest. The costs, or decrements in fitness, resulting from time and energy expenditure and risk of predation are normally offset by the benefits to be gained from the behavior. The benefits resulting from feeding, drinking, and incubation, although offset by the costs, nevertheless make these activities worthwhile. In the case of the activity of changing itself, however, there are no compensating benefits. The result is that when we look at a graph of net benefits (figure 4.19) we find that we cannot follow that normal rule that the animal performs the behavior that brings it the greatest benefit at each instant of time. If we follow this rule, the animal will never change to a new activity (where the cost of changing is above zero), because it will always be more beneficial to continue with the current activity than to take the drop in net benefit that changing involves. If we assume that the strength of an animal's tendency to do different activities matches the different net benefits (but see McFarland 1989b), we are in a similar conundrum. Thus, both functional and mechanistic approaches to the problem of changing from one activity to another involve difficulties. In the functional case, it can be argued that the cost of changing should be added to the cost of the activity to which the animal is about to change (Larkin and McFarland 1978). This has the effect of postponing the changeover. Empirical studies (McFarland 1971; Larkin and McFarland 1978; Larkin 1981; McFarland 1983) indicate that changes in behavior are postponed, or occur less frequently, when the cost of changing is raised. We will discuss this topic further in chapter 6.

## 4.5  Cost Functions

So far we have looked at various components of the cost function, including aspects of the cost of being in a particular state, the cost of performing a particular activity, and the cost of changing between activities. We now come to the problem of combining these components.

If the total cost, $C(x)$, can be represented as the sum of the cost associated with each $x$ in $x$, then $C(x)$ is said to be *separable*. Sibly and McFarland (1976) show that separability is approximately equivalent to probabilistic independence of the various factors. This means that the risk associated with the value of one variable (e.g., the mortar supply) is independent of the values of other variables. In assessments of the cost functions of animal behavior, separability has been assumed to hold in some studies but not in others. For example, Sibly and McFarland (1976) proposed the following cost function in their model of feeding and drinking in pigeons:

$$C(x, u) = k_1 x_h^2 + k_2 x_t^2 + k_3 u_f^2 + k_4 u_d^2,$$

where $k_1$, $k_2$, etc. are constants that weight the relative importance of being in a particular state $(x_n)$, or performing a particular activity $(u_n)$, and where $x_h$ is the hunger state, $x_t$ is the thirst state, $u_f$ is the rate of feeding, and $u_d$ is the rate of drinking. This cost function is quadratic and separable. A quadratic function implies that a given reduction in $x$ reduces the overall cost more when $x$ is large than when $x$ is small. Similarly, a given drop in the activity rate $u$ leads to a larger drop in costs when $u$ is large than when it is small. The separability implies that the risk due to one component is independent of the risk due to another. Thus, the risk due to hunger is independent of the risk due to thirst, and is also independent of the risk incurred in feeding or in drinking.

In general, the cost function "specifies the instantaneous level of risk incurred by (and reproductive benefit available to) an animal in a particular internal state, engaged in a particular activity in a particular environment" (McFarland 1977, p. 18). Sibly and McFarland (1976) defined the cost per unit time as the death rate minus the birth rate and claimed that minimizing the integral over time would give the trajectory that maximized the animal's Darwinian fitness. This is not really valid, because it fails to take account of the dependence of reproductive potential on survival. Freeman and McFarland (1982) developed the argument from first principles and showed that the "death rate minus birth rate" formulation is correct only when one of the rates is zero. They suggest an alternative formulation, but the Sibly-McFarland formulation remains valid for cases (such as feeding or drinking in pigeons) where reproductive strategy is not really relevant. (See also McNamara and Houston 1986.)

It is important to obtain an intuitive idea of the evolutionary argument here. Fitness has to do with reproduction, and mortality curtails reproduction. There is no intrinsic advantage in survival, except that it may permit future reproduction. The essence of the animal's problem is to decide between reproduction now and reproduction in the future (a topic which is the subject of considerable research; see e.g. Sibly and Calow 1986). Both the value of future reproduction and the probability of surviving to achieve it depend on the animal's choice of activities. (See McFarland and Houston 1981, pp. 146–148, for further exposition of this argument.)

It is also important to remember that cost functions deal with real risks, real costs, and real benefits (whereas utility functions and goal functions deal with notional costs and benefits). Therefore, the cost function is largely shaped by environmental forces—market forces in the case of robots and the forces of natural selection in the case of animals. Because of the difficulty of conducting the necessary field investigations, there have been few studies of cost functions proper. However, one such study is that carried out by Sibly and McCleery (1985), who conducted a long-term study of herring gulls at Walney Island (Cumbria, U.K.) during the incubation period. They describe a procedure for testing whether a particular set of decision rules maximize fitness, and they use it to identify optimal decision rules governing feeding, incubation, and the presence on territory of herring gulls during incubation. The characteristics of the optimal decision rules depend on the risks attendant upon each aspect of behavior. Therefore, in calculating the rules it is necessary to measure the risks an animal takes in carrying out its various activities. Using such estimates, Sibly and McCleery identify the characteristics of the optimal decision rules and use them as a basis for evaluating the fitness of the observed behavior.

The main risks of reproductive failure during the incubation period are egg death due to exposure or predation and parent death due to accident, disease, predation, or starvation. These risks can

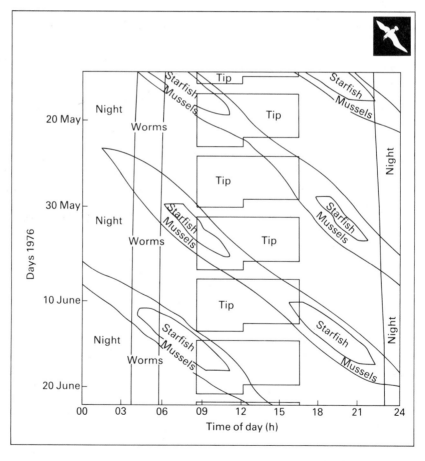

**Figure 4.20** Availability of major foods taken by herring gulls during incubation. (After Sibly and McCleery 1985.)

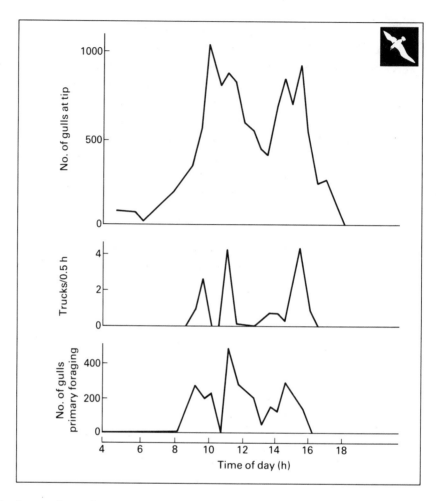

**Figure 4.21**  Opportunity profile for gulls foraging at a garbage dump. (After Sibly and McCleery 1985.)

be quantitatively evaluated by experiment (see figure 4.18). The opportunities relate mainly to feeding. Figure 4.20 shows the availability of the major foods taken by herring gulls at Walney. The various colony members specialize (to the extent of preferring certain sources of food) in feeding on different rhythmically available resources. These include refuse and earthworms (available on a circadian basis) and mussels and starfish (available on a tidal cycle). Each gull has to adjust its temporal pattern of incubation to permit both itself and its partner to take advantage of the feeding opportunity profiles that each is specialized in exploiting, without leaving the nest unattended. An opportunity profile is a function of time that represents the returns that the animal would obtain if it foraged at that time. An example is illustrated in figure 4.21. Successful incubation by a breeding pair requires complex cooperation and behavioral synchronization between the partners and with the prevailing circadian, tidal, and social rhythms.

Sibly and McCleery (1985) found that the feeding preferences of individual gulls were very important determinants of fitness. They

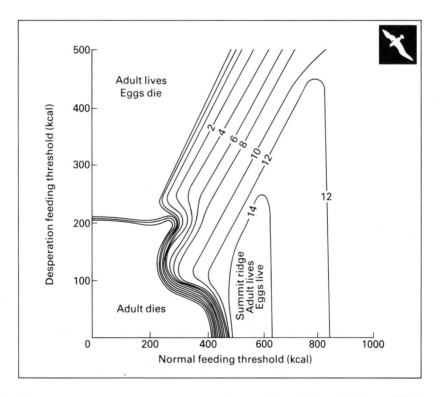

**Figure 4.22** Fitness landscape for a breeding pair of herring gulls. (After Sibly and McCleery 1985.)

constructed a fitness landscape for each breeding pair (an example is shown in figure 4.22) based on two important hunger variables, which they called *normal feeding threshold* and *desperation feeding threshold*. The former is the degree of hunger at which a bird would leave the territory to forage if one of its preferred foods became available, provided that its partner was present to take over incubation. The latter is the degree of hunger at which the bird would leave its nest to feed when a suitable opportunity arose, even if its mate was not available for incubation duty. On the basis of the fitness calculations, Sibly and McCleery (1985) identified various characteristics of the optimal behavior strategies. In particular, they predicted that energy reserves should be maintained between 500 and 1200 kcal; that the members of a mated pair should have complementary food preferences, at least one of these being a preference for feeding at the local refuse tip; and that a parent should desert its offspring if the parent's energy reserves fall below 200 kcal. They were able to test these predictions by observation and experiment.

### Points to Remember

- The combined physiological and perceptual state of an animal, as represented in the brain, is called the *motivational state*. It includes factors relevant to incipient activities as well as to the animal's current behavior.
- The motivational state of an animal at any particular time depends on its physiological state, on the cue state arising from its perception of the external world, and on the consequences of its current behavior.
- The behavior of an animal has consequences that depend on the situation in which the behavior occurs. These consequences influence the animal's motivational state in five main ways: by altering the external stimuli perceived by the animal, and hence altering the cue state; by direct feedback onto the motivational state; by altering the animal's physiological state; by preventing the animal from engaging in some other behavior; and by energy expenditure. Energy, and other physiological commodities such as water, are expended as a result of all behavior to a degree that depends on the level of activity, the weather, etc.
- The consequences of behavior can be represented in a motivational state space. The motivational state of an animal is portrayed as a

point in the space. As a consequence of the animal's behavior, the state changes, and so the point describes a trajectory in the space.

- A freely mobile robot is in a similar situation to an animal, in that its state is influenced both by environmental conditions and by the robot's own behavior.

- Some systems are better described in terms of discrete states and discrete time. It is possible to describe such a system as a finite-state automaton (a discrete-time system with finite input and output sets).

- One approach to the design of man-machine systems is to represent them as finite-state automata. Computer-aided design, using a language such as SL/R, can help here. This language facilitates the modeling and simulation of procedural knowledge in well-structured domains.

- It is also possible to arrive at a finite-state model by means of system identification procedures. These use observations of the input and the output of a system to determine its internal structure.

- An animal in a particular state runs a specifiable risk of incurring real costs. The cost of being in a particular state is a function of each state variable.

- Real cost can be defined as the contribution to fitness of an animal's life history after the (natural) period of study. The contribution to fitness is the expected future reproductive success after this period.

- Measurement of real costs requires experimental study in the natural environment. To obtain such information about a man-made machine would require risk and reliability studies in the working environment.

- There are three important aspects of cost: the cost of being in a particular state, the cost of performing an activity, and the cost of changing between activities.

- The cost function specifies the instantaneous level of risk incurred by (and the reproductive benefit available to) an animal or a machine in a particular internal state, engaged in a particular activity in a particular environment.

- Cost functions deal with real risks, real costs, and real benefits. Therefore, the cost function is largely shaped by environmental forces—market forces in the case of machines and the forces of natural selection in the case of animals.

# 5 Design and Decision

The essence of Darwinism is that form and function go hand in hand. Any present-day form in the animal kingdom is the outcome of compromise among various selective pressures. For example, the functions of vision in diurnal animals differ from those in nocturnal species. For nocturnal animals, sensitivity is at a premium and the eye must collect as much light as possible. The pupil should be large relative to the size of the eye as a whole, and this entails a big lens to avoid spherical abberation of the lens periphery. To maintain the image in focus on the retina, increased lens size must go hand in hand with increased lens curvature, producing a smaller image on the retina. Thus, many nocturnal animals have large lenses, which produce small bright images, whereas diurnal animals have smaller lenses, which produce larger images with con-p sequent improved acuity. Typical nocturnal eyes are found in the opossum, the house mouse, and the lynx, and also in deep-sea fishes (figure 5.1). In some other nocturnal animals, such as owls and bushbabies, the limitation on lateral expansion by the skull has led to tubular extension of the eyes. This simple example illustrates four important points about design:

- Design often involves tradeoffs among competing pressures. If the sensitivity of the eyes is to be increased, then it is inevitable that there will be some loss of acuity.
- There are nearly always constraints on design. For example, if the skull is not to become too wide larger eyes can be accommodated only by giving up the spherical shape and adopting a tubular shape. The disadvantage of this change is that animals with tubular eyes have very restricted eye movement and have to turn the head instead.
- Much can be learned about design by comparison of different species. The comparative approach has a long tradition in biology (see, e.g., Tinbergen 1959) and has recently become a sophisticated quantitative subject (see, e.g., Pagel and Harvey 1988).
- Implicit in design considerations is the notion of optimization. This is sometimes known as the "principle of optimal design."

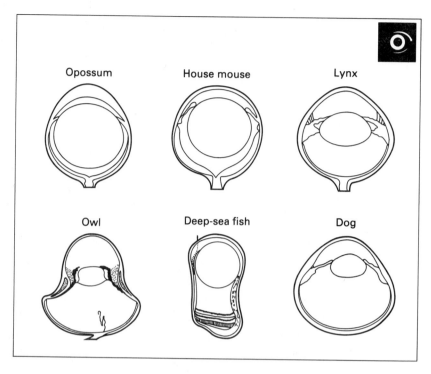

**Figure 5.1** Form and function in vertebrate eyes. The eye structures of various nocturnal animals, and of a deep-sea fish, are compared with that of a diurnal dog. (After Tansley 1965.)

Thus, if we ask what is the best form of eye for a particular situation, we are asking for the compromise that has the highest evolutionary survival value.

## 5.1 Optimal Design

In chapter 1 we saw that natural selection can be considered as a designing agent. Anyone who doubts this should read Dawkins 1986. The form of a biological structure can be seen as the outcome of a design operation that aims at the optimal form on the basis of certain criteria. A typical example is Murray's (1926) work on blood-vessel design. In considering the design of a simple blood vessel, we might ask what radius the vessel should have. Since all fluid flow involves frictional loss of energy, the pumping mechanism must maintain an appropriate power output if a steady flow is to be achieved. We might expect blood vessels to be designed to minimize power loss by presenting the least resistance to the flow of blood. Since resistance to flow rate falls as vessel radius increases, it would appear that the radius should be as large as possible. A large vessel radius implies a large volume of blood to be maintained and a large area of vessel wall to be maintained. We might, therefore, expect the benefit of large vessels to be offset by high maintenance costs. How should the benefits of low resistance to flow be offset against the maintenance costs of the blood vessels?

In chapter 4 we introduced the notion of a cost function in which cost is related to decrement in Darwinian fitness. It would be extremely difficult to evaluate the design of blood vessels in terms of fitness, but we can suggest an index of fitness based on our biological intuition. The metabolic energy cost involved in maintaining blood vessels must be obtained from the same source that supplies the heart's pumping energy. Our intuition tells us that power consumption is likely to be the overriding criterion in blood-vessel design. This is essentially a hypothesis; it may be incorrect; however, it does provide a basis for developing a theory, which can then be tested by observation. On the basis of this hypothesis, a number of authors have calculated and verified empirically the optimal angles and radii involved in vascular branching and bifurcation; see, e.g., Murray 1926; Cohn 1954, 1955; Rosen 1967; Milsum and Roberge 1973.

In this book we argue that, although the mechanism of machine design is different from the design mechanism pertaining in the animal kingdom, the principles remain the same. This is not a new idea. The parallelism between design in engineering and design in nature has been recognized for a long time (Cohn 1954, 1955; Milsum and Roberge 1973; Rosen 1967). The principle of optimal design simply asserts that a system, whether animate or inanimate, that is capable of modification in successive versions will tend to evolve toward an optimal configuration with respect to the selective pressures (or market forces) acting on the successive versions. This is not to say that optimal design is ever achieved; it is to say that optimality principles pertain (see also Maynard Smith 1978 and Alexander 1982).

The argument from optimal design can also be applied to behavior. In chapter 4 we saw that the costs and benefits attributable to an activity depend partly on the internal state of the animal and partly on the consequences of its behavior. The consequences are largely determined by the environment, so that the net benefit or fitness change accruing to the performance of a particular activity at a particular time will depend on the environmental circumstances. Figure 5.2 shows how fluctuating environmental circumstances can affect the advantages of performing various activities. Clearly, one sequence is better than the other, and it should be theoretically possible to attain the optimal behavior sequence. The question is, can the animal be so designed that it attains the optimal behavior sequence in a given set of circumstances?

We have to be careful, in answering this question, to distinguish between optimization with respect to the cost function and optimization with respect to the goal function (see chapters 3 and 4). No animal can be expected to attain an optimal behavior sequence that is perfect with respect to a real cost criterion. There are a number of reasons for this:

- Although natural selection is a designing agent, it acts slowly (generation by generation) in relation to changes in environmental circumstances. Except in a very stable environment, such as the deep sea, there is always an evolutionary lag. In other words, natural selection is a designing agent whose work is never finished, because the environment is always changing.
- When animals of different species use the same resources or have certain preference or tolerance ranges in common, niche overlap occurs. This leads to competition, especially when resources are in short supply. Competition may also occur among individuals of the same species for certain resources, such as food or territory. Competition may result in an individual's being displaced from its preferred habitat. Since this is usually the habitat to which the animal is best adapted, we can see that such an animal cannot be expected to perform to its best advantage.
- There is always some genetic variation among individuals of the same species inhabiting the same environment. Since this variation affects behavior, not all individuals can be equally well adapted.

A parallel here is the problem of designing the perfect automobile (i.e., one that everybody would buy). The criteria that appeal to motorcar buyers are continually changing, because of continual changes in the relevant environmental circumstances (the price of fuel, the crowdedness of the roads, etc.). By the time a new model is designed and launched, it is already out of date. Competition among car manufacturers may result in models being displaced from their ideal market. Thus, a cheap car designed for peasants

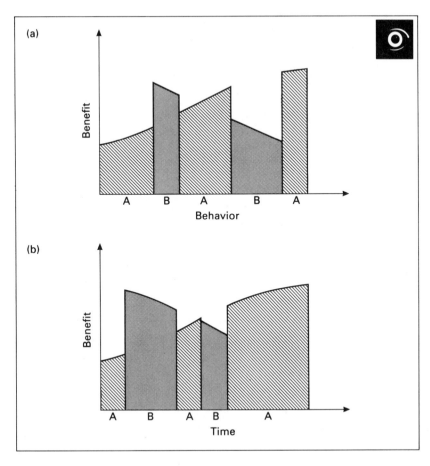

**Figure 5.2**   Benefits gained from two hypothetical behavior sequences under one set of environmental circumstances. The benefit gained from activity A, in a certain period of time,
is represented by the area under the curve. The benefit gained by area B is the area
under a different curve. These opportunity curves are characteristic of the environment, and are identical in parts (a) and (b) of this figure. The total benefit gained from
a behavior sequence of given length is obtained by summing the two shaded areas. Of
the two hypothetical sequences shown here, (b) yields greater benefit than (a), even
though they both occur under the same pattern of environmental change.

may end up being used primarily by students, because the peasants prefer some other model. Certain characteristics of the car, such as being high off the ground, may not be very relevant for student use. And there is always some "genetic" variation among cars from different manufacturers, which results more from the parentage of the car than from its current adaptation to the market. Even where different manufacturers aim at the same market, not all their products will be equally well adapted.

Optimization with respect to a goal function is an entirely different matter. As we saw in chapter 2, there are various arguments that lead us to expect animals to behave rationally. This implies that some entity (called *utility*) is maximized. As we saw in chapter 3, the utility function of economics is the inverse of the goal function of ethology. Therefore, on the basis that animal behavior is rational, we can expect an animal to behave optimally with respect to utility. This point can be illustrated by reference to our household robot (section 3.3).

We imagine a robot designed to carry out the cleaning and cooking chores in an American kitchen. The robot has to make decisions about its use of time: when to stop cleaning the floor, what chore to do next, etc. A well-designed robot will embody a goal function (McFarland and Houston 1981) that relates the different options to a common currency. That is, it specifies the extent to which adopting each option contributes to the maximized entity. We can suppose that the robot is designed to maximize some notion of efficiency, involving work done per unit time, per unit of energy expenditure, etc. The goal function is a design feature of the robot, but this does not mean that it is explicitly represented in the robot's brain. Many aspects of the design are relevant to the goal function, such as the diameter of the wheels, and the length of arms. In other words, the goal function is tacitly represented and is an emergent property of the design as a whole.

The robot can behave absolutely optimally, with respect to its goal function, only if it has complete freedom of action. In reality there will generally be constraints on the robot's behavior. The amount of energy available may be limited, so that energy spent on one activity is subtracted from that spent on another within a given time period. The rate at which chores can be performed may be limited by the nature of the environment and by the physical features of the robot.

The state of the robot in conjunction with the goal function specifies the optimal course of action. However, because of the constraints inherent in the situation, the robot may not be able to follow that course of action. Therefore, we have to distinguish between the optimal solution to the problem presented by a particular situation and the optimal attainable solution. The robot may be doing its best, but its best may not be the best possible behavior relevant to the situation.

The robot is designed to operate in a completely standardized American kitchen. The kitchen is an unvarying environment, except in a trivial sense, so the robot does not have to adapt its behavior by learning. If the robot is optimally designed, its goal function will be identical to the cost function that is characteristic of the American kitchen. In this example the cost function specifies the costs and benefits in terms of some measure of efficiency. The optimally designed robot is perfectly adapted to the American kitchen and will always carry out its duties in the most efficient manner. Suppose, now, that the robot is transferred to a French kitchen, and that the cost function characteristic of a French kitchen is different from that of an American kitchen. The robot will continue to behave in concordance with the notional costs and benefits embodied in its own goal function. It will still be an optimizing machine, but it will not be behaving optimally from the point of view of the French cost function. In French eyes it would not appear to be an efficient machine, and it would not do well in the French market.

When operating in the environment for which it is designed, the robot can maximize its efficiency by sequencing its behavior in an optimal manner, within the limits set by the constraints inherent in the situation. In an alien environment, we can expect the robot to adapt to a small extent, but its behavior will fall short of perfect because of the constraints on its behavior and because of the discrepancy between its goal function and the cost function characteristic of the situation.

## 5.2 Decision Variables

Implicit in our discussions of rationality, utility, and design is the notion of *decision*. We have now come to the point where we must spell out more precisely what is involved in this notion.

Both design and behavior involve decisions. In designing a wheel, an engineer has to decide what weight, radius, and strength the wheel should have. Similarly, in designing a bone, nature (through the process of natural selection) decides on the "best" combination of weight, length, cross-sectional area, etc. Behavioral decisions, which may involve movement of the wheel or bone, have to take account of the fact that these structural decisions have already been made. Thus, if the wheels are part of a bicycle, the rider takes account of their radius in deciding what gear to engage. (It would be better to say that the wheels' properties influence the rider's decision.) Similarly, the weight and length of a person's leg bones influence the natural frequency of his walking, and will inevitably affect the pattern of walking, running, and resting of a person traveling a long distance on foot.

Notice that the word *decision* is being used in a special, technical way. A person driving a motorcar with a manual gearshift makes decisions (in the normal everyday sense of the word) as to when to change gear. A person driving a car with an automatic gearshift makes no such decisions, but the behavior of the car may be the same. It makes no difference, in talking about the behavior of the car, whether the decisions to shift are made by the driver or by an automatic gearbox. What matters is the way in which the decision variables (speed, engine rpm, etc.) are deployed. A decision of a person, an animal, or a robot is simply the process by which the decision variables are changed. This process can occur as part as a design operation or as part of behavior. For example, a person making a bicycle can decide to change the radius of the wheels. A person riding a bicycle cannot do this, but can decide to change the speed of rotation of the wheels. The wheel radius is a decision variable in one case, the wheel speed in the other.

In chapter 2 we saw that decisions among mutually exclusive alternatives must involve a common currency. If the choice behavior is rational, then the choices will be transitive, implying a maximization (or minimization) principle. In mathematical terms, there must be a function (a currency function) that specifies the relationship between the currency and the decision variables. The role of the currency function is to translate all the decision variables into a single value (a real-valued function), so that all possible decisions can be ranked along a single scale. In chapter 3 we discussed decision-making from an economic viewpoint, with the currency is called *utility* and the currency function called a *utility function*. Note that utility functions are seen as properties of individuals, and the economic exercise attempts to specify what the individual ought to do to maximize utility. In chapter 4 we discussed decision-making from an ecological viewpoint, in which the currency is called *cost* and the currency function is called a *cost function*. Note that cost functions are seen as properties, not of individuals, but of the environment. The ecological exercise attempts to specify what the individual ought to do to minimize cost—that is, to minimize the threat from the environment, whether it be the natural environment or the market. From an ethological viewpoint, the currency is the (notional) cost and the currency function is the goal function. Note that goal functions are seen as (genetically determined) properties of individuals, and the exercise attempts to determine both what the individual ought to do to minimize the currency and how the individual might do this.

Some problems of terminology have arisen because similar concepts have evolved in different disciplines. In this book we will use the term *utility* for the decision currency employed by the individual, and *cost* for the ecological equivalent of this. We will use *utility function* for functions of a single decision variable, and *goal function* for functions of a decision vector. (Following McFarland and Houston 1981, we reserve the more general term *objective function* to denote the scientist's hypothesis about the goal or utility function). We reserve *cost function* for the ecological equivalent of the goal or utility function.

## 5.3  Designing Artificial Behavior Systems

The similarities between the design processes performed by evolution through natural selection and human design activities have been pointed out often. These similarities cover the selection process (i.e., the testing and evaluation of alternative designs or prototypes). The testing is based on an estimate of the contribution of overall fitness, or utility of design features (essentially the same processes for natural systems and artifacts). The design features selected for testing can be considered as hypotheses to be tested in respect of their contribution to the overall fitness of the design.

There is, however, an important difference in the process by which these design hypotheses are generated. Natural selection takes advantage of random variations by discriminating against design features that do not improve the system under development.

Such a process would be highly wasteful if used for the design of industrial products, and would greatly increase the cost of development and testing. Natural selection can, of course, be simulated on a computer, and such genetic algorithms are beginning to be used in the design of human artifacts (Koza 1991).

Both animals and the products of human design and manufacture can be analyzed in terms of their microscopic or macroscopic structure, their durability, and their performance in relation to their function. Analogies between animals and man-made products exist at several levels.

We are interested here in the design analogies between animals and products, and in the fact that design is judged by performance in relation to function. Animal design is coded for by genes, in the sense that different genes produce animals with different characteristics. The success of a design is measured by the success of the genes that produce it. This depends on the ability of those genes to spread in the population and on their ability, once established, to withstand competition from rival genes. This "spreading power" is most conveniently measured by the rate of increase of the gene. In evolutionary terms, those genes with the greatest rate of increase are the most successful, and are likely to persist longest in the population. Of course, once genes become established in the population, their long-run rate of increase is zero. Hence, after a period of evolution in a constant environment, we expect genes' rates of increase to be greater than those of possible competitors. We also expect their rates of increase to be zero. This means that possible competitors would have a negative rate of increase (i.e., would be selected against by the process of natural selection). The rate of increase of a gene depends intimately on its effects on the life cycle of the individual animals carrying it. Obviously, increasing fecundity and decreasing mortality will promote the spread of a gene, other things being equal.

How does this relate to product design? Suppose that a variety of products are under consideration, varying in the period required for product development, in the chance of total product failure in the market place, and in the expected returns from sales if the product is successfully launched. We can imagine an analogy between the life cycle of a product and the life cycle of an animal. This can be formulated as an exact mathematical analogy (McFarland 1991a).

The analogies in the design cycle are between the characteristics of the cycle and the criteria used to evaluate it. The development period is the period before any return on investment is achieved. For animals this is the period between birth and reproduction; for products it is the period before any financial returns accrue to the investor. Measures of the chance of a product's (animate or inanimate) surviving to enter the gene pool or the market lead to calculations about the return on investment. For animals this is the number of offspring produced when the individual reproduces (i.e., when the gene is copied into half the offspring on average, in accordance with Mendel's laws). In the case of man-made products, it is net income from sales. The success of the design is evaluated by the net rate of increase of the genes coding for it (in the case of an animal) or of the money invested in it (in the case of a man-made product).

In considering how the designer of a behavior system proceeds, let us assume that a human designer—an engineer—wants to build a system with specified behavior: an autonomous vehicle capable of moving around and transporting goods within a defined space, such as a kitchen or a shop floor. This example is simplified, but we assume that systems with much more complex behavior are also built this way. A similar design approach would be needed for the human-machine interfaces of large systems, such as process control systems in production plants for airplanes and spacecraft, where the behavior of the human operator is precisely prescribed and designed as part of the total system. Even operating instructions for consumer goods include some design of behavior in the form of instructions to the user.

Like all design exercises, the design of the behavior of an autonomous vehicle progresses through a number of versions, some of which will be tested only as prototypes. Others may make it to the market, where they will be judged by their success as products. Successive versions are improved as a result of the testers' and the users' experience with previous versions. Design can proceed by trial and error (thus incurring the disadvantage of unpredictable outcomes), or by the use of systematic design methods. Systematic design, based on analysis of the requirements and constraints of the application domain, proceeds through a sequence of design stages, from outline to detailed design, with checks after all stages.

We can consider the behavior of a system independently from the hardware or software that implements the behavior. Consider, as an analogy, the fact that the fully specified behavior of a computer program may be implemented in FORTRAN or in C. These implementations will appear the same if they conform to the abstract design of the desired behavior of the program, usually called the *specification*. A specification is comparable to the blueprint for a building, where the finished building is the implementation of the design. In man-machine systems, equivalent behavior may be implemented in hardware, or in software, or in instructions to a human operator.

In designing the behavior of a system, we can divide the relevant state variables according to whether they belong to one of three separate spaces: the environmental space, the behavior space, and the task space.

The *environmental space* defines the constraints, the topology, and the laws of movement within which the agent can move. The environment for our autonomous robot example is the kitchen or factory floor, including static and mobile obstacles to movement such as doorways, machines, and persons. The environment for a kitchen robot might look like figure 5.3.

The *behavior space* includes the variables to which the agent responds in its behavior and the variables that figure in the planning

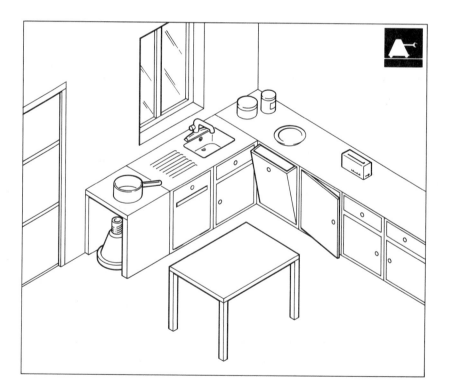

**Figure 5.3** Environmental space of household robot.

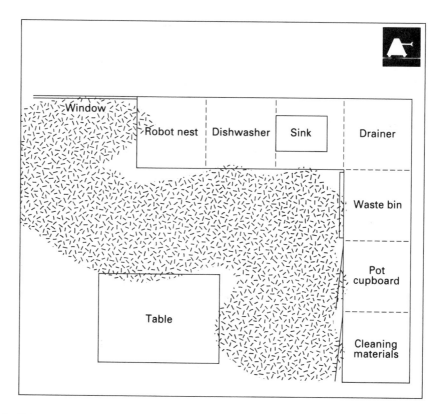

**Figure 5.4** Behavior space (stippled) of household robot.

of its behavior. The robot needs to respond only to those variables that are relevant to its behavior. Thus, the environment does not have to look to the robot as it looks to a human. The robot requires only a simplified view of the environment, indicating which behaviors and movements are possible. This selective view is sometimes called a *representation* in an artificial agent, or the *umwelt* (perceptual world) in an animal. For our kitchen robot, a layout in the form of routes around the floor, as shown in figure 5.4, suffices.

The *task space* includes the state variables that define the goals of the agent, including goal variables representing current states of planning. The task space of a robot designed to carry goods around a shop floor is defined by the possible states of all the goods which the robot may be asked to carry. A single task is defined by the initial location of an object and by the location to which it is to be taken. Not all possible combinations of initial and end states are meaningful tasks; most goods to be transported around the shop floor are found only at certain locations. The kitchen robot will be asked to transport dirty dishes to the dishwasher, but not to transport dirty dishes to the cupboard. This does not mean that the robot is not capable of putting dirty dishes into the cupboard; it just means that the designer does not anticipate that it will be asked to do this. The cupboard may be used as a temporary repository for dirty dishes in an emergency; however, the designer of the behavior does not need to include this state in the task space, either explicitly or implicitly.

Here is an example of a task for our kitchen robot:

Name of task: clean dishes

Initial state: robot in nest
        dirty dishes on table
        dishwasher empty

End state: robot in nest
        clean dishes in cupboard.

And here is an example of a task for a shop-floor robot:

Name of task: mail distribution

Initial state: robot in nest
        mail A in the out-tray at location I
        mail B in the receiving mail box
        in-tray empty

End state: robot in nest
        mail B in the in-tray at location J
        mail A in the post-office mail box.

Note that a task is described by the relevant parameters only. A small number of relevant state variables is defined by a task. Other states may be implied. For example, when the kitchen robot's task is complete the dishwasher is empty. Many irrelevant state variables, such as the location of cutlery, are not defined. (Dealing with the cutlery may be another task.) The task space is defined by the state variables that are relevant to a particular task.

## 5.4 Solving Tasks by Behavior

The behavior space of a robot is defined by the locations the robot can reach and by the transitions between those locations. In principle the robot may attain a nearly infinite number of states, but in designing a useful behavior space we can limit ourselves to a small number of states. This limited view of the situation, as represented in the behavior space of figure 5.4, is sufficient so long as the robot remains within the designated environmental and task spaces. The behavior space may be represented in many different equivalent forms, such as a graph, a state-transition network, or a set of propositions.

A task is solved by a sequence of movements in the behavior space of the robot. The behavior space implies that a constrained number of behavior sequences can lead from the initial state to the end state. A single sequence of operations, or state transitions, in the behavior space is called a *procedure*. In addition to being an ordered sequence of operations, a procedure is constrained by the dependencies between successive operations. It is not possible, for example, to put dirty dishes in the dishwasher when there are still clean dishes in there.

In addition to a description of the states, and in addition to the operations and state variables modified during the performance of a procedure, the procedure may also be characterized by the costs occurring during execution of the procedure. A procedure with a lower total cost is to be preferred over a more expensive procedure. In human behavior such procedures are called *skills*. Skills are well-defined and practiced sequences of behavior. (No variability is possible in skilled behavior as we have defined it so far, but this may be introduced in the form of conditional operations.) In order for a robot to exhibit useful behavior, it will require a set of procedures, or programs, corresponding to its typical tasks. Our kitchen robot might be designed with procedures for the following tasks:

clean dishes
clean floor
clean windows
clear dustbin
prepare tea.

Let us look at the task "clean dishes":

Initial state: dishwasher empty
          dishes on table

End state: dishes in cupboard

Procedures: open dishwasher,
       take dishes to dishwasher
       store dishes in dishwasher (repeat until dishwasher full or
         no dishes left)
       initiate dish wash
       wait for wash to finish
       carry dishes to cupboard (repeat until washer empty).

In addition, the robot must be instructed as to which tasks are to be carried out, and in which sequence. In an autonomous agent, decisions about task sequencing are made by the agent itself.

The behavior space must also be represented in the robot in an appropriate form. One possibility is to preprogram the robot with procedures for all the tasks that the designer foresees. Another possibility is to provide the robot with a map similar to that shown in figure 5.5. This would represent the linked behavior and task spaces of the robot. It would equip the robot with the ability to de-

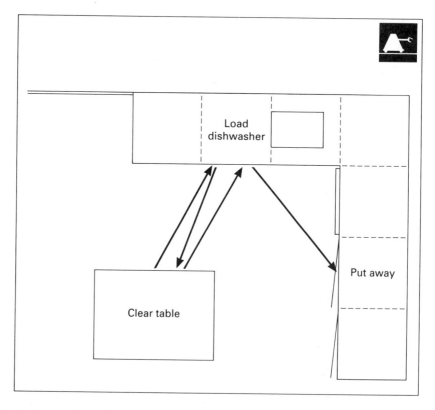

**Figure 5.5** Task space (arrows) of household robot.

velop a procedure for solving each task as it arises. This process is called *planning*.

The two approaches, preprogramming and planning, have their respective advantages and disadvantages. Storing all conceivable procedures (potential behaviors) has the advantage that the behavior of the robot will be well known and understood. Preprogrammed behavior has three main disadvantages:

- All tasks must be well known and anticipated by the designer, who must explicitly design the procedures for all the tasks that the robot will be required to solve.
- The storage space needed for a large behavior repertoire is prohibitively large.
- When it encounters unexpected states, the robot will behave inappropriately or arrive at deadlock.

The planning approach has three main advantages:

- Not all procedures have to be explicitly programmed.
- The robot has an improved ability to deal with unexpected or unknown states.
- The behavior repertoire of the robot can be modified without undue increase in the size of the memory.

The main disadvantages of planning are that it is time-consuming and likely to slow down the robot's behavior. The designer is faced with a tradeoff between rigid, fast, automaton-like behavior and slower, more flexible behavior.

Imagine a household robot with a wide range of possible activities. How would the owner instruct the robot from day to day? The owner could push some buttons in the morning, or use some fancy type of voice control, to instruct the robot in a set of tasks—for example,

Fix me a cup of coffee.
Wash the dishes.
Clean the floor.
Recharge your batteries.
Set the table for dinner for four people.

If this were the program for all Fridays, then it could be called FRIDAY and stored and called up under that name. Short-term contingencies could also be programmed, such as IF smoke is detected THEN call fire brigade. Similar programs could exist for other days of the week, with variations for the seasons. Similar contingency programs are known in animals, such as migratory birds (McFarland 1985).

## 5.5 Designing Procedures

Procedures are sequences of behavior that are recognizable by virtue of their repeated, efficient, and regular execution. They may be mental algorithms, which are abstract specifications of the steps taken by procedures that run in the mind. This view suggests that there are, in effect, mental programs similar to the programs written in a high-level programming language. Although they are only indirectly observable, either by inference from observed behavior or in verbal reports of mental events, it is claimed (Laird et al. 1987) that such procedures have a high degree of psychological reality, as opposed to being merely hypothetical.

Procedures are composed of basic operations that are not further divisible, and are combined into executable programs by a control structure. In the ACT* architecture of Anderson (1983) and in the SOAR architecture of Laird et al. (1987), the control structure is represented by a goal/subgoal decomposition with in a production-system architecture. The very same control structure may also be represented as a set of nested IF-THEN-ELSE statements, as a production system, or as a flow graph.

The similarity between computer programs and cognitive procedures suggests that the theory of computational complexity may be applied to cognitive procedures. Computational complexity is a measure of the cost of executing an algorithm on a given computer. The main cost factors are the use of resources such as the central processor, storage media, and input-output processors. Cognitive procedures appear to be limited primarily by the working memory available for intermediate storage and by the basic cycle time. However, the performance and the cost of executing cognitive procedures are dynamic, changing as a function of time and of repeated execution of the procedure. Fitts (1964) suggested that skills develop progressively from a cognitive stage, where procedures arise as a result of planning, to a stage where procedures are performed automatically. In the early stages, performing a procedure is a problem-solving process in which the goal, but not how to reach the goal, is known. After extensive learning and practice the procedure can be performed at higher speed, sometimes concurrently with other procedures, without step-by-step execution of the sequential operations.

In terms of computational complexity, procedures become less costly as a result of learning, but the learning process itself is slow and costly, as in animals (Tovish 1982). Cognitive architectures such as ACT* and SOAR include learning mechanisms which mimic learning processes by combining sequences of operations, and the control structure connecting them, into efficient subroutines. Automation makes the execution of procedures less costly, leaving more of the scarce resources of the central processor for the apparently sequential execution of the main program.

In practice, the skilled element in a human task domain can be quantitatively estimated by observing the learning time needed to acquire the procedures for a particular application. This time ranges from 50 to 100 hours for editing text with a text processor (Bösser 1987) to several thousand hours for acquisition of skills in mathematics, navigation, or language. Elio (1986) investigated the positive transfer between learning arithmetic procedures with equivalent elements and with equivalent sequential structures. He found that speed of transfer is a function of similar elements and similar structures.

A procedure is an underspecified plan. The prospective plan is an algorithm for attaining a goal state, anticipating to a certain extent variations in the states of the world that are to be encountered. The procedure is a retrospective protocol that instantiates such a plan. The utility of a plan derives to a large extent from its capability to respond adequately to variable conditions arising during execution of the plan.

## 5.6  Systematic and Computer-Aided Design of Behavior

Serendipity and selection by nature or by the market are effective and important mechanisms shaping the behavior of animals and artificial agents. In an industrial environment it is important that design progress more systematically, with greater predictability of effort and output. Such design of behavior applies not only to the design of artificial behavior systems but also to the design of man-machine systems, where the behavior of the user is implicitly designed into the product.

The range of technical products available today includes few systems with complex behavior. Most automate some functions only, mostly in the form of preprogrammed procedures and feedback control mechanisms. The design of a technical product defines the behavior of the product and the procedures the user can perform (i.e., the behavior space of the user) to benefit from the product. In effect the user delegates part of the control to the machine, retaining part of it under his control.

Traditionally, machine design progresses through the development and testing of a succession of prototypes. Some of these may be selected for production and be tested further in the market. This whole process can be accelerated if the initial design and testing can be carried out by computer simulation, now common practice in some industries.

In chapter 4 we saw that designing a device that forms part of a man-machine system can be computer-aided using the SANE language, developed by Bösser and Melchior (1990). The SANE language and an associated set of software tools facilitate the modeling and simulation of behavior. The principle adopted by the SANE approach is to represent the behavior space as an automaton and the task space as a set of desired end states.

The functionality of a technical system must be designed to match the tasks of the user. The procedures that an operator uses to execute tasks are a function of the task (the state changes to be achieved) and the tool used. The user is assumed to have task-related knowledge, which can be seen as knowledge of the job to be done that is independent of the means of doing the job. Note that a task should be defined by an initial state and an end state, not (as is often done) in terms of the procedures used. Thus, the operator's task-related knowledge is really knowledge about desirable changes in the state of the operator. It is separate from tool-related knowledge, which includes the procedures that may be used to solve a given task.

At this point it may be helpful to return to an example described in chapter 4. Suppose that we are designing a secure entry system for a laboratory. Each legitimate laboratory worker is issued a magnetically coded card and a code number. To enter the building it is necessary to have the card read by the appropriate machine and to enter the code number that corresponds to the card. The man-machine system is described as a finite-state machine. The user's task is to enter the building. The user starts in an OUTSIDE state and ends in a LAB state (see figure 4.14). These can both be seen as states of the user, in the sense that the user's perception (of being in a certain place) is part of the user's overall state. The user has to know that being outside is not the same as being inside the laboratory, that a particular building is the laboratory, and so on. This task-related knowledge is independent of the tool-related knowledge that the user requires to enter the building.

To enter the building via the card system, the user needs knowledge of the procedures for entering the building. After repeated practice, this knowledge develops into a skill. The user has to know how to insert the card into the machine, how to enter the code number, etc. How the user acquires the skill does not concern us at the moment (but see chapter 11). Once acquired, the skill becomes a procedure for using the tool. In other words, the use of the tool requires knowledge that is largely procedural. This tool-related knowledge is tied closely to the use of the tool. Some of the functions involved are embedded in the user procedures, and others in the functions of the automatic system. The tool-related knowledge is specific to the tool used and is separable from the task-related knowledge, as illustrated in figure 5.6.

The important feature of the SANE (Skill Acquisition NEtwork) architecture is that the task is described independently of the tools that may be used to accomplish it. In fact, the user may have alternative tools for accomplishing a task. Our laboratory user may arrive at the building equipped with a valid card, a hammer, a jimmy, and a picklock, and equipped with the tool-related knowledge required to use a hammer to break a window. It is open to the user to choose between using the card-entry system as a tool for entering the building and using any other tools for the same purpose. The circumstances that would prompt the user to use either of these modes of entry are not our concern here; we merely wish to point out that the user will often have alternative tools available, as illustrated in figure 5.7.

The objective of building technical systems is to support the user or owner of these systems in accomplishing tasks, either by taking over tasks previously performed by the user or by extending the user's abilities to perform complex tasks. Ideally the design of a device that is to be of maximum benefit to the customer should proceed in the following sequence:

1. Tasks and constraints are analyzed.
2. Task decomposition and device functionality are specified.
3. The complexity of user procedures is evaluated.

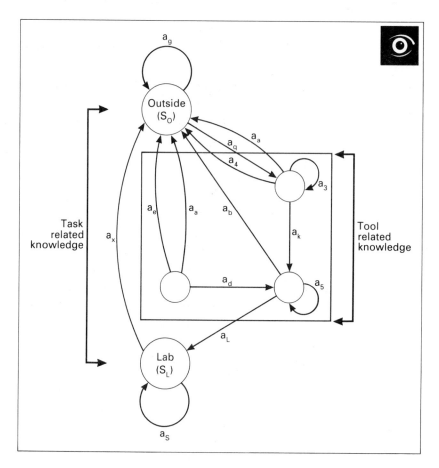

**Figure 5.6** Distinction between task and tool-related knowledge, portrayed in terms of the finite state automaton of figure 4.14.

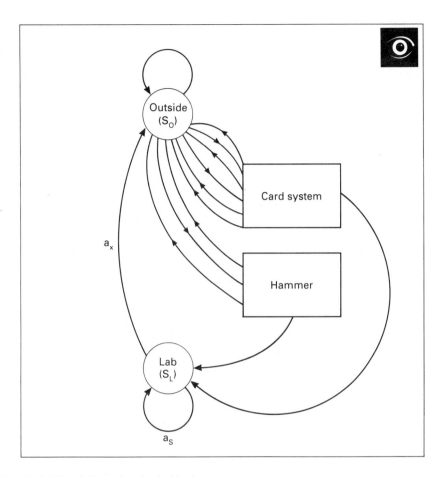

**Figure 5.7** Availability of alternative physical tools.

4. Design modifications are specified, possibly after repeated test/redesign iterations.
5. The detailed design is completed and implemented as a product.
6. Prototypes are built and evaluated, or the product is tested on the market.

In order to illustrate the generality of this approach, let us consider the design of a road map. Road maps are tools used by drivers in tasks which involve driving from one place to another. In terms of the above design sequence: (1) The tasks can be defined in terms of moving from one state (being in place A) to another state (being in place B). The constraints relate to the fact that automobiles are confined to roads and so on. (2) The general task (driving from one place to another) can be decomposed into specific tasks (driving from one particular place to another on a particular occasion). The device functionality relates to the desirability of having specific places (that might be required for a particular task) marked on the map, of having the roads clearly marked, etc. (3) The complexity of the user procedures relates to the requirement of using the map while driving. The way the map is folded and the symbols used on the map will be important here. Steps 4, 5, and 6 have to do with the map production and evaluation. In the production process, proofs will be checked for errors, color veracity, print clarity, etc. Prototypes will be evaluated by experts, and marketplace trials will be conducted by salesmen.

A paper map allows a ariver to search for more efficient routes and to correct errors, but it requires some additional map-reading skills. An automatic route-guidance system could make the task easier for the driver, as it requires little knowledge, but it limits the driver to the use of those functions and locations which are programmed into the system. There may be a new road not included in the system, or the system may be unaware that a certain road is blocked.

In addition to a paper map or an electronic guidance system, a driver may employ a mental map. The navigation skills of the Polynesians and the Inuit illustrate that equivalent functionality may be available from cognitive skills and technical tools. Complex navigational techniques are required to travel by boat between the widespread islands of the Pacific, or between points on the snow-covered Arctic land mass. Among the indigenous peoples, this is achieved by the development of extensive and sophisticated skills representing comprehensive understanding of natural phenomena (Thomas 1987; Gladwin 1970; Irwin 1985; Lewis 1972). Such abilities involve implicit maps and various procedural skills. Models of these could be in SANE, or in sets of ACT* production rules, or in SOAR architectures.

Plans are also tools that can be employed in particular tasks, as illustrated in figure 5.8. Another example may help to make this point. Noble (1989, p. 275) notes that "a chess player may, during an end game, have seen that if his opponent makes a particular move, he will certainly be able to force a checkmate. The realization itself and the planning of possible future action is independent of whether or when the opponent actually makes the move in question. It depends only on the rules of chess and the ability of the player to achieve a fully rational analysis of the possibilities

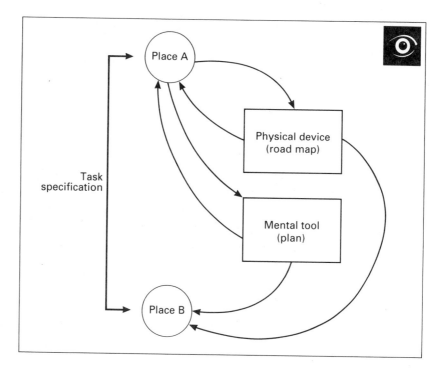

**Figure 5.8**  Alternative tools may be physical or mental.

within those rules." In planning future moves, the player is devising a tool that may or may not be usefully employed in the task of winning the chess game. To the extent that the plan is independent of the progress of the game, it conforms to the definition of a tool within the SANE architecture. In devising the tool, the player is conducting a design operation that must (to be successful) have certain attributes:

- The relevant tasks (winning chess games) and constraints (within the rules of chess) must be defined.
- The task decomposition (i.e., a particular game) and the tool functionality (the rationality of the plan in relation to the game in question) must be specified.
- The complexity of the user procedures (e.g., in terms of memory load) must be evaluated.
- Design modifications must be specifiable if the plan is to be adaptable to changed scenarios or different games.
- If the plan is to be successful in the market (e.g., be published in chess books), prototypes must be evaluated.

The main point is that the SANE architecture can encompass mental as well as physical tools. The principles of good design remain much the same for these different types of tools.

## 5.6 Tradeoff in Design

At the beginning of this chapter we asked how the benefits of low resistance to flow should be offset against the maintenance costs of blood vessels. The quantitative relationship involving the radius of the vessels, the resistance to flow, and the energy costs of maintenance can be calculated from simple physical considerations. A common currency is achieved by expressing both radius and cost in terms of the power requirements, The optimum radius of a single vessel can then be calculated (Milsum and Roberge 1973). This is the radius at which least energy is required to transport the blood.

As we saw in chapter 4, a general feature of optimization is that it results from a tradeoff process in which the costs and benefits of different aspects of the process are counterbalanced. Indeed, it can be said as a matter of principle that tradeoff is the essence of good design. This principle applies just as much to behavior as it does to anatomical or morphological design. As an introductory example, let us take an everyday human situation.

Let us consider a motorist on a long journey, keeping an eye on the fuel gauge. At what point (on the fuel gauge) should the motorist stop for fuel? To answer this question we need to know the risk of running out of fuel as a function of the position of the fuel gauge. In other words, we need to know cost as a function of state. This depends largely on the ecology of the situation—in particular, the distribution of petrol stations. If there were a gasoline station every 10 miles, then the motorist could allow the fuel to deplete until there was just 10 miles' worth of fuel left (a simple threshold policy). If, on the other hand, the stations were distributed normally, then the risk of running out of fuel would increase as the square of the depletion (for the reasons given in section 4.4), and if the distribution conformed to some other function then the risk function would also be different. The evaluation of the risk function by the motorist would depend on the seriousness of running out of fuel (in terms of lost time, extra expense, etc.). In other words, much would depend on whether the motorist was risk-averse or risk-prone. Thus, the function employed by the motorist in decision-making (a component of the goal function; see chapter 4) would

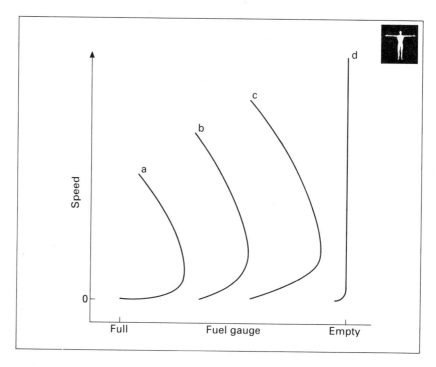

**Figure 5.9** Tradeoff between speed and fuel supply for a motorist. Isoclines a, b, c are for increasing distance.

depend partly on the ecology of the situation (as appreciated by the motorist) and partly on various aspects of the motorist's makeup and internal state.

If the motorist stopped for fuel whenever the gauge reached a simple threshold, then time and energy would be wasted if the threshold was set too low (because the stops would be more frequent than was necessary), and unnecessary risks would be taken if the threshold was set too high. Moreover, a simple threshold would be insensitive to the ecology of the situation (unless the gas stations were placed at regular intervals). The most important disadvantage with the threshold model, however, is that it takes no account of the face that fuel consumption varies with speed. Figure 5.9 shows the distances that can be covered as a function of speed and fuel supply. The exact shape of the functions will vary with the characteristics of the car, but usually there is a particular cruising speed at which the rate of fuel consumption per distance covered is minimized. If there is an urgency factor (desired journey time), then the motorist will want to drive as fast as possible (ignoring safety considerations for the moment), provided there is

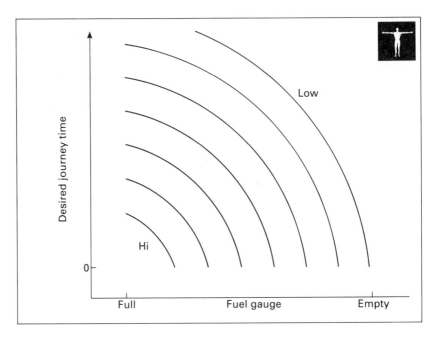

**Figure 5.10** Tradeoff between journey time and fuel supply for a motorist. Isoclines are for speed of travel.

sufficient fuel. When the fuel supply is low, the motorist has to sacrifice speed in the interests of economy (figure 5.10). In other words, in deciding at what speed to drive, there is a continual tradeoff among a number of variables.

Tradeoff considerations are important in animal behavior, and many examples have been investigated. For example, Zach (1979) discovered a simple tradeoff in the foraging behavior of crows that feed on shellfish on the west coast of Canada. The crows hunt for whelks at low tide, usually selecting the largest ones. When they find one, they hover over a rock and drop the whelk so that it breaks open to expose the edible inside. By dropping whelks of various sizes from different heights, Zach discovered that the number of times a whelk has to be dropped in order to break is related to the height from which it is dropped (figure 5.11). The crows have to expend energy in flying up to drop a whelk, so Zach calculated the total amount of upward flying that a crow would have to do to break a whelk from a given height. He showed that the lowest flying cost is incurred if the whelks are dropped from about 5 meters, as figure 5.11 shows. Thus, there is a tradeoff between the number of drops required to break the whelk and the height of

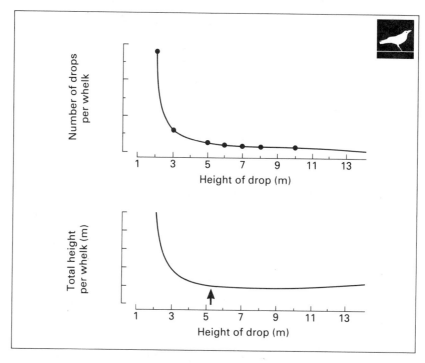

**Figure 5.11**  Tradeoff between number of attempts and cost per attempt for a crow breaking open a whelk. Upper graph shows number of times crow must drop shell to break it as function of height of the drop. Lower graph shows that total amount of upward flight (number of drops × height of each drop) is minimal at the height (arrow) usually used by crows. (After Zach 1979.)

drop. Calculations based on this tradeoff reveal that there is an optimal dropping height (figure 5.11). Zach found that the height from which crows usually drop their whelks corresponds closely to the calculated optimal drop height of 5 meters. Thus, it appears that the crows somehow have been programmed to exploit this particular feature of the foraging situation.

The tradeoffs inherent in animal behavior will be embodied in the goal function. In chapter 4 we saw that the goal function includes those properties of the animal that are relevant to the notional costs associated with the various state variables and with the various aspects of behavior. These may include physical properties of the animal as well as evaluations represented in the brain. For example, a person traveling across town on foot has to make decisions as to when to rest, to walk, to jog, to pause, etc. The goal function will include factors associated with the person's energy reserves, the risks of crossing roads, etc. It would also include some more physical factors, such as the length of the person's legs (which affects the natural walking pace). Optimal decisions between jogging, walking, pausing, and resting will inevitably be affected by all these factors, and will result in a tradeoff between the rate of energy expenditure and the speed of travel.

An inevitable consequence of the optimality approach to animal behavior is that there will be tradeoffs among alternative courses of action. The logic of this conclusion is fairly simple. If the conditions relevant to only one activity pertain at a particular time, then the optimal policy is straightforward: The animal engages in that activity and optimizes its pattern of behavior with respect to the use of energy, time, etc. For example, the optimal behavior for a hungry pigeon faced with a source of food is to eat at a negatively accelerating rate (Sibly and McFarland 1976; McCleery 1977). If the conditions relevant to two or more activities apply simultaneously, the animal has to choose between them. Moreover, its state when one activity is possible is not the same as its state when two activities are possible, and so the optimal behavior for one activity in the presence of the other possibility is not the same as the optimal behavior for that activity on its own.

Recent applications of "optimality thinking" to animal behavior indicate that animals do not usually concentrate on one task until it is finished, but tend to interleave tasks. This is what would be required for an animal to trade off among all important criteria. For example, pigeons that are both hungry and thirsty, and placed in a position where they can work for food or for water, do not complete one task before starting the other; they interleave the two in a manner required by the optimal tradeoff between the cost of carrying high deficits and the cost of consuming at a high rate (Sibly and McFarland 1976). Similarly, foraging sticklebacks change their pattern of predation when there is danger from predators; they achieve an optimal trade off between attention to prey and attention to predators (Milinski and Heller 1978; Heller and Milinski 1979). And great tits, when their territory is threatened by intruders, increase their vigilance at the expense of their food intake rate (Ydenberg and Houston 1986; Stephens and Krebs 1986).

### Points to Remember

- Any present-day natural form or biological structure is the outcome of compromise among various selective pressures. Such forms can be seen as the outcome of a design operation that aims at the optimal form on the basis of certain criteria.

- Although the mechanism of machine design is different from that pertaining in the animal kingdom, the principles remain the same. The principle of optimal design simply asserts that a system (whether animate or inanimate) that is capable of modification in successive versions will tend to evolve toward an optimal configuration with respect to the selective pressures (or market forces) acting on the successive versions.

- The argument from optimal design can also be applied to behavior. An animal can be so designed that it attains the optimal behavior sequence in a given set of circumstances.

- It is important to distinguish between optimization with respect to the cost function and optimization with respect to the goal function. No animal can be expected to perfectly attain an optimal behavior sequence with respect to a real cost criterion.

- Optimization with respect to a goal function is possible. On the basis that animal behavior is rational, we can expect an animal to behave optimally with respect to utility.

- Both design and behavior involve decisions. A decision (of a person, an animal, or a robot) is simply the process by which the decision variables are changed. This process can occur as a part as a design operation or as a part of behavior.

- In this book we use the term *utility* for the decision currency employed by the individual, and *cost* for the ecological equivalent of this. We use *utility function* for functions of a single decision variable, and *goal function* for functions of a decision vector. We reserve the more general term *objective function* to denote the scientist's hypothesis about the goal or utility function. We reserve *cost function* for the ecological equivalent of the goal or utility function.

- In designing the behavior of a system, we can divide the relevant state variables according to whether they belong to the environmental space, to the behavior space, or to the task space.

- The traditional processes of machine design can be accelerated if the initial design and testing can be carried out by computer-aided design. This can help with the design of systems that involve dynamic behavior of animals, robots, and man-machine systems.

- The procedures that an operator uses to execute tasks are a function of the task (the state changes to be achieved) and the tool used.

- The user is assumed to have task-related knowledge, which can be seen as knowledge of the job to be done that is independent of the means of doing the job. Note that a task should be defined by an initial state and an end state, and not (as is often done) in terms of the procedures used.
- Plans are mental tools that can be employed in particular tasks in a manner analogous to the manner in which physical tools are used.
- A general feature of optimization is that it results from a tradeoff process in which the costs and benefits of different aspects of the process are counterbalanced. It can be said as a matter of principle that tradeoff is the essence of good design.

In robotics, opinions vary as to the distinction between an automaton and a robot. Heiserman (1981) states that true robots are characterized by adaptability and autonomy, but he finds the latter hard to define. A machine that is controlled directly by a human operator or indirectly by means of a prescribed program is not autonomous. Such machines are essentially mechanical extensions of human activity, requiring control via a radio link or an umbilical cord. Even so-called industrial robots are not true robots according to Heiserman, because they require indirect human intervention when it is time to change the task.

Other roboticists are content with the usual dictionary definitions of a robot as a machine that is capable of performing near-human tasks, an intelligent and obedient machine that is capable of some behavior, and so forth. According to Hall and Hall (1985), there is only one definition of an industrial robot that is internationally accepted. It was developed in 1979 by a group of industrial scientists at the Robotics Industries Association who defined an industrial robot as a reprogrammable, multifunctional manipulator designed to move materials, parts, tools, or specialized devices through various programmed motions for the performance of a variety of tasks. Each of these definitions begs a number of questions, but it seems to us that the most important issue is the nature and definition of autonomy. Before addressing this issue, let us look at some aspects of nonautonomy.

## 6.1 The Robot as Automaton

Originally, an automaton was a clockwork machine in the form of a doll or an animal that performed particular operations in a life-like manner (Cohen 1966; McCorduck 1979). In strict scientific terms, it is extremely hard to define an automaton. At one extreme, an automaton is a mechanism that acts automatically, without human intervention, and performs a preset routine regardless of the circumstances. The point here is that such automata act unconditionally. Some automata, however, are capable of acting conditionally. That is, when in one state they behave in one way and when in another state they behave in a different way. The change in state may result from the accomplishment of a particular task, as in the automatic car wash mentioned in chapter 4, or it may result from a change in environmental circumstances.

As a example, let us look at a design given by Heiserman (1981) for a robot which is capable of moving around a room and extricating itself when it encounters an obstacle. This machine also monitors its own battery level and begins to seek out a nest when the level reaches a prescribed low point. The nest houses a battery charger and a bright light which aids the robot in finding it. Upon noting that its battery is low, the robot searches for the nest, activating its response-to-stall mechanism if it encounters an obstacle on the way. It is evident that the robot uses some kind of positive phototaxis in homing in on the light that indicates the nest. Upon reaching the nest, the robot connects itself to the charger and begins monitoring the current. When this current falls below a prescribed level, the robot ignores the light and treats the nest as any other obstacle. The main flow chart for this behavior is shown in figure 6.1.

The operating routine begins with a forward-motion program, which starts the machine running across the floor in a straight-ahead fashion. Once under way, the program checks the MAN switch to see whether the operator wishes to take over manual control. If this is not required, the program then checks for a stall condition. This is the only provision for sensing contact with an immovable object. If there is a stall on either the drive motor or the steering motor, then a stall-response routine is implemented. Finally, the program checks for the battery level, and enters a nest-search routine if the battery is low.

Heiserman (1981, p. 387) writes: "This is a rather high-level parabot machine. It is capable of caring for its own needs and surviving rather well without human intervention. The only feature that knocks it out of the realm of real robots is the fact that all its responses to the environment are prescribed in its memory. It makes no decisions independent of the program specified earlier by the programmer that gave birth to the creature."

We have here two different issues. The first is whether the machine is capable of learning to perform new responses not prescribed by the programmer. It is important to note that learning

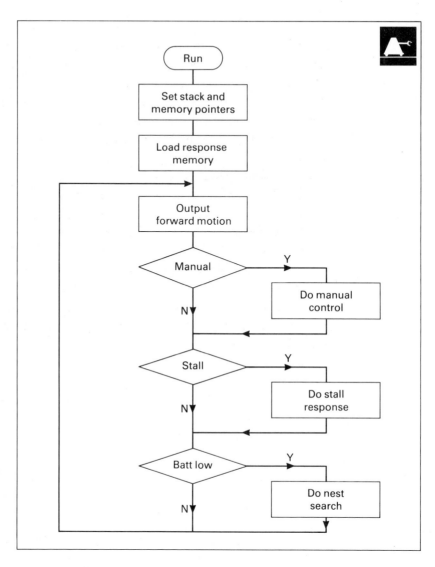

**Figure 6.1**  Main program flowchart for robot with nest search. (After Heiserman 1981.)

can encompass many degrees of autonomy, ranging from simple conditional adaptation to truly cognitive innovation. The second issue concerns the extent to which a machine can be motivationally autonomous. In our opinion, Heiserman's machine is not motivationally autonomous, because its changes in behavior are simply contingent upon fixed thresholds.

If we look closely at the mechanism responsible for deciding when to initiate nest search, we discover that the decision is entirely dependent on a battery-checking subroutine, which compares the actual voltage level with some prescribed low-level trigger voltage and then returns to the calling program. As soon as the battery threshold is passed, the machine implements the nest-search and battery-recharge subroutines, as indicated in figure 6.2. This is a very unsophisticated and unsatisfactory way of organizing behavioral priorities. Moreover, a robot based on such threshold-crossing principles is simply an automaton with some built-in contingency routines. It is a robot without motivational autonomy.

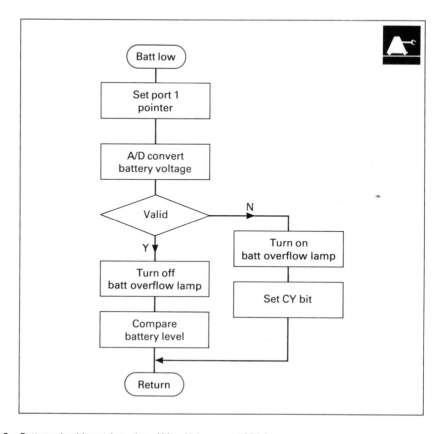

**Figure 6.2**  Battery-checking subroutine. (After Heiserman 1981.)

## 6.2  Control

Why do we maintain that a robot with built-in contingency routines lacks autonomy? The reason is that such robots are controlled by an outside agent. They do not have self-control. This issue has both conceptual and technical aspects.

The conceptual issues have been admirably addressed by Dennett. He points out that we want to be in control, and to control both ourselves and our destinies. "But," he asks, "what is control, and what is its relation to causation and determinism? Curiously, this obviously important question has scarcely been addressed by philosophers." (1984, p. 51)

In ordinary terms, "A controls B if and only if the relation between A and B is such that A can drive B into whichever of B's normal range of states A wants B to be in . . . for something to be a controller its states must include desires—or something "like" desires—about the states of something (else)." (Dennett 1984, p. 52)

It follows that, for an agent to be self-controlled, its states must include desires. In other words, a self-controlling agent must have some kind of motivation. Moreover, writes Dennett (1984, p. 116), "The robot has interests (if some what contrived and artificial interests). . . . So events bearing on those interests can be, and should be, recognized as having a special interest for the robot. Then it is clear what a robot-opportunity would be: The robot has a robot-opportunity whenever it is caused by such special-interest events to 'consider', and if it so decides, to plan and execute, a timely project designed by it to further its interests in the light of those events." (Note that, for Dennett, robot = autonomous agent.) In other words, the autonomous robot can recognize opportunities and exploit them.

We must now consider the notion of autonomy in a more technical sense. Two important concepts here are *observability* and *controllability*. These concepts, first developed by Kalman (1963), have proved to be very important in control systems. In 1968 Kalman suggested that these concepts might also be important in biology, and they have proved to be particularly relevant to behavior studies (McFarland 1971; McFarland and Houston 1981; McFarland 1989b). As Kalman (1963) notes:

*A system is said to be completely controllable if it is possible to move any state to any other state in a finite time by a suitable choice of input.*

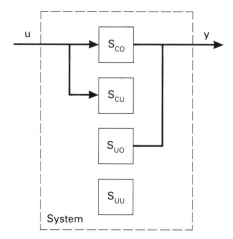

**Figure 6.3** Partitioning a system on the basis of controllability and observability criteria. co: controllable and observable; cu: controllable but unobservable; uo: uncontrollable but observable; uu: uncontrollable and unobservable.

*A system is said to be completely observable if observation of the inputs and outputs for a finite time enables the state to be determined.*

*A system may be partly controllable and partly observable. In fact, we may classify a system into subsystems on this basis. There are four possible classes, as shown in figure 6.3.*

Consider some theoretical implications of these concepts. The relationship between the inputs and outputs of a system may be described by the transfer function of the system. If the transfer function remains the same, irrespective of the input, the system is said to be *linear*. Many nonlinear systems behave linearly for a given range of inputs. If this is their normal operating range, they may be said to be *normally linear*.

Kalman showed that for linear systems the transfer function is equivalent to those states of the system that are controllable and observable. This result has two important implications:

- If a technique for obtaining a transfer function is applied to a system, any uncontrollable or unobservable parts of the system will not be represented.
- If a completely controllable and observable model were to be constructed, there would be no grounds for objection to the state variables, because they would be mathematically derived from the transfer function. (This is of importance in the behavioral sci-

ences, where there is often disagreement about the way a system is described.)

Kalman's results apply only to linear systems. However, we can extend them to nonlinear systems by making use of the close correspondence between the dynamical systems theory (which Kalman used) and the theory of finite automata. Kalman (1963) compared his theorems with Moore's (1956) results on automata, and Arbib (1966, 1969) investigated this relationship in considerable detail. The advantage of finite-automata theory is that the question of linearity does not arise unless extra structure is added. That is, unless the system switches between modes which have different structures (see chapter 4 above and pp. 85–88 of McFarland and Houston 1981). We do not propose to enter into details here, but we hope that it will be sufficient for our purposes to note that the concepts of observability and controllability apply to those nonlinear systems that can be analyzed in terms of the theory of finite automata.

Certain types of robots, including those with simple threshold devices for switching from one activity to another, will be controllable. That is, if the controller knows enough about the state of the robot, the robot can be made to behave as the controller wishes. Other types of robots will not be controllable. The would-be controller may be able to exercise some type of influence over the robot, but the extent of this control will depend on the robot's motivational tendencies. Presumably robots will differ in this respect. A man is usually more successful in influencing a dog's behavior than a cat's, because the dog is more amenable. Dogs like to be cooperative; cats do not. Uncontrollable robots, like dogs and cats, are autonomous.

Certain aspects of the system may not be observable, and certain aspects may not be controllable by the investigator. This unobservability and this uncontrollability pose problems in the interpretation of scientific data. For example, a model that contains no redundant elements is said to be *minimal*. A model that is the only one that can account for the data is said to be *unique*. Kalman (1963) showed that a model is minimal if and only if it is completely controllable and completely observable. Moreover, a minimal model is unique. An autonomous robot would not be completely controllable and observable. Therefore, an investigator's model of such a robot would not be minimal or unique. In other words, an investigator cannot expect to be able to produce a complete (minimal and unique) model of an autonomous robot, and for this reason he should not expect to be able to control the autonomous robot.

## 6.3 Motivational Autonomy

In everyday language, the term *motivation* is used to describe the experience of desiring to act in particular ways in order to achieve certain ends. Thus, if a man wants sexual satisfaction, we say he is sexually motivated. The scientific study of motivation is diverse in its origins and methods of approach, but motivation is not difficult to define in scientific terms. Changes in behavior may be due to any one, or any combination of, the following five factors: external stimuli, maturation, injury, motivation, and learning. Motivation can be defined as including reversible processes that are responsible for changes in behavior. This definition distinguishes motivation from the other four types of process responsible for behavioral change, which are all irreversible. The definition is purely classificatory in nature (it comes from the Latin for *movement*). It invokes no material or mechanistic explanation of the processes involved.

Motivation is best described in terms of the state of the system. As we saw in chapter 4, the motivational state of an animal at any particular time depends on its physiological state, the cue state arising from its perception of the external world, and the consequence of its current behavior. A mobile robot is in a similar situation to an animal, in that its state is influenced both by environmental conditions and by the robot's own behavior. The robot does not have a physiology as such, but it has some equivalent state variables, such as fuel supply and operating temperature. The robot will be designed to operate within certain upper and lower temperature limits, analogous to the tolerance limits of animals (figure 4.9).

Changes of state do not themselves cause changes in behavior; however, they should be thought of as analogous to mechanical displacement or electrical charge, requiring some compliance or capacitance mechanisms to exert an effort (force or voltage) on the mechanisms responsible for behavior. In the case of robots there will presumably be monitors for the fuel deficit, and temperature, equivalent to the physiological monitors of animals (see chapter

4). It is important to recognize that there are two stages in this monitoring process, as illustrated in figure 4.12. The first involves monitoring the state variables with appropriate sensors; the second involves some sort of calibration of the monitored message. Obviously, the same monitored diplacement in state will differ in significance for different robots or animals. Moreover, decisions have to be made among various different displacements in state, all monitored by different kinds of sensors. Clearly, these parallel messages must all be calibrated in terms of their significance, or importance, to the robot or animal making the decisions.

As we saw in chapter 4, where decisions are to be based on displacements in state there must be some assessment of the cost (or importance) of the value of each state variable. Moreover, where there is a difinite (lethal) boundary to the state variable, the cost is likely to be quadratic. For example, as the voltage of the battery in Heiserman's parabot declines, the associated cost should increase as the square (figure 6.4). This function corresponds to the risk of running out of fuel (figure 4.16). Similarly, we can imagine that the robot will cease to operate if its temperature rises to high, so that there is also a similar function for temperature (figure 6.5). When

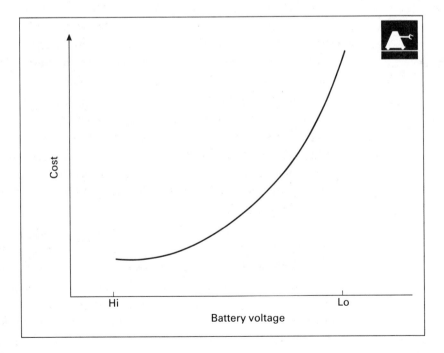

**Figure 6.4** Cost associated with fuel supply as function of battery voltage.

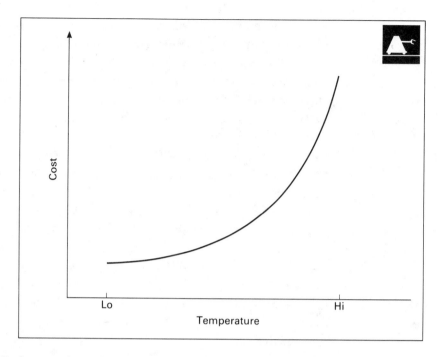

**Figure 6.5** Cost associated with temperature as function of temperature.

we combine figures 6.4 and 6.5, we obtain a plane in the state space with the cost isoclines superimposed, as illustrated in figure 6.6. Let us suppose that the robot is in a particular state $\mathbf{X}$ (figure 6.6). As the robot goes about its business the battery's voltage will fall, and the temperature will rise (we assume this for the purposes of illustration), giving the trajectory $\mathbf{X}_0 - \mathbf{X}_1$ (figure 6.6). According to Heiserman's (1981) threshold model, the robot should start seeking its nest when the battery level reaches the particular threshold B (state $\mathbf{X}_2$ in figure 6.6). This may be satisfactory under some circumstances; but suppose the robot's temperature increase were much steeper, as shown by trajectory $\mathbf{X}_1' - \mathbf{X}_2'$ in figure 6.7. It is possible that by the time the temperature reached the battery threshold (state $\mathbf{X}_2'$) the trajectory would be dangerously high. No doubt it would be possible to incorporate a temperature threshold, above which the robot would switch to cooling behavior. But there might not be enough fuel to accomplish this cooling behavior (this would depend upon the cooling opportunity profile). It is not difficult to see that, as soon as there are more than one or two important state variables, the threshold model becomes totally unsatisfactory. The designer will find it difficult to find a suitable

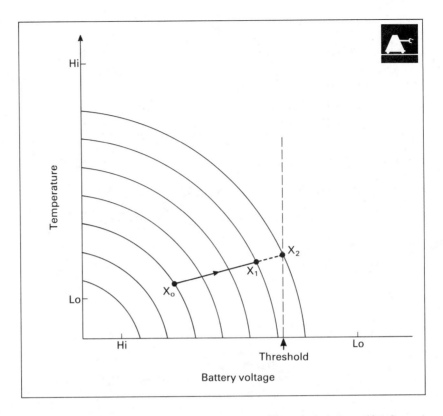

**Figure 6.6** Cost isoclines for temperature and battery voltage. The robot starts seeking its nest when the trajectory crosses the battery-voltage threshold (dashed line).

location for each threshold. If the designer plays it safe and places the thresholds low, the robot will inevitable be very inefficient. On the other hand, to place the thresholds high is very risky. A alternative design would allow for tradeoffs among the important variables.

We now need to consider what factors should be taken into account in deciding when to seek the nest. Assuming that the robot has a measure of its current fuel supply, and that this measure can be calibrated in terms of its importance, or value, we (as designers) must ensure that the calibration results in units which will enable the robot to compare its need for fuel with its other needs. It is clear that such measures are best expressed in terms of utility (see chapter 3). In other words, we should design our robot so that it compares the merits of differing activities in terms of their utility. Figure 6.8 shows a likely utility function for the fuel supply.

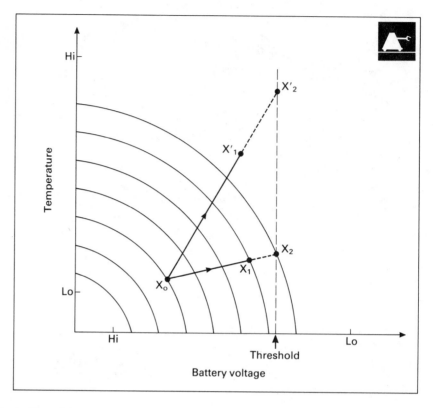

**Figure 6.7** As figure 6.6, but with alternative trajectory which reaches the battery threshold when the temperature is dangerously high.

In order to recharge its batteries, the robot must cease its ongoing behavior. The ongoing behavior will also have a utility function associated with its consequences, as shown in figure 6.9. This may relate to the way in which the ongoing behavior affects the current state of the robot, or, if a task is involved, it may reflect progress with the task (as appreciated by the robot and therefore, strictly, represented as part of the state). In deciding when to recharge its battery, the robot takes all relevant utility functions into account.

This evaluation of utilities is what makes the robot motivationally autonomous. If we were to try to make Heiserman's robot motivationally autonomous, then we would alter the main program flow chart (fig. 6.1) to look something like figure 6.10. In other words, the motivationally autonomous robot decides for itself what activity to implement at any time, on the basis of an evaluation of the utilities of the alternatives. To do this the robot

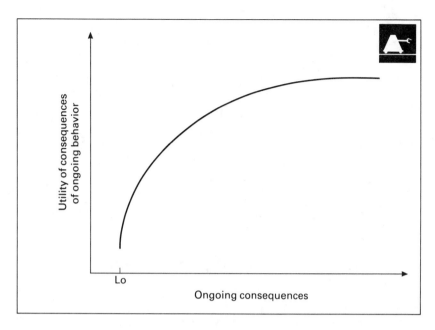

**Figure 6.8**  Utility function for robot's power supply.

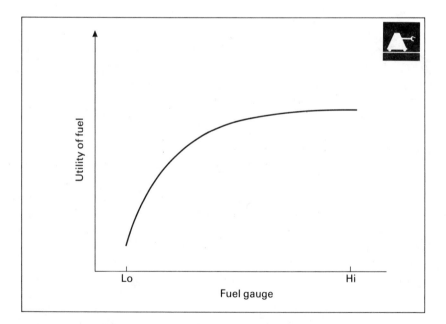

**Figure 6.9**  Utility function associated with consequences of robot's ongoing behavior.

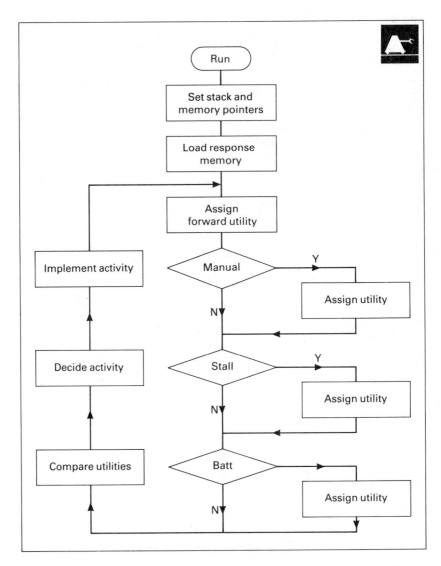

**Figure 6.10** Modification of main program flow chart (figure 6.1) to introduce motivational autonomy.

must have access to a set of values (the set of utility functions) derived from its overall goal function.

We are not advocating a robot designed along the lines of figure 6.10, because a number of problems remain to be sorted out. Indeed, the remainder of this book is devoted to these problems. What we are trying to do here is define motivational autonomy. Our definition is inevitably somewhat arbitrary, because the difference between a motivationally autonomous robot and an automaton with elaborate conditional subroutines is a difference of degree. Nevertheless, it seems useful to define a motivationally autonomous robot as one in which changes in behavior are the results of decisions based on evaluation of the circumstances. In a well-designed autonomous robot such evaluation will be related to functional questions, such as efficiency, costs, and benefits.

To cope with the concept of autonomy, we must redefine the traditional ethological view of motivation (outlined above and in chapter 4). (See McFarland 1991b for a discussion.) If we ask whether automata have motivation, the answer must be yes, according to the criteria outlined above. The motivational state of a clockwork mouse is simply the part of the state of the machine that influences its behavior. Does this mean that an automaton is self-motivating? Here the answer must be no, because an automaton is, by definition, controllable by an outside agent. There seems to be a paradox here. On the one hand, motivation is whatever moves the machine; on the other hand, automata are not self-motivating.

Clearly, the above definition of motivation is not adequate to distinguish between an automaton and an autonomous agent. The problem lies with the consequences of behavior. The motivational state of an automaton is affected, willy nilly, by the consequences of its behavior. The motivational state of an autonomous agent, on the other hand, is affected by the expected consequences of its behavior. In the case of a well-designed automaton, such as an animal, the likely consequences of each activity have been anticipated at the design state. In the case of an autonomous agent, it is the agent that does the expecting. It is this feature that gives the autonomous agent its self-motivating property.

An autonomous agent, before engaging in a new activity, takes account of the expected consequences of the alternatives. To do this the agent requires knowledge of the probable consequences. In other words, it must have some memory of past consequences of

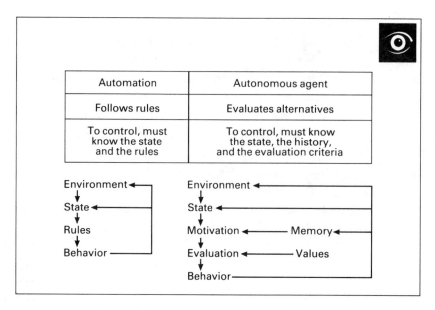

**Figure 6.11** Some distinctions between automata and autonomous agents.

similar activities. On the basis of its knowledge of the likely consequences of alternative activities, the agent is able to perform some evaluation of the situation. (See McFarland 1991b.)

The motivation of an autonomous agent depends not only on its state but also on its assessment of the likely consequences of future activity. As figure 6.11 shows, this redefinition of motivation plays a key role in defining autonomy. As Dennett (1984) pointed out, the autonomous agent, to be self-controlling, must want something.

## 6.4  Changing from One Activity to Another

We must discuss a number of problems associated with changing from one activity to another before proceeding with the topics of motivation and autonomy.

First, the utility gained from an activity depends partly on environmental factors. The utility is influenced by the consequences of the behavior. For example, the utility gained from picking blackberries depends partly on the availability and accessibility of berries on the bushes. These parameters determine how the rate of picking (in attempts per minute) is translated into returns in grams per minute. The *availability* $(r)$ of blackberries is a function of their number and size (i.e., grams per square meter of bush surface).

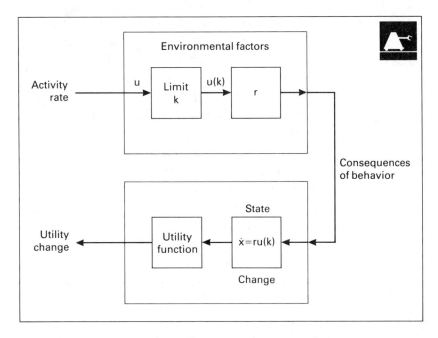

**Figure 6.12** Consequences of behavior in terms of accessibility (k) and availability (r) of resources.

The *accessibility* (k) of blackberries is related to the difficulty of picking them, and includes such factors as the berries' height above the ground, the number of intervening thorns, and the degree of adherence of the berries to the bush. The availability is usually represented as a parameter and the availability as a constraint, as illustrated in figure 6.12. The utility associated with the returns will depend on the number of blackberries already picked (the relevant state variable).

The environmental factors that determine the consequences of behavior often vary with time. For example, herring gulls often feed on garbage dumps. The gulls studied at Walney Island (see figure 4.21) visited the dump only when food was available. The normal routine was for the trucks to arrive at the site at about 1100 hours and 1600 hours, having just collected domestic rubbish from houses. The trucks tipped their contents onto the site, and this (consisting largely of waste food) was then covered with inorganic matter by a bulldozer. The availability of food for gulls was severely restricted by this routine, because the food was not accessible to them after it had been buried by the bulldozer. The returns that a gull could obtain from a time unit of foraging at different times throughout the day constitutes the *opportunity profile* for that activity.

The utility to be gained from a particular activity depends on the change in state that will result from the activity. This, in turn, depends on the initial state and the consequences of the behavior. The current opportunities determine the consequences that can accrue from a given unit of behavior. The rate and intensity of the behavior will determine the extent of these consequences. In a situation where there are alternative possible activities, a decision has to be made. The intelligent solution is to make such decisions on a rational basis, as we saw in chapter 2.

Rational decision making boils down to maximizing utility at each and every decision. In other words, a rational animal or robot should change from one activity to another only when the change will result in an increase in marginal utility. To do this, the decision must take account of the current state and of the change in state that would be expected to result from each alternative. Each alternative will have various costs and benefits associated with it. For example, in changing from its ongoing behavior to battery-recharging behavior, the mobile robot is likely to incur the cost involved in battery recharging, the benefits gained from battery recharging, the cost of not doing the ongoing behavior, and the cost of changing itself. Before seeing how these combine to give the overall change in utility, let us look at each in more detail.

- Normally, batteries have to be recharged slowly to avoid damaging them. If the robot does not turn itself off, there will be a low rate of energy expenditure throughout the period of recharging.
- There will be a continual change in state during recharging, due to the increase in battery voltage. The net benefit will be a function of the increased voltage minus the voltage loss due to energy expenditure during recharging.
- The cost of not performing the ongoing behavior will depend on the nature of the behavior. If the behavior is of the type that normally replenishes a deficit (like feeding and drinking in animals), the deficit may grow during the period of inactivity. If the behavior is of a type that accumulates some external material (such as bricklaying or nest-building), then there may be costs associated with postponement of the project.
- The cost of changing from one activity to another presents considerable problems. We saw in chapter 4 that when an animal changes from one activity to another it usually has to pay for the change in energy and time. Thus, an animal that becomes thirsty

as a result of feeding may have to travel to find water to drink. We would expect this animal to change from feeding to drinking when the net benefits to be gained from drinking exceed those gained from feeding. The problem is that there are no benefits gained from the activity of changing itself, so we cannot follow the normal rule that an animal engages in the activity that brings the greatest net benefit at each instant of time.

When the time comes for our autonomous robot to recharge its batteries, we expect the net benefit to be gained from recharging the batteries to be greater than that gained from the ongoing behavior (see above). However, our robot cannot suddenly change to recharging batteries, because it must first seek the nest. The robot expends energy and time in seeking the nest, but it gains no benefits. It is true that it gains benefits from recharging its batteries, but this is a different activity. It may be thought by the reader that nest-seeking should be part of battery-charging behavior. Indeed, in animal behavior circles, nest seeking would be called the *appetitive behavior*, and battery charging the *consummatory behavior* (McFarland 1981). The problem is that simply changing the name of the activity does not alter the fact that there is a period of time during which the robot is gaining no benefits from its behavior. We have to account for the fact that the robot changes from its ongoing behavior, from which it obtains benefits, to a new activity (nest seeking) from which it obtains no benefits. Exactly the same cost-of-changing problem occurs in animal behavior theory, as we saw in chapter 4.

A solution to the cost-of-changing problem has to be found in both functional and mechanistic terms. That is, we need a satisfactory functional argument to account for the fact that the robot (or animal) apparently violates an important functional principle. We also need some hypotheses that are capable of providing a mechanism for changing from one activity to another. Empirical studies on animals (see chapter 4) indicate that changes in behavior are postponed, or occur less frequently, when the cost of changing is raised. This suggests that the cost of changing is added to the cost of the activity to which the animal is about to change, since this has the effect of postponing the changeover (figure 6.13).

We now have to consider further problems. For the animal (or robot) to postpone changing activity in accordance with the magnitude of the cost of changing, it must have foreknowledge about the

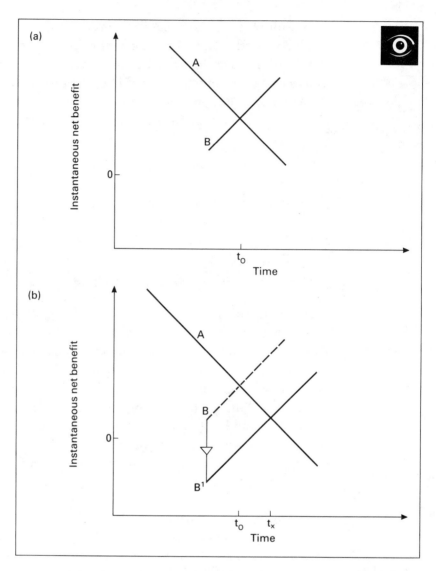

**Figure 6.13** Cost of changing from one activity (A) to another (B). (a) When the cost of changing is zero, the changeover occurs at $t_0$. (b) Increasing the cost of changing has the effect of reducing the benefit due from B from B to B, thus postponing the changeover from $t_0$ to $t_x$.

cost of changing. How does it "know" how large the cost of changing is going to be? Moreover, there will often be a number of activities that the animal could change to, each with a different cost of changing. How can it assess these different costs? The first part of the answer is that the animal does not have genuine foreknowledge of the costs of changing. It can only have estimates. Second, it has been suggested (McFarland 1989b) that animals obtain these estimates as part of their assessment of the opportunity values of the alternative activities. The first step is to stop thinking about costs and benefits and start thinking in the equivalent motivational terms. In chapter 4 we saw that we can equate the net benefit of an activity with its utility, and we can identify this with the animal's motivational tendency to perform the activity.

Suppose that an animal engaged in activity A is likely to change to activity B. The strength of the tendency for B will depend on the internal state relevant to B in some combination with the cue state (see chapter 4). The cue state will be influenced by cues indicating the opportunity value (e.g., the likelihood of obtaining food per unit time if the animal were to spend time feeding) of the activity in question. It is not difficult to envisage that the opportunity value could include an assessment of the cost of changing. Cues indicating a high cost of changing would diminish the opportunity value, because the time and energy spent changing would diminish the net returns per unit time gained from activity B. There would be a lowering of the B tendency to a degree depending on the strength of these opportunity cues, and this would lead to postponement of the A-B changeover. Once the change had taken place and the cost of changing had been paid, the inhibiting effect of the opportunity cues would no longer be effective, and there would be a consequent rise in the B tendency (figure 6.14). In other words, the tendency to perform an activity increases soon after the animal starts to perform the activity, and thereafter declines as the consequences of the activity have their normal effect. McFarland (1989b) has pointed out that this is exactly what we would expect from a model in which the tendency is initially enhanced by positive feedback and subsequently diminished by negative feedback (figure 6.15). Thus, it may be that positive feedback provides the cost-of-changing mechanism.

In assessing the cost of changing among a number of alternatives, animals presumably evaluate the alternatives. But how many

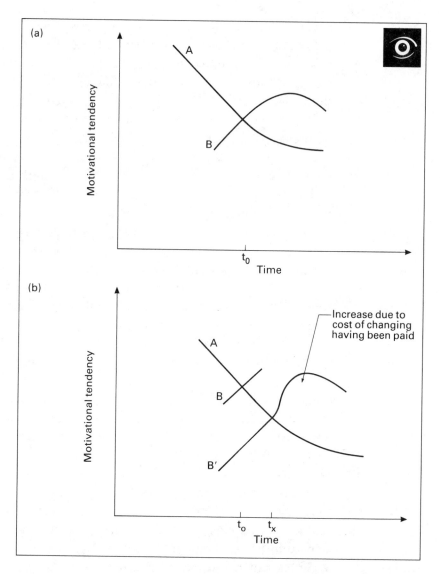

**Figure 6.14** Increase in tendency to perform behavior B as a result of the cost of changing's having been paid. (a) Zero cost of changing. (b) Nonzero cost of changing.

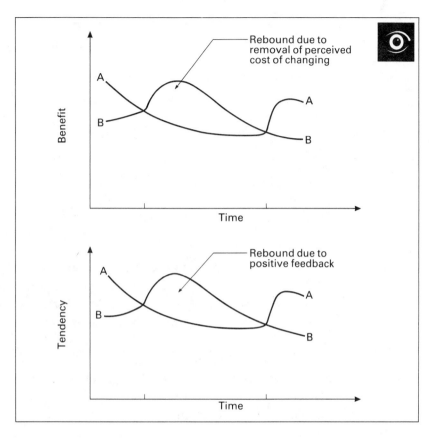

**Figure 6.15** Comparison of functional (above) and mechanistic (below) models of changing from one activity to another. (After McFarland 1989b.)

alternatives are taken into account? To answer this question we need to explore the topic of motivational evaluation.

## 6.5 Motivational Evaluation

Motivational evaluation involves the assignment of (expected) utility to behavioral alternatives. Once the utilities have been assigned, a decision can be made. This is the essence of autonomous behavior.

The first problem we have to address is the very large number of behavioral alternatives. Does motivational evaluation imply assignment of utility to all alternatives? In the case of our nest-seeking robot (above) we assumed that all alternatives were reviewed sequentially and that utility was assigned appropriately (see figure 6.10). Such an arrangement may be satisfactory where there are only a few alternatives, but it would be very time-consuming and inefficient if there were many. For an animal, the number of alternatives would seem to be very high, so a sequential search of all possibilities would seem unlikely. Moreover, our robot example implies that the alternatives are serviced in a particular order (i.e., check manual control, check for motor stall, check battery level). A sequential procedure of this type would not only be very cumbersome; in addition, it would rarely service the alternatives in the best order. An important aspect of motivational evaluation is to provide for flexible decision-making.

How many alternatives there are and how they should be evaluated are questions relevant to both animal behavior and AI. In animal behavior, it is important to remember that motivation includes factors relevant to incipient activities as well as to current behavior. At any given time, an animal's motivational state is usually capable of supporting more than one activity. Thus, if an animal is thirsty and water is available, its motivational state can support drinking behavior; if it is hungry and there is some evident prospect of finding food, it can support foraging behavior; if a potential mate is present but the animal is not in the right stage of its reproductive cycle, its motivational state cannot support mating behavior. In such an animal, drinking and foraging would be incipient activities, or candidates for behavioral expression, but mating behavior would not be a candidate. If the animal were an automaton, then which candidates gained behavioral expression would depend on the rules, or other mapping, relating motivational state to behavior. If the animal were an autonomous agent, we would expect it to take account of the likely consequences of the behavioral alternatives.

In AI the problem of evaluating the numerous candidates for behavioral expression is sometimes seen as a breadth-of-search problem and sometimes a problem of selecting actions from a fixed repertoire (Maes 1991). Whatever the decision-making mechanism employed by an animal, it must cope with the following tasks:

- The numerous behavioral alternatives must somehow be reduced to a manageable number of candidates for behavioral expression (the breadth-of-search task).
- To evaluate the alternatives, the animal must have some knowledge of the probable consequences of the alternative activities (the depth-of-search problem).

If the animal is an automaton, these two tasks are accomplished by means of built-in procedures. The breadth-of-search task is circumvented, because the animal simply performs that activity dictated by its current state. The depth-of-search task does not arise, because the possible consequences of an activity are not evaluated but are simply assumed as part of the design process. If the animal is autonomous, these two tasks become problems for the individual. In AI terminology they are both aspects of *planning*, which can be defined as generating of a sequence of activities designed to achieve a particular end without performing those activities.

The search procedures involved in planning generate knowledge (Anderson 1983b; Newell 1980). Most cognitive scientists assume that planning and actual performance of behavior generates procedural knowledge (roughly speaking, the knowledge of what sequences of operations are appropriate in given situations and to what results they lead). As a result, the agent will know under what conditions a particular activity can be applied and to what consequences it is likely to lead. In a sense, an automaton also has this type of knowledge, but in a less explicit form. In an automaton, the information concerning the behavioral options and their consequences is implicit in the design. In an autonomous system, some of the equivalent information may also be explicit. For example, a person may know how to ride a bicycle. Part of the information required for this activity is stored as procedural knowledge, or skill, but part of it is implicit in the person's physical makeup, leg length, stance on the bicycle, etc. A person mounting a bicycle knows which skill routine is appropriate, and what consequences are likely to follow. The person knows *how* to ride a bicycle, and they know *that* he has the skill to ride a bicycle.

The distinction between *knowing how* and *knowing that* is important. These concepts, which originated with Ryle (1949), have been absorbed into human cognitive psychology (Anderson 1976) in the guise of *procedural* and *declarative* representations of knowledge. A procedural representation directly reflects the use to which the knowledge will be put in controlling the agent's behavior, whereas a declarative representation corresponds to a statement describing relationships among events in the agent's world. (In the latter case, the statement does not commit the agent to any particular course of action.) These terms were introduced into animal behavior studies by Dickinson (1980), who cites experimental evidence for the validity of the distinction.

As we have seen, the ability to take account of the expected consequences of alternative activities is the hallmark of an autonomous agent. If consequences occur with a certain probability, rather than with certainty, then an automaton will simply take the consequences as they come. But an autonomous agent could base its decisions on the mean (or expected) outcome. This does not necessarily imply that the agent should opt for the outcome with the highest mean return; as we know from economics, decisions may be based on maximization of expected utility. Thus, the mathematical apparatus used in accounting for attitude toward risk in humans can be, and has been (Stephens and Krebs 1986), successfully applied to corresponding phenomena in animals. However, this has been done in the context of behavioral ecology—in other words, the theory has been applied to the attitude toward risk of the designer of the agent, not to that of the individual agent.

In thinking about the individual, recall from chapter 3 that economic theory tells us that, if outcomes are transformed through a utility function, the operation of an Expected Utility Criterion will identify that activity with the highest Certainty Equivalent that is coherent with the preference attitude of the decision-maker as revealed in the derivation of the utility function. The point here is that the decision-making mechanism has to operate on real quantities (either electrical potentials or transmitter substances). A decision has to be made at each and every moment in time, and these decisions are, in effect, based on the certainty equivalent relating to some uncertain ecological process or to uncertain consequences of the behavior.

In terms of an individual autonomous agent (animal, robot, or economic consumer), decisions that are designed to maximize expected value or expected utility may be based either on average payoffs as perceived by the designer or on some notion of expectancy on the part of the individual. In the former case we are dealing with a well-designed automaton, in the latter with some process of judgement and decision.

Rachlin (1989) has reviewed the many views of the mechanisms involved in judgement and decision-making in his attempt to reconcile behaviorist and cognitive approaches to choice. Since we are primarily interested in the borderline between automata and autonomous agents, it is not really necessary to review these theories here, because they go far beyond the primitive essence of the difference between automata and autonomous agents in their attempts to account for the judgements and decisions made by humans. Our program is not so ambitious.

In essence, an autonomous agent makes some assessment of the possible alternatives, whereas an automaton simply has its actions dictated by its state. The autonomous agent is able to make an assessment because it is capable of planning and because the results of its planning affect its motivational state.

## 6.6  Planning

To plan is to generate a sequence of activities, designed to achieve a particular end, without performing those activities. Basically, a planned sequence of activities is generated by reviewing alternatives, drawing up a short list of feasible possibilities, and assessing these possibilities in terms of the particular end that the planning system is designed to achieve. This three-stage process is illustrated in figure 6.16.

The first stage of planning is to review the alternatives—but how many? In AI terminology, this is the *breadth-of-search problem*. For example, there are 792 somatic muscles in the human body. In theory, since these are supposed to be voluntary muscles, one could decide to contract any one of them, or any combination of them. Does this mean that, in planning what movement to make next, one must review 792! alternatives? This is obviously computationally impossible. The breadth of the search must somehow be limited. One possibility is that it is limited by motivational state. The agent simply does not consider an alternative that has no current motivational relevance. In other words, the planning system comes up with a short list of behavior candidates not as a result of exhaustive search, but as a result of motivational filtering. (See also McFarland 1992.)

The second stage of planning is to evaluate the consequences of performing each of the candidate activities. This review of the consequences must be based on knowledge of the probable outcomes, and the results of the review must be stored. This aspect of planning requires some form of cognitive evaluation. It is cognitive because some of the knowledge manipulated in the review is declarative knowledge. For example, I know that the likely consequence of pushing this switch is that the picture on my word processor's screen will change.

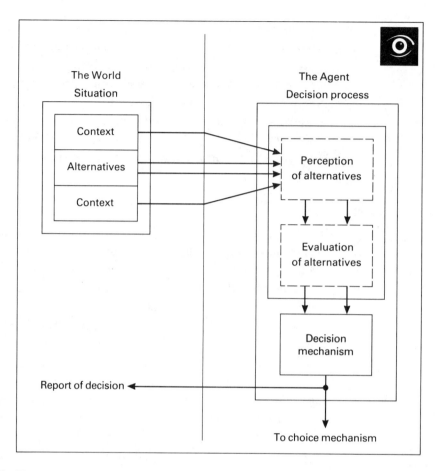

**Figure 6.16**   Three stages of planning. (After Rachlin 1989.)

The third stage of planning is to decide among the evaluated alternatives on the basis of some criterion. There are many ways in which such a decision may be made (see Rachlin 1989 for a discussion). For an intelligent agent to be well adapted, the decision-making mechanisms must be related to some criterion of fitness or utility. This means that the decision-making mechanism must be able to refer to some representation of the goal function (see also McFarland 1991b). With decision-making mechanisms left aside for the time being, the decision-making task amounts to choosing the alternative with the highest expected utility.

Thus, a motivationally autonomous robot must (1) review the options and reduce them to a manageable number of candidates, (2) estimate the consequences of the alternative activities, (3) assign a utility to each of the consequences, and (4) choose the candidate whose consequences yield the highest expected utility. We tend to view these operations as a sequence, but this does not necessarily mean that they are performed sequentially. It may be that they occur in parallel. Once again, this is a question of architecture.

## 6.7 Autonomy and Artificial Intelligence

We have argued that one essential ingredient of an autonomous agent is planning. Planning requires searching among possible alternatives, and the problems this introduces are among the core problems of AI. We do not offer immediate solutions; indeed, solutions for search problems as they are traditionally formulated may not even be possible. We think, however, that considerations along the following lines may bring us closer to some solutions:

- The planning of behavior, (that is, generating behavior plans and projecting them into the future) is done at a cognitive level, using search procedures (often formulated in a problem space). It is generally agreed that this search procedure generates knowledge (Anderson 1983a; Newell 1980). Most cognitive scientists assume that planning and actually performing behavior generates procedural knowledge (roughly speaking, the knowledge of what sequences of operations are appropriate in given situations and what results they lead to). As a result, the agent will know under what conditions a particular activity applies and what sequences of operations and their consequences it is likely to lead to. In addition, as a result of the assessment of the resulting environmental situation (in relation to the goal function), the agent obtains additional knowledge in the form of an assessment of the situation attached to the resulting state of affairs. This additional knowledge may be a form of declarative knowledge.

- The major problem with behavior planning based on search procedures is the amount of computation required for a thorough search. The amount of search can be reduced by the application of appropriate heuristics. Heuristics can be rules of thumb indicating solutions that may work but are not optimal. This is the type of heuristic on which rule-based systems rely. Heuristics may also be based on the goal function, which by definition is known in total to the agent. In addition, the agent requires the ability to assess the potential of the current situation relative to the goal function, and the potentials of the next reachable states. Search can be reduced by canned, prepacked procedures or by appropriate evaluation of the consequences of behavior relative to the goal function. (See McFarland 1992.)

- The degree of autonomy of an agent will be highly correlated with the amount of cognitive search the agent can deploy in making decisions. Consider as an example the car-driver system and the gear changes it makes. In a car with an automatic transmission, the decisions to change gears are based entirely on fixed rules, resulting in complete predictability of the behavior of the system and zero autonomy. In a car with a manual transmission, driven by a person who has learned simple fixed rules for shifting gears and who applies them in a stereotyped manner, behavior similar to that of the automatic system will be generated. In a car with a manual transmission, a professional rally driver will use rules which are considerably more complex than those used by an inexperienced driver. In addition, the rally driver is capable of estimating the likely results of unconventional gear shifts, which violate some of the more general rules. Because he can make a more detailed and precise estimate of the benefits and disadvantages of certain actions, he has greater autonomy within his behavior space.

- An autonomous robot needs the capability to choose the right behavior at the right time, taking as many of the ensuing consequences as possible into account. Therefore, both the system generating behavior (including planning, search, and heuristic rules) and the motivational system (based on the goal function and the cost function) must be well designed. The amount of cognition and planning using search will be seriously limited in any robot. The design must therefore be based on a judicious compromise between decision making based on cognition and decision making based on rules. It may be possible to rely on rules in some situations and on cognition in others. Therefore, autonomy is a multi-dimensional entity.

- The problem in designing autonomous robots is to deploy a compromise between decision making by rules and decision making by cognition. Since there will be many dimensions involved, it may be possible to rely on rules in some situations and on reasoning in others. Therefore, we need to think about autonomy in a multi-dimensional context.

**Points to Remember**

- Most robots are automata in the sense that their behavior is entirely state-dependent.
- Autonomous agents are self-controlling in the sense that they have some kind of motivation. This makes them relatively uncontrollable.
- Motivations can be defined as reversible internal processes that are responsible for changes in behavior.
- A motivationally autonomous robot can be defined as one in which changes in behavior are the results of decisions based on evaluations of the circumstances. In a well-designed autonomous robot, such evaluation will be related to functional criteria (efficiency, costs and benefits, etc.).
- The utility gained from an activity depends partly on environmental factors, because the utility is influenced by the consequences of the behavior.
- Parameters such as availability $(r)$ and accessibility $(k)$ determine the returns (change of state) due to the consequences of behavior. The utility associated with the returns will depend on the current value of the relevant state variable. The changes in this variable over time provide the opportunity profile for that activity.
- The utility to be gained from a particular activity depends on the change in state that will result from the activity. This, in turn, depends on the initial state and the consequences of the behavior.
- The current opportunities determine the consequences that can accrue from a given unit of behavior. The rate and the intensity of the behavior will determine the extent of these consequences.
- Motivational evaluation involves the assignment of (expected) utilities to behavioral alternatives. Once the utilities have been assigned, a decision can be made. This is the essence of autonomous behavior.
- The numerous behavioral alternatives are somehow reduced to a manageable number of candidates for behavioral expression.
- To evaluate the alternatives in terms of utility, the agent must have some knowledge of the probable consequences of the alternative activities.
- Generally, the type of knowledge obtained as a result of assessment of the environmental situation will be declarative knowledge, as opposed to procedural knowledge. Roughly speaking, procedural

knowledge is knowing *how* and declarative knowledge is knowing *that*.

- The main problem in designing autonomous robots is to strike the best compromise between decision making by built-in rules and decision making by cognition.

# 7 Goals and Behavior

Apparently purposive behavior can be achieved by a variety of mechanisms, ranging from simple goal-achieving behavior to complex intentional behavior. In this chapter we review these mechanisms and establish a terminology.

## 7.1 Goal-Achieving Behavior

A goal-achieving system is one that can recognize the goal once it is arrived at (or at least change its behavior when it reaches the goal), but the process of arriving at the goal is largely determined by the environmental circumstances. What happens at each point in the causal chain depends partly on what has just happened and partly on the environmental circumstances. A similar principle can be seen in immunological systems and in other biochemical systems in which there is some form of template recognition. In such systems the significant events occur when one molecule recognizes another (a kind of lock-and-key mechanism) within a suitable environment, or medium. These systems are goal-achieving by virtue of the fact that the necessary environmental features are generally present at the appropriate stage in the causal chain.

Bertrand Russell (1921, p. 32) put forward a goal-achieving type of theory as a general theory of purposive behavior: "A hungry animal is restless until it finds food: then it becomes quiescent. The thing which will bring a restless condition to an end is said to be what is desired (its purpose)." The implication here is that the animal is in an environment in which the restless behavior is appropriate. When it encounters and recognizes the relevant (food) stimuli, the animal changes its behavior. This simple goal-achieving view of animal behavior does not, in fact, accord with modern knowledge of foraging behavior.

A chaffinch usually learns the song to which it is exposed as a nestling. Chaffinches reared in isolation will sing only a crude and simplified version of the normal song. The development of the full song requires both exposure to the song and the opportunity to practice singing it. Thus, there is a phase of perceptual learning during which the nestling stores a description of the complete song, which is followed by a stage when the year-old bird learns to reproduce a song matching this stored description. In nature, chaffinches achieve the goal of storing the song that is typical of their species as a result of being in their parents' nest. Chaffinches reared in the laboratory and exposed to the song of a different species do not produce chaffinch song in later life. Thus, the first stage of song learning is a goal-achieving stage, which is usually successful because the necessary environmental circumstances are present at the crucial stage of development. In many species, this type of perceptual learning, often called *imprinting*, is important in learning the characteristics of the habitat, the parents, and future mates (McFarland 1985).

Goal-achieving behavior in humans is probably more commonplace that we tend to imagine. Consider a collector of matchboxes, or any other artifact with a long and varied history. The collector does not deliberately set out to search for matchboxes, but relies on serendipity—the habit of making happy and unexpected discoveries by accident. The main characteristic of goal-achieving behavior is preprogrammed recognition. The goal is achieved by being in the right place at the right time and recognizing this state of affairs.

### 7.2  Goal-Seeking Behavior

A goal-seeking system is one designed to seek a goal that is not explicitly represented within the system. Many physical systems are goal-seeking in this sense. For example, a marble rolling around a bowl will always come to rest in the same place. It may take various routes, depending on the starting conditions. The marble appears to be goal-seeking because the forces acting on it are so arranged that the marble "is pulled" toward the goal. In some goal-seeking systems that are designed to maintain a particular level or direction, a dynamic equilibrium is maintained by self-balancing forces. Such systems may be based on osmosis, gyroscopic forces, etc. The goal-seeking system achieves its effects by virtue of the forces acting on and within the system. There is no internal representation of the goal-to-be-achieved, nor does the system depend for its working on being in a particular environment (as does a goal-achieving system).

A stone thrown through the air obeys a "least action" law, minimizing a particular function of kinetic and potential energy. The stone behaves as if seeking an optimal trajectory, although its behavior is in fact determined by forces acting in accordance with Newton's Laws of motion. This is an example of an extremal principle.

Historically, the first extremal principle is Fermat's Principle of Least Time, which states that a ray of light moving through a medium (whose refractive index may vary from point to point) will follow, of all possible paths, the path for which the transit time is a minimum. In the seventeenth century Willebrod Snell discovered an algebraic law linking incident and outgoing angles. Pierre Fermat soon pointed out that, in traveling from A to B, light does not necessarily travel the path of minimum distance, but rather that of shortest time. Richard Feynman (1964, pp. 26–27) explains why this is a somewhat disconcerting view: "With Snell's theory we can 'understand' light. Light goes along, it sees a surface, it bends because it does something at the surface. The idea of causality, that it goes from one point to another, and another, and so on, is easy to understand. But the principle of least time is a completely different philosophical principle about the way nature works. Instead of saying it is a causal thing, that when we do one thing, something else happens, and so on, it says this: we set up the situation, and *light* decides which is the shortest time, or the extreme one, and chooses the path. But *what* does it do, *how* does it find out? Does it *smell* the nearby paths, and check them against each other? The answer is, yes, it does, in a way."

As Feynman goes on to explain, there is a quantum-mechanical view of Snell's Law that gives considerable justification to Fermat's Principle.

The mechanical analogue of Fermat's Principle is Maupertuis' Principle of Least Action. Both these principles were generalized by Hamilton in the nineteenth century and incorporated into Hamilton's Principle, one of the major unifying concepts of theoretical physics (Rosen 1967, 1970). The behavior of any physical system can be accounted for both in terms of certain rules, such as Newton's Laws, and in terms of Hamilton's Principle. Thus, the behaviour of a stone thrown into the air is determined by Newtonian forces, but at the same time it conforms with Hamilton's Principle in minimizing the "action" (a function of the potential and kinetic energy).

Extremal principles may be regarded as teleological statements (Nagel 1961), but the systems whose behavior they describe would not normally be regarded as goal-directed. Many a physical system comes to a natural equilibrium, in a minimal-energy configuration, simply as a result of the resolution of counteracting forces. To regard such minimal states as goals would be to trivialize the usefulness of the concept (see also Woodfield 1976, pp. 67–68). A ball that comes to rest after rolling down a hill would not normally be said to have reached its goal, or to have rolled down the hill in order to achieve a certain state. It is, nevertheless, goal-seeking in the sense described above. The behavior of the ball conforms to an extremal principle which is analogous to the principles used to account, for example, for the optimality principles that are employed in the explanation of animal behavior (McFarland 1993). In other words, there is an analogy between the extremal principles of physics and the optimality principles of biology (Rosen 1967, 1970).

An animal may behave as if seeking an optimal trajectory through the state space (Sibly and McFarland 1976; McFarland and Houston 1981), but such an account says little about the mechanisms involved. Optimality principles are, in effect, functional explanations which describe how the animal ought to behave in order to attain some objective. For a causal explanation, the equivalent of physical forces must be established. These will presumably take the form of a set of rules of thumb governing behavior, or of some equivalent mechanism. Examples of rules of thumb in animals can be found in Stephens and Krebs 1986.

## 7.3  Goal-Directed Behavior

A goal-directed system involves an explicit representation of the goal to be achieved, which is instrumental in directing the behavior. In this book we reserve the term *goal-directed* to indicate behavior (of a human, an animal, or a machine) that is directed by reference to an internal representation of the goal to be achieved. By *directed* we mean that the behavior is actively controlled by reference to the (internally represented) goal. The behavior will be subject to outside disturbances, which will usually be corrected for. Thus, by *directed* we mean that the behavior is guided or steered toward the goal, despite disturbances.

A *goal representation* is a physically or physiologically identifiable (in principle) representation that is "explicit" in the sense of Dennett 1983. In this category are included the *set point* of simple servomechanisms, the *Sollwert* and *search image* of classical ethologists, and any form of explicit mental representation that functions as a source of comparison is a goal-directed system. Although it can always be said of a goal-seeking system that the goal must be somehow represented, since there must be features of the system that are responsible for the goal-seeking behavior, such representation is merely implicit, or tacit (Dennett 1983). This tacit form of representation is purely a way of naming the parameters of the system (which we normally think of as "distributed" throughout the system), which may be said to "represent" the goal by virtue of their role in the design of the system. Note that this is true of any system that does what it does by virtue of its design (see chapter 5). It is not equivalent to the type of goal representation that involves an explicit representation that is capable of directing behavior.

What do we mean by *goal-directed behavior*? Since the goal of behavior is achieved at the end of the relevant behavior sequence, it is obvious that the goal itself cannot direct the behavior. By *goal-directed behavior* we mean that a representation of the goal directs the behavior. If there is no explicit representation of the goal, then the behavior cannot be goal-directed.

In the paradigm case of goal-directed behavior, the difference between the "desired" state of affairs and the actual state of affairs (as monitored in the negative feedback pathway) provides the error signal that actuates the behavior-control mechanism, as shown in figure 7.1. The behavior may also be affected by disturbances, including influences from other systems. The exact nature of the input to the behavior-control mechanism will vary from system to system. In *proportional control* systems the actuating signal is proportional to the error. In more sophisticated systems the control may be very complex.

An essential feature of a goal-directed system is that some of the consequences of the behavior are monitored and this information is made available to the control mechanism. Few or many features of the behavior consequences may be monitored, and the information gained may influence the control system in various ways. If, for some reason, it is not possible to monitor the consequences, then it is not possible to attain goal-directed behavior. This may be

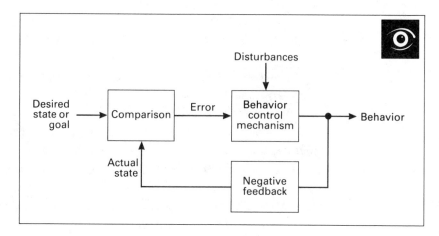

**Figure 7.1** The paradigm case of goal-directed behavior. A comparison between the desired and actual state of affairs provides the (error) information that actuates the behavior.

the case if the consequences are not completely observable in the sense discussed in McFarland 1989b (see also chapter 6 above).

A simple example of a goal-directed system is provided by the thermostatic theory of temperature regulation in animals. True thermal homeostasis is found in birds and mammals, which are able to maintain a constant body temperature despite fluctuations in environmental temperature. These animals are called *endotherms* because their high metabolic rate provides an internal source of heat, and their insulated body surface prevents uncontrolled dissipation of this heat. (Animals that gain heat primarily from external sources, such as sunlight, are called *ectotherms*.) Endotherms maintain a body temperature that is usually higher than that of their surroundings. The brain receives information about the temperature of the body and is able to exercise control over mechanisms of warming (such as shivering) and cooling (such as panting). According to the thermostatic theory, when the brain gets too hot (relative to some reference temperature) the cooling mechanisms are activated, and when it gets too cold heat losses are reduced and warming mechanisms may be activated.

The essential features of the thermostatic theory are as follows: (1) There is an internally represented reference temperature (often called the *set point*) with respect to which the body temperature is judged to be too low or too high. (2) There is a mechanism (called a *comparator*) for comparing the set temperature with the body temperature. (3) The output of the comparator actuates the heating

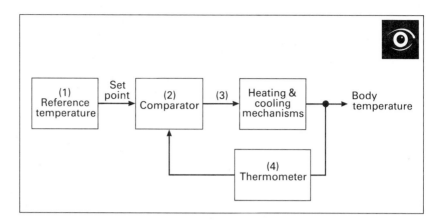

**Figure 7.2**    The four essential features of a thermostatic theory: (1) the reference temperature, (2) the comparator, (3) the error signal, and (4) the measurement of body temperature. (After McFarland 1989b.)

and cooling mechanisms. (4) The resulting body temperature is measured by appropriate sense organs (which we will call *thermometers*), and the comparison between the set point and the body temperature is based on this information. The overall principle of operation is called *negative feedback*, since the comparator essentially subtracts the measured body temperature from the set temperature, and the difference (called the *error*) provides the actuating signal, as illustrated in figure 7.2.

To recapitulate: A system can be goal-achieving or goal-seeking without being goal-directed. A goal-achieving system is one that can recognize the goal once it is arrived at (or at least change its behavior when it reaches the goal), but the process of arriving at the goal is largely determined by the environmental circumstances. A goal-seeking system is one that is designed to seek the goal without the goal's being explicitly represented within the system. A goal-seeking system can be based on a dynamic equilibrium of various forces operating within the system. A goal-directed system involves an explicit representation of the goal to be achieved, which is instrumental in directing the behavior. The distinctions among these different types of purposive behavior are sometimes blurred, and it is not always easy to see which is important in a particular case.

Passive control (Milsum 1966), or goal-seeking, systems have often been suggested as alternatives to the goal-directed explanation of physiological regulation. An example is temperature regulation in mammals, in which the principle of operation is usually likened to that of a thermostatically controlled domestic heater, with a set point representing the desired temperature (see figure 7.2). The alternative theory is that the thermoregulatory system is so designed that the processes controlling heating and cooling balance each other over a wide range of conditions, without any representation of a set point. This alternative view has led some to argue that the concept of a set point has little more than descriptive value (McFarland 1971; Mogenson and Calaresu 1978).

In the case of thermoregulation, the set-point concept seems intuitively satisfying but may be misleading. In other cases, it may be counter intuitive but useful. For example, physiologists often refer to a set point for the body weight of an animal. Many animals are able to regulate body weight with considerable precision, and the set-point concept provides a useful means of portraying the regulatory system. It is difficult, on the other hand, to imagine that an animal has a device for telling it how heavy it should be, or that it has a means of measuring its own weight. Considerable controversy has arisen over the use of the set-point concept in this context (Wirtshefter and Davis 1977). It may be that the alternative theories of physiological regulation cannot be distinguished at the control-systems level of explanation. When the data can be interpreted in two different ways, it is possible that the alternative theories could be intertranslated. If this is the case, then only physical (or physiological) identification of the goal representation (or set point) could settle the issue.

## 7.4 Action Theory

Action theory has its origins in attempts to provide a psychological role for the will. Ach (1910, p. 256) defines action as an object-oriented act of will. The action is related to an anticipated result (the goal), and to an intention (will) to reach the goal. For the early German psychologists (Wundt 1907; Ach 1910; Lewin 1935), and for Tolman (1932), the concept of goal-oriented action (*Handlung*) was fundamental. In the more behavioristic American psychology, the concept can be traced from Watson (1913) to the cybernetic view of Miller, Galanter, and Pribram (1960) (see Silver 1985).

Historically, the cybernetic approach began with Rosenblueth, Wiener, and Bigelow (1943), who defined purposeful behavior in terms of negative feedback systems. The behavior of such a system

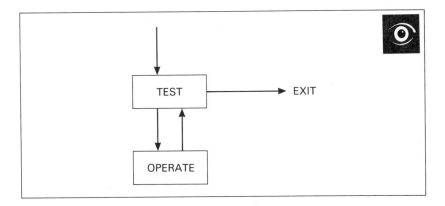

**Figure 7.3** A simple TOTE system.

is controlled by the difference between the present state of the system and the "intended" state, or goal. Miller et al. (1960) developed this idea and proposed that action can be understood in terms of Test-Operate-Test-Exit (TOTE) units, such as that illustrated in figure 7.3. According to this model, the actions that an animal performs are continually guided by the outcomes of various tests. The "image" of a goal supplies the criteria that must be met before the test is passed. Comparison of test outcomes continues until the incongruity between test outcome and criterion is zero. TOTE units can be arranged hierarchically into larger tote units. Miller et al. (1960, p. 34) suggest that "the compound of TOTE units unravels itself simply enough into a coordinated sequence of tests and actions, although the underlying structure that organizes and coordinates the behavior is itself hierarchical, not sequential."

We can illustrate this approach by reference to the problem of using a map. The conventional approach is to suppose that the person selects a goal, such as Madison Square Garden, and then uses the map, together with information about his current position on the map, to select a route to the goal. The map is then used to guide the person along the route. There are various possible versions of this approach, but all require that a (mental) representation of the goal is compared with information about the current position, and that the outcome of this comparison is the main variable controlling the behavior, so that a feedback loop is created, as shown in figure 7.3. Figure 7.4 illustrates a possible TOTE model of the Manhatten map problem. Starting from the Guggenheim Museum, the task is to drive to Madison Square Garden. The subject pinpoints his current position on the map (either a real map or a cognitive

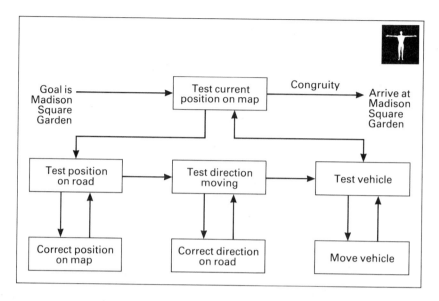

**Figure 7.4** A TOTE system for driving through Manhattan to Madison Square Garden.

map). If he does not think he is at Madison Square Garden (the goal), he checks his position on the road. If this does not correspond to his position on the map, he corrects his position on the map. The subject then tests his direction of movement. If this is not toward the goal, he corrects the desired direction of movement. Then he tests the vehicle (e.g., by making a turn) until the vehicle is moving in the right direction. The loop is now closed, and it is time to test the current position on the map again. This is not a perfect illustration, but it is the kind of thing that Miller et al. (1960) envisage.

The TOTE model is concerned with the guidance and monitoring of ongoing behavior, and has much in common with the action theory. There are, however, many forms of action theory (Brand 1970, 1984), and it is not possible to give a single, generally agreed-upon, precise definition of an action. Probably the most widely held view among philosophers is the *causal theory*, which maintains that the difference between a movement pattern and an action is that the latter is accompanied by a particular kind of mental event, which plays a causal role, whereas the latter is not so accompanied. For example, in putting his hands forward to break a fall, John may follow the same pattern of movement as when he puts his hands forward to perform a somersault. The latter is an action, because some mental event (the nature of which depends on the variety of action theory) played a causal role in the behavior. The former is not an action, because this (special) kind of mental event is lacking (note that there must have been some kind of neural event that caused the hands to move). In ordinary language we might say that the former was a reflex, while the latter was deliberate. This type of theory was held by Hobbes, Locke, and Hume, and has recently been advocated by Davidson (1963, 1978), Goldman (1970, 1976), Sellars (1966, 1973), and Searle (1979, 1981). Basically, all are goal-directed theories, because they envisage a mental state of affairs that is related to the goal (i.e., some form of knowing about the likely consequences) that is instrumental in guiding the behavior.

Among psychologists there is also a variety of approaches to action theory. For some (see, e.g., von Cranach 1982), goal-directed action refers to a person's goal-directed, planned, intended, and conscious behavior. For others, actions need not be intentional, but must involve some sort of mental representation that guides the behavior; these representations include schemata (Bartlett 1932; Neisser 1976), frames (Minsky 1975), and scripts (Schank and Abelson 1977). Thorndyke (1984) discusses the essential similarities underlying these terms. Without going into detail at this stage, we can give a simple example. Bartlett (1932, p. 202) observed that, when playing cricket or tennis, "When I make a stroke I do not, as a matter of fact, produce something absolutely new, and I never merely repeat something old. The stroke is literally manufactured out of the living visual and postural 'schemata' of the movement and their interrelationships."

The word *schema* is used in many contexts in psychology. We are interested here in the movement schema, a knowledge structure that provides the outline of a movement pattern but does not contain specific information about a particular movement pattern. For example, Pew (1974) observed that a sorter in a post office stands near a source of packages of a variety of shapes and sizes. A set of 25 mailbags stands between 2 and 4 meters away. As each package appears, it is examined and then tossed into the appropriate mailbag. The accuracy in getting the package into the mailbag is very high, even though the mailbags are at differing distances from the sorter and the posture of the sorter is different during each throw. It appeared to Pew that the sorters had developed through experience a general schema for the movement patterns they used while sorting, and that this enabled them to do the job more quickly and efficiently than they could otherwise. Schmidt (1975) suggested that there are several stages involved in employing movement schemata. First the overall situation has to be evaluated and the appropriate type of action selected. Then the initial conditions, such as the weight of the mailbags and the distance they have to be thrown, are assessed and incorporated into the appropriate schema. This involves calculating specific values for parameters, such as force and time, and employing these in the movement-control program.

## 7.5 A Critique of Action Theory

Action theory is a body of theory that sets out to account for purposeful behavior by providing a model that is essentially goal-directed. We have doubts about this type of theory on various grounds (see also McFarland 1989a). At the outset we should point out that, in our view, action theory is incompatible with the principles of good design of behaving agents, and there is a viable alternative to it.

In the case of animal behavior, the argument may be summarized as follows: Natural selection has designed animals, not to pursue a single goal at a time, but to pursue a course of action that is optimal in relation to a large number of internal and external factors. Thus, there a continual tradeoff among the costs and benefits of various possible activities. The result is that behavior is directed, not by any goal representation, but in a holistic manner that takes into account all relevant aspects of the animal's internal state and of the perceived external situation (McFarland 1989b). This is essentially an argument from design. The assertion that behavior is not controlled by goal representations implies that behavior is not goal-directed. There are various reasons for this assertion (see McFarland 1989a), but the most important one is that the notion of goal-directedness is incompatible with the tradeoff principle.

The problem becomes apparent when we consider what is to make an agent stop a particular task and start another. One scenario, with which the goal-directed approach has no difficulty, is that the agent changes to a new task if another goal suddenly becomes more important than the goal it is currently pursuing. In the normal course of events, however, we have to ask whether the well-designed agent should (1) finish one task before starting another (this is difficult to engineer because it requires a lockout mechanism which may prevent the agent from responding to emergencies), (2) change to a new task when the importance of the current task drops (as a consequence of the agent's behavior) below the level of an alternative goal (this means that tasks will rarely be completed), or (3) change to a new task when the balance of considerations, including the cost of changing to another task, favors the change. A sophisticated version of this arrangement employs a complex set of tradeoff rules (see chapter 5). Their implementation makes the goal representation redundant; it has no role to play, since the behavior is governed entirely by tradeoff mechanisms in which all variables have equal status. Goal-directed behavior is defined (above) in a way that requires the goal representation (a variable with special status) to be instrumental in guiding the behavior. If the behavior is determined entirely by tradeoff considerations and the goal representation has no role to play, then it is not guiding the behavior, and the behavior cannot be goal-directed.

At this point, we should perhaps reiterate our basic argument. Animals are rational beings. This means that the individual is designed to behave in such a way that some entity is maximized (subject to certain constraints). We may call this entity *utility*. Now, there must be some mathematical function with respect to which the utilities of particular states and activities are judged (i.e. the dynamic equivalent of utility functions). We call this mathematical function the *goal function*. It describes the notional costs and benefits attributable to all possible states and activities of the animal (the actual costs and benefits are described by the cost function). The goal function specifies the motivational design of the individual. (Individuals have different goal functions.) Specifying the goal function tells us nothing about the mechanisms by which animal behavior is controlled, but it does tell us the design criteria. If certain proposed mechanisms violate the design criteria, then those mechanisms cannot be responsible for the control of behavior. An important aspect of the design criteria is the *tradeoff* principle, which we regard as the essence of good design.

If it is correct that goal-directed behaviour, a mechanism proposed for the control of behavior, violates the tradeoff principle, then goal-directed behavior (as defined in this chapter) cannot be a viable model for the control of behavior. Since action theory is a goal-directed theory, we are inclined to reject action theory as a model for the control of apparently purposeful behavior.

It might be helpful to elucidate these arguments by discussing a specific example. Allen (1984, p. 126) uses the example of turning on a light to illustrate the problem of the relationship between actions and intended effects:

*There are few physical activities that are a necessary part of performing the action of turning on a light. Depending on the context, vastly different patterns of behavior can be classified as the same action. For example, turning on a light usually involves flipping a light switch, but in some circumstances it may involve tightening the light bulb (in the basement) or hitting the wall (in an old house). Although we have knowledge about how the action can be performed, this does not define what the action is. The key defining characteristic of turning on the light seems to be that the agent is performing some activity which will cause the light, which was off when the action started, to become on when the action ends. An important side effect of this definition is that we could recognize an observed pattern of activity as "turning on the light" even if we had never seen or thought about that pattern previously.*

What Allen calls an action we call a *task*. The task here is to move from one state (light off) to another (light on). The task is a property of the situation that can be recognized by an outside observer and by the agent, but this does not mean that the task is involved in the control of the behavior in a teleological manner. Furthermore, implicit in Allen's formulation is the notion that the agent has in mind an intended effect (or goal), which is instrumental in guiding the behavior. (In other words, the behavior is goal-directed.) In ordinary (folk psychology) terms, the agent wants the light to be on, forms the intention (a representation of the goal to be achieved) to put the light on, and seeks a way to achieve that end. Allen identifies the indeterminate relationship of intended effect to behavior as a problem for planning or plan recognition.

We depart from Allen (and from any other goal-directed formulation) in one important respect. For Allen the problem is a closed one, whereas for us it is an open one. Allen's problem is closed because it begins with one state of affairs (light off) and ends with another (light on). For us it is open, because the two states (light off and light on) are simply states in a series of possible states of the world that an observer (including the agent) can identify as a task. In other words, in Allen's system knowledge of the task is instrumental in guiding the behavior, whereas we maintain that this goal-directed aspect is not necessary.

An anthropomorphic scenario may help to provide an intuitive understanding of our position. In this scenario the agent enters the room and recognizes that things would be better if the light were on. In other words, the state "light on" is a desirable state of affairs (but so are many other states). In ordinary terms, the agent wants the light to be on. (Up to this point we agree with Allen.) Having entered the room, the agent reviews the behavioral options. Let us say that these are (a) turn on light, (b) pick up book, and (c) exit room. The consequences of each are then evaluated, and the option with the most beneficial consequences is then chosen. Let us suppose that this is option a. The agent then starts to walk toward the light switch; however, at the same time he is reevaluating the options, which now include (d) avoid chair in middle of room. This type of reevaluation is a frequent (unconscious) occurrence, and the agent simply chooses the most beneficial option each time. This may or may not result in the agent's turning on the light. If the agent does turn on the light, we may say that a task has been accomplished, but at no point does the goal (accomplishing the task) control the behavior of the agent. (For a similar anthropomorphic scenario see McFarland 1989a, p. 287.)

## 7.6 Intentional Behavior

Human behavior can be said to be intentional when it involves some representation of a goal that is instrumental in guiding behavior. Thus, if a man has a mental picture of the desirable arrangement of items on his desk, and if this mental representation guides his behavior in placing books the desk, then he can be said to place them intentionally. If, however, he places items on the desk haphazardly, or on the basis of simple habit rules, then his arrangement of the items may not be intentional. In order for his behavior to be intentional, the mental representation of the book arrangement does not have to be a conscious one. Although consciousness and intentionality are sometimes linked, it is better to treat them separately (Dennett 1978).

On this type of definition, intentional behavior is a form of goal-directed behavior. It is close to our everyday notion of intentional behavior, but once we start to define our terms rigorously we find that we deviate from the everyday view. Matters are complicated by the fact that the term *intention* is used differently in different disciplines.

Ethologists have long recognized *intention movements* in animals as indications of what the animal is about to do. Both human observers and members of the animal's own species can often predict the future behavior of an animal from its intention movements, and it may seem silly to assume that the animal cannot anticipate the next steps in its own behavior (Griffin 1976). It is more likely, however, that intention movements are merely the initial stages of behavior patterns that are terminated prematurely, either because the animal is in a motivational conflict or because its attention is diverted to other possible aspects of behavior. Indeed, it is difficult to imagine how such incipient behaviorial fragments could be avoided in an animal with a complex repertoire of activities (McFarland 1985).

Another aspect of animal behavior that has the appearance of intentionality is the injury-feigning distraction display of certain birds. When an incubating sandpiper (*Ereunetes mauri*) is disturbed by a ground predator, it may leave the nest and act as though injured, trailing an apparently broken wing and luring the predator away from the nest. When the predator has been led a safe distance from the nest, the bird suddenly regains its normal behavior and flies away (Skutch 1976). While most ethologists are content to account for this type of behavior in terms of ritualized display, some (see, e.g., Griffin 1981, p. 135) wish to keep open the possibility that the birds are behaving intentionally. Many ethologists see little difference between the deception practiced by injury-feigning birds and that evident in primate behavior (Kummer et al. 1990; McFarland 1989b), but others are less skeptical (Mitchel and Thompson 1986).

In philosophy the term 'intention' is often used to signify 'aboutness'. An intentional statement is a statement that is about something. According to Dennett (1978, p. 271), "An intentional system is a system whose behavior can be (at least sometimes) explained and predicted by relying on ascriptions to the system of beliefs and desires (and other intentionally characterized features)—what I will call intentions here, meaning to include hopes, fears, intentions, perceptions, expectations, etc. There may, in every case be other ways of predicting and explaining the behavior of an intentional system—for instance, mechanistic or physical ways—but the intentional stance may be the handiest or most effective or in any case a successful stance to adopt, which suffices for the object to be an intentional system." As Dennett (1978) notes, in considering the behavior of a complex system we can take a number of different stances that are not necessarily contradictory. One is the design stance, which we adopted in chapter 5; another is the physical stance, which bases predictions on the physical state of the system; another is the intentional stance, which Dennett is adopting in the above quotation. This assumes that the system under investigation is an intentional system, possessing certain information and beliefs and directed by certain goals. In adopting this stance, Dennett is attempting, not to refute behavioral or physiological explanations, but to offer a higher level of explanation for the behavior of systems so complex that they become unmanageable.

## Points to Remember

- A goal-achieving system is one that can recognize the goal once it is arrived at (or at least change its behavior when it reaches the goal), but the process of arriving at the goal is largely determined by the environmental circumstances.
- A goal-seeking system is one that is designed to seek a goal without the goal's being explicitly represented within the system. A goal-seeking system can be based on a dynamic equilibrium of various forces operating within the system.
- A goal-directed system involves an explicit representation of the goal to be achieved, which is instrumental in directing the behavior.
- In the paradigm case of goal-directed behavior, the difference between the "desired" state of affairs and the actual state of affairs (as monitored in the negative feedback pathway) provides the (error) signal that actuates the behavior-control mechanism
- There are many forms of action theory, and it is not possible to give a single, generally agreed-upon, precise definition of an action. Probably the most widely held view among philosophers is the causal theory, which maintains that the difference between a movement pattern and an action is that the latter is accompanied by a particular kind of mental event, which plays a causal role, whereas the latter is not so accompanied.
- Basically, action theories are goal-directed theories, because they envisage a mental state of affairs that is related to the goal (i.e.,

some form of knowing about the likely consequences) that is instrumental in guiding the behavior.

- According to the TOTE (Test-Operate-Test-Exit) theory, the actions that an agent performs are continually guided by the outcomes of various tests. The "image" of a goal supplies the criteria that must be met before the test is passed.

- Movement schemata refer to a knowledge structure that provides the outline of a movement pattern but does not contain specific information about a particular movement pattern.

- Action theory is incompatible with the view that behavior-control mechanisms are designed in accordance with tradeoff principles.

- Action theory sees a task as closed, in the sense that it begins with one state of affairs and ends with another. The alternative is that tasks are open, because the apparent beginning and end states are simply states in a series of possible states of the world that an observer can identify as a task.

- In ordinary language, human behavior is said to be intentional when it involves some representation of a goal that is instrumental in guiding behavior. In ethology and in philosophy, the term 'intention' can have other meanings.

In this chapter we discuss some of the more philosophical issues involved in the concepts of task and tool. We find it necessary to abandon the conventional view of a task, which is anthropocentric and some what misleading in the AI context. A task is accomplished when a particular state is reached as a result of behavior. How the task is accomplished is a question that should be distinct from questions about the definition of a task. Tools are often seen as aids in accomplishing tasks, but we must be careful to define tools independently of the tasks to which they relate.

We suggest, for example, that a cognitive map is a tool. It represents declarative knowledge of the world, which can be used in a variety of ways. It is not part of a procedure for finding one's way around, nor does it provide a representation of the goal to be achieved in any goal-directed or intentional process. A road map of Manhatten is an analogy with real life. At every turn, a person, an animal, or a robot has to decide what to do next. In our view the current theories that purport to deal with this problem are inadequate, because they cannot handle the subtleties of decisions taken in the face of major and minor disturbances of the situation. Rather than tinker with a theory that is flawed in principle, we are attempting a radical departure from the generally accepted view that intentions (or goal representations) play a causal role that differs from the roles of other influences on behavior.

## 8.1  The Nature of Tasks

In ordinary life, tasks are not defined in an absolute sense. For a small child to pick up a glass is a task. For a person to fix a drink for another person is a task. For a waiter to take orders for drinks, and then serve them, is a task. In artificial intelligence and robotics, a task is what is achieved by an action. In task planning (formally the same as automatic program generation), the user supplies the input-output requirements of a desired program, and the program generator then creates a program that will produce the desired input-output behavior (Fu et al. 1987). In psychology, tasks are often defined in terms of the activities involved; however, it is more satisfactory to define a task in terms of the state change involved (Bösser 1989a).

In chapter 5 we saw that the procedures an operator uses to execute tasks are a function of the task (the state changes to be achieved) and the tool used. The user is assumed to have task-related knowledge, which can be seen as knowledge of the job to be done that is independent of the means of doing the job. A task is defined by an initial state and an end state, so the operator's task-related knowledge is really knowledge about desirable changes in the state of the operator. This task-related knowledge is independent of the tool-related knowledge that the user requires to accomplish a particular task. The latter is largely procedural, and is restricted to the use of the tool; in this way, it differs from task-related knowledge.

In our view, a task is a property of the situation that can be recognized by an outside observer, but this does not mean that the task is involved in the control of the behavior in a teleological manner. A task involves movement from one state to another, but identification of these states is fairly arbitrary. Let us take a simple example: When an adult asks a small child to pick up a cup, the adult is setting a task. The task can be identified by the initial state (cup on table) and the end state (cup grasped in child's hand). It is important to realize that this task identification occurs in the mind of the adult, not in the mind of the child. To the child, the adult makes a request, which is to be weighed against all the other motivational inputs that impinge on the child; getting praise may be a desirable state of affairs, but it is only one among a number of desirable future states. The child may be motivated, by the adult's request, to start to pick up the cup, but the task (as identified by the adult) may or may not be completed. Some other activity may suddenly seem more appealing to the child, so that the task is not accomplished. Even if the task is accomplished, we are not justified in concluding that the end state (cup in child's hand) was instrumental in guiding the behavior of the child. In other words, we are not justified in concluding, simply from observing the behavior, that the activity of picking up the cup was goal-directed (see chapter 7). We argue below that the state (cup in hand) has a status no different from that of any other motivational state.

In the case of an adult fixing a drink for another person, it may seem that the task must be identified as such in the mind of the actor. When asked, the actor can say "I am fixing a drink for Tom." This might seem to be good evidence that the task 'fixing a drink' is identified as a task in the mind of the actor, and even that it has the status of an action, in the sense that the actor's behavior becomes goal-directed. We are willing to accept that, in some sense and in some circumstances, the adult may be able to identify the task (see below). We are not willing to accept that a task can ever have the status of an action, or that it can ever come to represent a goal in a goal-directed system.

The circumstances in which an actor may identify a task are those in which the actor recognizes that there is some bonus to be gained from accomplishing the task as a whole. For example, in fixing a drink, the actor may recognize that the payoff from serving the recipient of the drink can be gained only by completing the task. Not only is a half-fixed drink not as acceptable as a fully fixed drink, but its presentation to the would-be recipient is a kind of insult. So any benefit to be gained by offering a half-fixed drink is likely to be offset by the violation of social convention. (Note that a small child may not realize that a cup half-grasped is not as good as a cup fully grasped.)

An observer identifies tasks in terms of changes in the state of the world. (We call this *first-order task recognition*.) To an actor in a first-order system, the same task remains unidentified and simply appears as a request. A more sophisticated actor may identify the task in terms of changes in the actor's motivational state. The actor perceives the changes in the state of the world that are brought about as results of the actor's own behavior, and this perception changes the actor's motivational state. Thus, in identifying the task recognized by another person, the actor identifies the particular change in motivational state that corresponds to the change in the state of the world that is important to the other person. We call this *second-order task recognition*.

The sense in which the actor identifies the task (in the second-order sense) is utilitarian. In deciding what to do, the actor weighs the consequences of the alternatives. In considering the consequences of fixing a drink, he recognizes that a fully fixed drink is worth something (in terms of utility) whereas a partly fixed drink is worth nothing (for the sake of argument). In identifying the task in this way, the actor is recognizing what the other person regards as a task. Thus, task identification by the actor is the process of recognizing what state of affairs will satisfy or please another person.

Our attitude may be summarized as follows: To an observer, a task is identified in terms of changes in the state of the world. To an actor, the same task may be identified in terms of changes in the actor's motivational state. The actor perceives the changes in the state of the world that result from the actor's behavior, and this perception changes the actor's motivational state. Thus, in identifying the task recognized by another person, the actor identifies the change in motivational state that corresponds to the change in the state of the world that is important to the other person.

So far we have focused on defining and recognizing tasks in relationships among people. What about human-robot interactions? In cases where the robot is an automaton, such as those discussed in chapter 5, there is little difference between the robot tasks and the design objectives. In other words, the designer of the automaton arranged the state-behavior rules so that the automaton inevitably accomplishes those tasks that were defined at the design stage (see chapter 5).

In the case of an autonomous robot, the designer cannot dictate the behavior of the robot. If the designer wishes the robot to accomplish certain tasks, then the robot must become the kind of agent that wants to perform such tasks. Thus, the relationship between a person and an autonomous robot will be similar to that between a person and a dog: the person must induce in the robot a change in motivational state that corresponds to the task that he wishes the robot to perform.

## 8.2 Specifying Tools

In chapter 5 we saw that the task is identified independently of the tools that may be used to accomplish the task. In SANE, the state variables are conveniently divided into three types: determinators, task attributes, and costs. The determinators are the state variables of the device (or tool) that determine which operations are possible. For example, in the building-entry example discussed in chapter 4, the variable "enter correct code" determines whether or not the green light comes on (figure 4.14). Task attributes are state variables of the task in hand. In terms of the same example, the variable "OUTSIDE building" is a task attribute. Determinators and task attributes are mutually exclusive classes, because tasks and tools are defined to be independent of each other. Costs are universal state variables, such as fuel or energy. In terms of the building-entry example, the electricity used by the system and the energy used by the operator are costs.

The user sets up operations for accomplishing tasks, using physical devices or mental tools. In the study of man-machine systems, physical devices are usually taken to be man-made equipment, such as hammers or typewriters. They can be modeled in the conventional physical manner, or they can be modeled functionally (as in chapter 5).

In animal behavior studies, tool use is defined as the use of an external object as a functional extension of the body to attain an immediate goal (van Lawick-Goodall 1970). This definition excludes some cases of manipulation of objects by animals and includes others. For example, the Egyptian vulture (*Neophron percnopterus*) is known to break ostrich eggs by throwing them against stones. This does not count as tool use, because the stone is not an extension of the vulture's body. However, a vulture also may carry a stone into the air and drop it onto an ostrich nest, or pick up a stone in its beak and throw it at an egg (figure 8.1). These uses of a stone do count as tool use, because the stone can be regarded as an extension of the vulture's body.

An animal that scratches or rubs itself against a tree is not using the tree as a tool, but an elephant or a horse (figure 8.2) that picks up a stick to scratch itself is using the stick as an extension of its body for a short-term purpose. However, a bird that carries twigs to build a nest is using each twig as material and not as an extension of its body. A nest normally is not regarded as a tool for raising the young, because it achieves a long-term rather than a short-term objective.

There has been much debate as to whether tool use by animals is a sign of intelligence (see McFarland 1985, pp. 510–514, for a review), but this is not the issue that concerns us here. The question is, what counts as a tool for a human, an animal, or a robot?

An agent may use one of a set of alternative types of tools in accomplishing a task. For example, as an aid in the task of driving from A to B, a driver may use, as a tool, a physical device such as a road map. The driver could, alternatively, employ a mental map, or plan, for the same purpose. Plans are tools that can be employed in particular tasks. Alternatively, the driver might have traveled from

**Figure 8.1** An egyptian vulture about to throw a stone at an ostrich egg. (After van Lawick-Goodall 1970.)

A to B many times before. Suppose that driving along a particular route from A to B had become habitual. The driver does not drive in precisely the same way each time, but the general scheme remains the same. We have here something akin to a movement schema (i.e., a knowledge structure that provides the outline of a movement pattern but does not contain specific information about a particular movement pattern). Our point here is that a driver can employ such schemata as tools in accomplishing driving tasks.

Another type of tool is a sign. Following Peirce (1931) and Cherry (1957), we defined a sign as a transmission or a construct designed to enable an animal to affect the state of another. In other words, a sign is a tool that can be employed to move from one state of the world to another. A sign can be employed as a means of manipulating the behavior of other individuals. For example, many species of moths and butterflies suddenly expose eye-like spots on their hind wings when they are disturbed while resting (figure 8.3). These "eye spots" startle predatory birds, giving the moth a chance to escape. The display of eye spots is a form of mimicry of the sign

**Figure 8.2** A horse using a stick for scratching. (After van Lawick-Goodall 1970, from a photo by J. Chapman.)

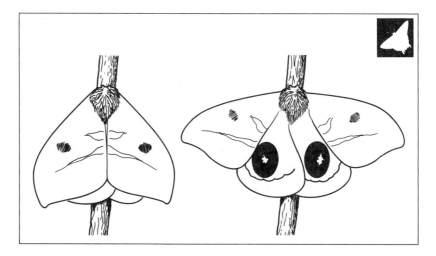

**Figure 8.3** An *Automeris* moth in the resting position (left), with forewings held over hindwings. When the moth is disturbed by a bird, the forewings are pulled forward to expose the eyelike spots on the hindwings (right). (After Alcock 1989, from a photograph by Michael Fogden.)

stimuli used by other species. Thus, they have a deterrent effect, presumably on account of their resemblance to the birds' predators. It may be objected that the moth's response is simply a reflex, and not an instance of tool use. Certainly it does not conform with the definition of tool use employed in animal behavior studies (see above). Note, however, that we define tools in terms of achieving tasks rather than goals. Our definition of a tool is entirely functional; it says nothing about the mechanisms (goal-directed or otherwise) involved in tool use. It does not matter, from the functional viewpoint, whether the moth acts in a reflex manner or whether cognition is involved.

In specifying the function of deterrence and in labeling signs as tools, we are saying that using a sign is a means of accomplishing a task. This need not imply that a tool is used *in order* to accomplish the task; it may simply imply that a tool is, as a matter of fact, a means of accomplishing a task. Remember that we see a task, in functional terms, as a property of an observer, not of an actor. Thus, the moth does not use the eye-spot sign in order to frighten away a predator, but it is recognized (by design or otherwise) that a consequence of using this tool is that the predator is likely to be frightened away. Our position here is similar to Suchman's (1987, pp. 51–52) position with respect to actions and plans:

> *Most accounts of purposeful action have taken this relationship to be a directly causal one. . . . Given a desired outcome, the actor is assumed to make a choice among alternative courses of action, based upon the anticipated consequences of each with respect to that outcome. Accounts of actions taken, by the same token, are just a report on the choices made. The student of purposeful action on this view need know only the predisposition of the actor and the alternative courses that are available in order to predict the action's course. The action's course is just the playing out of these antecedent factors, knowable in advance of, and standing in a determinate relationship to, the action itself.*

> *The alternative view is that plans are resources for situated actions, but do not in any strong sense determine its course. While plans presuppose the embodied practices and changing circumstances of situated action, the efficiency of plans as representations comes precisely from the fact that they do not represent those practices and circumstances in all of their concrete detail.*

We differ with Suchman in some respects. In particular, whereas she preserves actions as units of behavior, we abolish them by assuming that they exist in the eye of the beholder only. Nevertheless, it is worth reiterating Suchman's observations in our terminology: The actor is assumed to make a choice among alternative possible activities, based on the anticipated (by design or cognition) consequences of each with respect to utility. The student needs to know the predisposition of the actor and the alternatives that the actor sees to be available in order to predict the actor's behavior. Plans (and signs and other tools) are resources for behavior in particular situations, but do not in any sense determine its course.

We can envisage the actor as having a tool kit from which a tool can be chosen that is appropriate to the current situation. The actor can (by design or cognition) choose a of tool on the basis of the anticipated consequences (in terms of utility) of using the tool. In the case of the moth mentioned above, the following alternatives are available when it is disturbed by a predator: (1) continue with the previous behavior, with the likely consequence of being eaten; (2) fly away, with the likely consequence of being caught if the predator is a bird; and (3) display eye spots, with the likely consequence of frightening away the predator if it is a bird. In this case, we assume, the choice is made on a predesigned, hard-wired basis, maybe of a contingent kind (e.g., "if a 'bird' choose (3); otherwise choose (2)"). In other cases, planning may be involved. The actor is presented with a limited set of operations. The likely consequences of these are examined, and they are evaluated in terms of the built-in goal function. Examination and evaluation are aspects of planning. The actor may implement one plan and store some of the others for possible future use.

We have now moved some way from the definition of tool use found in animal behavior studies. A tool is indeed an extension of the body; however, what is the body but a tool (or set of tools) for moving from one state of the world to another? In other words, the body of a person, an animal, or a robot, together with its ready-to-hand equipment, is a set of tools that can be used in accomplishing tasks. These tools include parts of the body capable of physically manipulating the world (which we call *limbs*), mental tools (which may be *schemata* or *plans*), communicative tools (which we call *signs*), and physical equipment (which we call *devices*).

### 8.3  Accomplishing Tasks

In this section we compare the conventional view of task accomplishment with our alternative view, as developed over the last few chapters. We do this by analyzing a particular scenario from each of the two standpoints.

Consider the problem of using a map. The argument is much the same for real maps as for cognitive maps. Suppose we imagine a driver who is in possession of a map of Manhattan. The conventional approach to using a map is to suppose that the subject (an animal, a robot, or a person) selects a location (such as Madison Square Garden) as a goal and then uses the map, together with information about its current position on the map, to select a route to the goal; the map is then used to guide the subject along the route.

There are various possible versions of this approach (e.g., means-end analysis and action theory); however, all of them require that a mental representation of the goal be compared with information about the current position, and that the outcome of this comparison be the main variable controlling the behavior, so that a feedback loop is created. In chapter 7 we saw that Miller et al. (1960) developed this feedback idea, and they proposed that action can be understood in terms of Test-Operate-Test-Exit (TOTE) units, such as that illustrated in figure 7.3. According to this model, the actions that the subject performs are continually guided by the outcomes of various tests. The "image" of a goal supplies the criteria that must be met before the test is passed. Comparison of test outcomes continues until the incongruity between test outcome and criterion is zero. This model provides a way of carrying out a plan given as a hierarchy of goals. A number of TOTE units can be arranged hierarchically into a larger TOTE unit, as can be seen in figure 7.4.

This TOTE model is concerned with the guidance and the monitoring of ongoing behavior, and has much in common with the various forms of action theory. All are, basically, theories of intentional behavior (see chapter 7). Thus, Brand (1984, p. 201), despite his many criticisms of the TOTE model, maintains that "intentional action is an action both planned and guided to completion."

In our view, theories of this kind, which assume that behavior is goal-directed, are inadequate (see chapter 7). Hierarchically organized and goal-directed behavior-control systems lock the subject into the chosen course of action. For example, Heckhausen and

Kuhl (1985, p. 152) recognize that "if two or more intentions have been activated, a decision has to be made as to which alternative has priority in access to behavior and how the execution of two or more intentions should be combined or scheduled in a sequential order. . . . A second class of control processes consists in sticking to a goal once it has been chosen for imminent action. The activated intention is shielded from competing intentions or action tendencies. Neither those authors nor other proponents of intentional-action theory or its variants (as far as we have discovered) seem to appreciate the fundamental contradiction here.

Action theory is flawed because the notion of rational choice among alternative courses of action is basically incompatible with the notion of sticking to a course of action once it has been chosen (McFarland 1989a, b). An extreme version of this view is the script theory of Schank and Abelson (1977), according to which "a script is a predetermined, stereotyped sequence of actions that defines a well-known situation" (p. 41). Scripts come from plans, which "compete for the same role in the understanding process, namely as explanations of sequences of actions that are intended to achieve a goal. The difference is that scripts are specific and plans are general." (p.72) Some philosophers regard this as the essence of human intentionality. Brand (1984, pp. 260–261) writes: "Scripts are stored in declarative memory. A script is selected by means of a motivational system. . . . Each scene, or each segment of a scene, calls forth a production set stored in production memory. Production sets interact with working memory, which results in the activation of motor schemata. These motor schemata guide bodily movements." The problem with this type of theory, as with any goal-directed theory (in which a representation of the goal to be achieved directs the behavior) is that it is hopelessly unadaptable. To survive in the real world, the system that controls behavior must be able to adapt to changing circumstances, whether they be emergencies or subtle changes in the balance of advantage.

To illustrate our point, let us briefly return to the problems faced by a person driving through Manhattan on the basis of the goal-directed (or action-theory) principle. Starting at the Guggenheim Museum, the best route is to drive along 88th Street and then turn right at Madison Avenue. We can imagine that our driver formulates a plan on the basis of his knowledge of the map of Manhattan and proceeds to allow the plan to control his behavior. In other words, the driver forms an intention to drive to Madison Square

Garden along a certain route. (In some versions, the driver is following a script derived from the map.) Suppose that as the driver approaches the junction with 65th Street, he finds that the police have blocked off Madison Avenue because of an accident. Our driver can turn right or left along 65th Street or can attempt to proceed down Madison Avenue despite the roadblock. Obviously the driver should deviate from the planned route, but this requires jumping out of the original program and giving control to a different plan. It might be thought that such a contingent jump should not be too difficult to engineer. For example, attention could be switched to alternative courses of action when the discrepancy between the expected and attained progress reached a particular threshold. Consider, however, the lesser problem of the progress down Madison Avenue becoming very slow because of heavy traffic. Should the driver now make a deviation? Suppose there is a strange noise coming from the engine; should the driver stop because of that? What about discomfort caused by a stone in the driver's shoe? The question of whether or not to stop and remove the stone difficult for a goal-directed or TOTE-type model to handle, especially if it is hierarchically organized. The stone represents a low-level interference. The tendency to remove the stone may build up over time, but at what level does it interrupt the ongoing behavior? Does the driver attempt to remove the stone while moving, or attempt to stop in the fast-moving traffic, or deviate from the planned route? To handle this type of problem, some kind of jump-out contingency program has to be introduced into the goal-directed model. (Indeed, there must be as many conditional escape routines as there are future possible contingencies.) Such a mechanism can only be arbitrary, because there is no way of judging what threshold levels are appropriate for the necessary jump-out routines. The only appropriate levels would be those based on a cost-benefit evaluation of the ever-changing situation. In other words, it is a question of tradeoff between the merits of continuing the journey and the disturbance caused by the stone. Such tradeoff can only be inherent in the design of the system as a whole.

To summarize: The basic objection to goal-directed theories and their derivatives (see, e.g., von Cranach and Kalbermatten 1982; Hacker 1982) is that they are poorly designed. Real systems, being the products of evolution by natural selection, are not poorly designed. This conclusion gives a clue to an alternative approach.

The alternative we prefer is based primarily on the argument that efficient tradeoff principles are an essential feature of optimal design in a multi-task being (see chapter 7), and that the goal-directed principle is incompatible with this tradeoff principle. These are, primarily, functional arguments, or arguments from design. The essence of the argument, then, is that goal-directed mechanisms violate certain design criteria. We should now take a closer look at these mechanisms and their alternatives.

If the map representation of the chosen route through Manhattan does not act as a goal to be achieved, then what is its role? To answer this question let us start at the beginning. Our driver is at the Guggenheim Museum. He attaches utility to being at Madison Square Garden, but he also attaches utility to other things, such as walking in Central Park. The driver has to decide whether to drive to Madison Square Garden or to walk in Central Park. In the weighing of pros and cons, some utility is attached to using the map of Manhattan. If the driver is a stranger in New York, he will have no mental map (we assume), but he will have a physical map. A physical map is difficult to read while one is driving an automobile, so its utility is not that great. It might be better to memorize the map before setting out. On the other hand, the quickly memorized map is fallible, and its utility is limited. The point we are making is that utility is attached to the operation of using the map. This is single variable, traded among other variables in the decision as to whether to drive to Madison Square Garden or walk in Central Park. If the map's utility is high, then the balance may be tipped in favor of driving to Madison Square Garden, and vice versa.

Once the driver is en route to Madison Square Garden, there is still the possibility of parking the car and walking in Central Park. The utility of this option may be unchanged, but it will be somewhat offset by the cost (in time, energy, and risk) of parking the car. In addition to this option, the driver has the options of different routes through Manhattan. At every point, the driver could, for example, continue straight on, do a U-turn, turn left, turn right against the one-way traffic, or park the car and take a walk in Central Park. We assume that the driver will take the option with the highest net utility. This will depend partly on his reading of the map.

In making a decision, the driver evaluates the consequences of each possibility. In doing this he takes account of many factors, including the speed and density of the traffic and the factors gained by consulting the map. The map gives some indication of the possible courses of action and of their associated utilities. In other words, the map is simply a tool for estimating the utility of each of the alternatives. Thus, the driver approaching the junction of Madison Avenue and 65th Street sees that Madison Avenue is blocked by the police because of an accident. As was mentioned above, the obvious alternatives are to turn right or left along 65th Street and to attempt to proceed down Madison Anenue despite the roadblock. By consulting the map the driver can see that turning left at this point will bring him into a state that leaves open many routes to Madison Square Garden. He may also be able to see that this route is likely to be more beneficial that the other alternatives. If he has a stone in his shoe, the driver can decide, simply by comparing the consequences of the alternatives, whether to stop the car and remove the shoe immediately or whether to drive further. By consulting the map he might be able to see that if he drives a little further he will come to a place where he can safely stop. The map in no way controls the behavior. It can be used or discarded at any point. Its status is the same in the decision-making process as the immediate stimulus provided by the stone in the shoe.

We are suggesting that the cognitive map represents declarative knowledge of the world, which can be used in a variety of ways. It is not part of a procedure for finding one's way around, nor does it provide a representation of the goal to be achieved in any goal-directed or intentional process. (See McFarland 1989a for the view that intentions do not guide behavior.) We are not alone in being dissatisfied with the conventional action-theory view. For example, Suchman (1987, p. 28) notes that "The planning model in cognitive science treats a plan as a sequence of actions designed to accomplish some preconceived end. The model posits that action is a form of problem solving, where the actor's problem is to find a path from some initial state to a desired goal state, given certain conditions along the way (see Newell and Simon 1972 for the seminal formulation of this view)." However, Suchman (ibid., pp. 47–48) objects that "to characterize purposeful action as in accord with plans and goals is just to say again that it is purposeful and that *somehow*, in a way not addressed by the characterization itself, we constrain and direct our actions according to the significance that we assign to a particular context. How we do that is the outstanding problem. Plans and goals do not provide the solution for that problem, they simply re-state it." She proposes (ibid., pp. 49–50) that "common-sense notions of planning are not inadequate versions of scientific models of action, but rather are resources for people's practical deliberations about action. As projective and retrospective accounts of action, plans are themselves located in a larger context of some ongoing practical activity.... To designate the alternative that ethenomethodology suggests—more reformulation of the problem of purposeful action, and a research program, than an accomplished theory—I have introduced the term *situated action*. The term underscores the view that every course of action depends in essential ways upon its material and social circumstances."

## 8.4 Reporting on Tasks

In everyday life we continually announce our intentions in various subtle and not so subtle ways. In addition, we continually interpret the behavior of others in intentional terms. Exactly what is going on in such social interactions is a matter of considerable current debate (see, e.g., Montefiore and Noble 1989), much of which does not concern us here. In some respects, however, these teleological aspects of social interchange do have a direct bearing on problems of cooperation among autonomous robots.

Let us return, for the moment, to the problem of driving through Manhattan. It would be reasonable to suppose that our driver could talk about his intention to proceed to a particular place on the map. This suggests that he has some representation of the goal to be achieved. In ordinary life we would regard the statement "I am going to Madison Square Garden" as evidence of a particular intention on the part of a driver. Conventional action theory has little problem with this scenario, because it envisages the actor's behavior as being guided by a representation of the goal to be achieved in the form of an intention, a plan, or a desired goal. For the actor to use this representation as a basis for communication presents few problems. Indeed, teleological communication of the kind "I am driving this way in order to reach Madison Square Garden" is often taken as evidence for intentional behavior.

In the alternative (tradeoff) theory, every choice variable (i.e., every option) has equal status in the decision-making process. There is no special status given to a variable (or vector) repre-

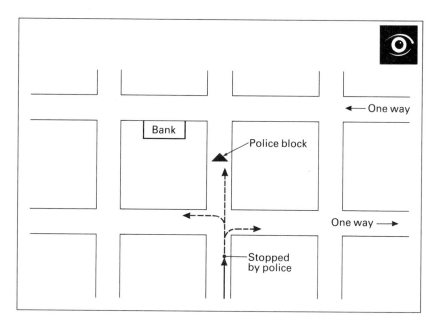

**Figure 8.4**  A motorist (arrow) approaching a choice point.

senting the goal, as is required by most versions of action theory. Indeed, it is the essence of a tradeoff that the alternatives should all have equal voice, even though the relative loudnesses of the alternatives will vary from one occasion to another (see also McFarland 1989a, p. 144). The problem is this: If each of the alternative possible activities has the same status, how does the subject single out one in making a verbal report of his behavior?

It is important to realize that the subject does not give an accurate report of his intentions or his behavior. We can illustrate this by reference to a specific example. Figure 8.4 shows a typical situation for our driver in Manhattan. Let us assume that the driver attaches high utility to visiting a certain bank. The alternatives open to the driver are shown in the figure. Arguments for and against the four alternatives are listed in figure 8.5. The driver weighs these pros and cons (either cognitively or otherwise), and this process of evaluation results in the set of net utilities shown in the right-hand column. The driver chooses the potential activity with the greatest net utility.

Suppose that the driver is stopped by a policeman and asked "Where are you going?" What is the driver to say? Two truthful answers are "I am going to the next intersection and then I will decide where to go next" and "I am going from the cradle to the

| Alternative | Points for | Points against | Net utility |
|---|---|---|---|
| a Straight ahead | Short distance to bank | Police arrest | 3 |
| b Turn right | Easy turn | Long distance to bank | 8 |
| c Turn left | Short distance to bank | Risk having car smash | 2 |
| d Stop | Can remove stone from shoe | Annoy other motorists | 9 |

**Figure 8.5**  Utilities of alternatives open to the motorist of figure 8.4.

grave." These are unsatisfactory to the policeman because they impart no information of any use to him. The policeman already knows that the driver is bound to proceed to the next intersection and is eventually bound to proceed to the grave. A somewhat untruthful answer is "I intend to go to the So-and-So Bank." A completely untruthful answer is "I intend to go to the So-and-So Bank to cash a check (when really my top priority is to rob it)." These last two answers are more informative than the first two; however, they are not (in our view) entirely truthful, because, taken literally, they imply that the subject has an explicit representation of, and gives absolute priority to, the goal to be achieved (the bank), and that this representation is instrumental in controlling his behavior. Note also that the statement "I plan to rob the bank" is dishonest in implying that the plan is controlling the driver's behavior, whereas "I have a plan to rob a bank" would be honest to the extent that he might have declarative knowledge of a plan. The plan opens up behavioral possibilities that would not be available without the plan. To the extent that these have utility, the plan itself may be said to have a certain utility, which may or may not enter into the driver's evaluation. Lest this seem an exaggerated scenario, we should remind ourselves that similar phenomena occur in animal behavior and in marketing (see figure 8.6).

The question of honesty in animal communication has received considerable attention (Trivers 1985; de Waal 1982, 1986; Mitchel and Thompson 1986; Rohwer and Rohwer 1978). It is clear that, from an evolutionary point of view, there are situations in which animals are designed to deceive others, as the moth (figure 8.3) deceives the predatory bird. Within a species, deceitful communication is frequently used in gaining sexual, social, or political

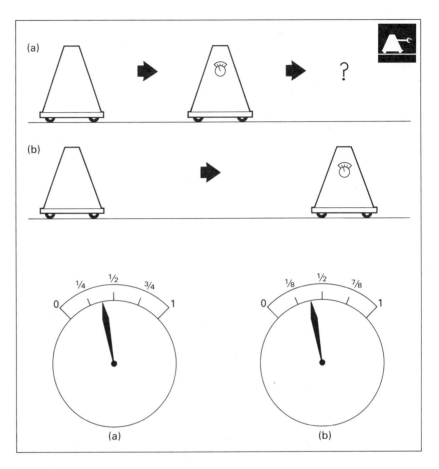

**Figure 8.6** Development of two robots made by rival companies. To enhance customer appeal, company a introduces a gauge displaying battery charge. Company b retaliates with a slightly different gauge. The scale on gauge a is an honest representation of the charge, while that on gauge b is designed to give the impression that robot b is more economical than it really is.

**Figure 8.7**  A frigate bird inflating its air sacs during courtship display and thereby making itself appear larger.

advantage, as when an individual makes itself appear larger to bluff a rival (figure 8.7). Manipulative communication is widespread in the animal kingdom, and is seen by many as evolutionarily inevitable. Indeed, it has been suggested that self-deception—hiding the truth from one's conscious mind the better to hide it from others—has evolved in humans to fulfil such functions (Trivers 1985).

This line of reasoning has a number of implications for our concept of intention. In ordinary parlance, we may deceive others fortuitously or deliberately. Fortuitous untruthfulness is careless, or negligent; deliberate untruthfulness is usually regarded as dishonest. We are now suggesting that a certain degree of untruthfulness is part and parcel of our normal social intercourse.

McFarland (1989a, p. 214) has suggested that our evolutionary inheritance predisposes us to interpret the world in terms of meanings and purposes, as if the rivalries of our political life were relevant to the inanimate world: "This is the teleological imperative. The result is that we attribute purpose where there is no purpose, and seek for meaning where there is no meaning. To insist that there must be a meaning to life, a purpose behind our suffering, an intent behind every action, is to take up a political stance. It is saying, in effect, that a satisfactory explanation must be made palatable to me, as a linguistic, purpose-assuming, teleological-thinking human being." The suggestion here is that the teleological imperative has evolved as part of a communication package designed to circumvent exploitation, manipulation, and discounting by conspecific rivals. By communicating in a teleological mode, the actor can avoid being judged as honest (and exploitable) or dishonest (and discountable). Moreover (following Trivers), the (evolutionary) strategy is more effective if the actor is self-deceiving.

The evolutionary argument underlying these suggestions can be illustrated in terms of a futuristic robotics scenario (adapted from McFarland 1989b, pp. 144–145):

*Imagine two robots sharing the household chores. To do this effectively, they would have to communicate with each other. Suppose they were designed to communicate in the English language. What would they have to say to each other?*

*Much would depend on the type of cooperation involved. If the robots were automata, then the modes of communication would depend directly on each robots' state. To some extent there would be a difference of interest between the robots' designers and their customers, as there is in selling any manufactured product. If the robots were autonomous, then there would be more scope for manipulative communication. If one robot had full information of the internal state of the other, it could behave as though the other's state were part of its own state, and it could organize its behavior accordingly (if the two robots' goal functions were the same). This would be the ideal situation for cooperating robots, but not for competing robots. As in animal behavior (Dawkins and Krebs 1979), it is in the interests of competing robots to control the information about internal state that is made available to others. Honesty is not always the best policy. It is in the interest of the individual robot to save time and energy by allowing the other robot to carry the greater burden of the household chores. As in the case of the single robot, we can expect there to be a tradeoff between the benefits of keeping the house clean (to prevent competitive invasion from another species of robot) and the benefits of economizing (and thus costing less than a rival of the same species). "What are you going to do next?" says robot A to robot B. An honest robot might reply: "My top priority, as determined by my internal state and my perception of the kitchen, is to wash the dishes. My second priority is to make the beds, and my third priority is to clean the kitchen floor. However, because of the cost of going upstairs, I will probably do the washing up, and then clean the kitchen floor before making the beds." A less honest robot might reply "I intend to do the washing up." If this were a complete lie, then robot A would soon learn that B was not to be believed, and B's utterances would become devalued. If the washing up were indeed B's top priority, then it might be better for B to say "I intend to do the washing up" than to be completely honest. If B did not complete the washing up, and was challenged by A, then B could say that the statement of intention had been genuine but that B had subsequently realized that some other job should be done instead. In fact, B may have known all along that the washing up would not remain B's top priority for long.*

*The honest robot would be at a disadvantage in the robot community. It would be less efficient than its competitors, and it would be discriminated against in the market. It would be less efficient because less honest robots would manipulate it into taking bad decisions, in the apparent spirit of cooperation. The transparently dishonest robot would be discriminated against by other robots, who would soon learn (or their designers would learn) to recognize a cad in the community. They would be unable to cooperate with others, and so they would be less competitive in the marketplace. The somewhat dishonest robot would sell well in the marketplace.*

The point here is that the teleological mode of communication is somewhat dishonest. It can summarize what the actor is likely to do, but it leaves room for maneuvering. Thus, a robot that says "I intend to clean the floor next" is not revealing its true state. The statement may be true at the time, but the robot knows that when the time comes it will have to refuel. Moreover, if cleaning the floor ceases to be the most advantageous task, the robot can easily make an excuse for not doing it: "I intended to clean the floor, but. . . ." Thus, the suggestion is that the honest robot is exploited, the dishonest robot is avoided, and the teleological robot is the most successful at cooperating with other robots.

In summary, the argument is that we frequently deceive others as part of our normal (evolutionarily designed) behavior, but sometimes we construe this as being intentional. The behavior of others seem to us to be goal-directed, because we communicate in teleological terms—partly as a shorthand and partly as a cover for our true motives. Our own behavior seems to us to be intentional, because we are designed to think in teleological terms. This mode of thinking is useful in interpreting the behavior of our political rivals, but it is inherently self-deceiving.

## 8.5  Tasks for Autonomous Robots

In a simple autonomous robot, only first-order task recognition would be possible. An observer could identify the task in terms of changes in the state of the world, but this identification would not be apparent to the robot (see above). To induce the robot to accomplish first-order tasks, the user must motivate the system appropriately (as one would with a dog). Thus, a truly autonomous robot is different from a conventional AI decision-making system. It has no internal representation of goals to be achieved or tasks to be accomplished. It simply maximizes its behavior (subject to constraints) with respect to a particular mathematical function, called the goal function (or the set of utility functions).

Social communication among autonomous robots would be necessary for cooperative behavior. As in the more advanced animals, the members of such a society would be essentially selfish, each acting in accordance with its own motivational priorities. It is up to the designer of the cooperative enterprise to ensure that the tasks that require cooperation arise, as an emergent property (see chapter 12), from the combined behaviors of essentially selfish agents. The most useful design, from the human viewpoint, would have autonomous robots capable of second-order task recognition.

To accomplish second-order task recognition, an autonomous robot would have to be able to perceive the changes in the state of the world that were brought about as a result of the robot's own behavior, and this perception would necessarily change the robot's motivational state. This would enable the robot to identify tasks in terms of changes in its own motivational state. Now, in identifying the task recognized by another agent (whether a person or a robot), the robot identifies the change in motivational state that corresponds to the change in the state of the world that is important to the other agent. Thus, second-order task recognition implies that the motivational state of the other agent is taken into account in the planning and utility estimates.

In a man-made autonomous system, the "other agent" may be the customer. The system is designed to produce (as far as is possible) the state of affairs that will please the customer. If the customer wants many tasks running concurrently, then the pleasing state

of affairs is definable in a state space. A particular state is identified by the customer in one way (e.g., so much of each task done),
but it is identified in a completely different way by the autonomous robot, because the robot is designed to attach utility to
those state of the world that please the customer. Similarly, cooperating autonomous robots should be designed to please each
other while each maintains its individual (selfish) integrity.

### Points to Remember

- An observer identifies tasks in terms of changes in the state of the
  world. This is first-order task recognition. To an actor (in a first-
  order system), the same task remains unidentified and simply
  appears as a request.
- In identifying the task recognized by another person, the actor
  identifies the change in motivational state that corresponds to the
  change in the state of the world that is important to the other person. This is second-order task recognition.
- In studies of animal behavior, tool use is defined as the use of an
  external object as a functional extension of the body to attain an
  immediate goal.
- We can define tools in terms of achieving tasks rather than goals.
  This definition of a tool is entirely functional; it says nothing about the mechanisms (goal-directed or otherwise) involved in tool
  use.
- Tools may include parts of the body capable of physically manipulating the world (which we call limbs), mental tools (which may be
  schemata or plans), communicative tools (which we call signs), and
  physical equipment (which we call devices).
- Action theory is flawed, because the notion of (rational) choice
  among alternative courses of action is basically incompatible with
  the notion of sticking to a course of action once it has been chosen.
- Manipulative communication is widespread in the animal kingdom and is seen by many as evolutionarily inevitable. Indeed, it
  has been suggested that self-deception—hiding the truth from
  one's conscious mind the better to hide it from others—has
  evolved in humans to fulfil such functions.
- We may often deceive others as part of our normal (evolutionarily
  designed) behavior, but sometimes we construe this as being intentional. The behavior of others seem to us to be goal-directed, be-

cause we communicate in teleological terms (partly as a shorthand and partly as a cover for our true motives). Our own behavior seems to us be intentional, because we are designed to think in teleological terms. This mode of thinking is useful in interpreting the behavior of our political rivals, but it is inherently self-deceiving.

- Social communication among autonomous robots would be necessary for cooperative behavior. As in the more advanced animals, the members of such a society would be essentially selfish, each acting in accordance with its own motivational priorities.

In this chapter we outline the stages that are involved in specifying the design of the decision-making processes of a Multi-task Autonomous Decision-making (MAD) robot. For a robot to be a MAD robot, its decision-making processes must conform to certain criteria, tailor-made for the environment in which it is to operate. It is the specification of these criteria that we are concerned with here.

We envisage an exercise in designing a mobile robot with behavior that results from rational decision-making. Another way of saying this is that the robot makes transitive choices among mutually exclusive behavioral options (see chapter 2). These options are the decision variables of the system. In our example (below), the decision variables are constrained in the sense that not all options are open simultaneously. Thus, choice at any particular time is restricted to a certain number of candidates.

The activity resulting from the choice of a particular candidate has characteristic consequences that alter the state of the robot. The utility of the activity to the robot depends on these consequences.

In chapter 5 we saw that a currency function specifies the relationship between the currency and the decision variables. The role of the currency function is to translate all the decision variables into a single value (a real-valued function), so that all possible decisions can be ranked along a single scale. In this book we use the term *utility* for the decision currency employed by the individual and the term *cost* for the ecological equivalent of this. We use the term *utility function* for functions of a single decision variable and the term *goal function* for functions of a decision vector.

The goal function is the prime feature of the design exercise we set ourselves in this chapter. We assume that we are given a particular robot with a particular behavioral repertoire and with the consequences of each of its possible activities already prescribed. The problem is: How should the robot deploy its behavioral options in time? This is not simply a matter of optimal time allocation, because questions of stability, reliability, and customer appeal also have to be considered.

## 9.1 Outline of a Housekeeping Robot

Suppose we are given a robot with a certain behavioral repertoire but with no decision-making capability. The design of a decision-making capability will be crucial for the robot's success in the market. Before considering the factors that are likely to be of importance in this design, let us take a look at our robot.

Figure 9.1 (a finite-state diagram) shows the major activities of our housekeeping robot. There are four primary command states: kitchen (K), nest (N), floor (F), and window (W). All transitions between these command states are possible, but the robot must be in

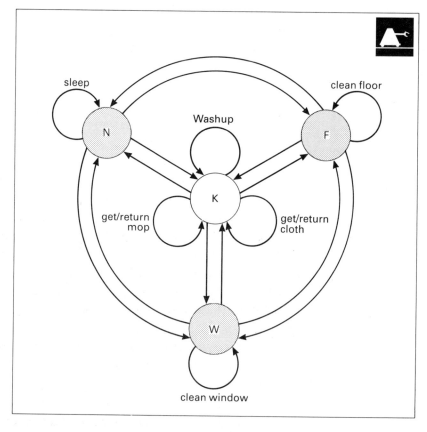

**Figure 9.1**  Finite-state diagram for a housekeeping robot. N = nest, F = floor, W = window, and K = kitchen.

certain command states to perform certain activities. To do the activity **washup** (British for "wash the dishes") must be in the kitchen (K). To fetch or return tools for window and floor cleaning, it also must be in the kitchen. To recharge its battery (an activity we call **sleep**), the robot must be at the nest (N). To clean the floor it must be at the floor (F), and it must also be in possession of a "mop," obtained from the kitchen. To clean the windows, the robot must be at the window (W) and be in possession of a "cloth," obtained from the kitchen.

Most of the robot's activities (**gotoN, gotoK, gotoF, gotoW, getmop, returnmop, getcloth, returncloth, windowclean, floorclean,** and **sleep**) are simple activities with relatively simple consequences. The activity **washup**, however, is more complex. The dishes are stored in a cupboard, and through use they are left around the kitchen, creating clutter. The robot can **collect** the dishes, one at a time, and place then in a washpile. It can **wash** dishes from the wash pile, and place them to dry (drypile). It can take dishes from the dry pile and put them into the cupboard (**putaway**). This cycle of three subactivities is illustrated in figure 9.2. Ideally, the use of dishes would not be under the control of the robot but would result from the activities of other agents. For modeling purposes, it is convenient to deem that dishes are used whenever the robot's back is turned. In practice, this means that clutter is increased (and cupboard contents decreased) each time the robot leaves the nest or enters the kitchen, unless the clutter is already maximal.

The state of the system can be described in terms of the state variables **Battery** (B), **Window** (W), **Floor** (F), **Clutter** (C), **Washpile** (L), **Drypile** (D), and **Cupboard** (P). Each activity has consequences

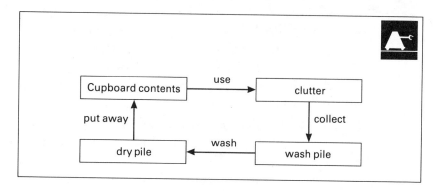

**Figure 9.2**  Cycle of subactivities involved in washup.

| Activity | B | W | F | C |
|---|---|---|---|---|
| goto N | +1 | +1 | +1 | −1 |
| sleep | −5 | +2 | | −1 |
| goto KWF | +2 | +1 | +5 | −1 |
| get cloth | +1 | +1 | +1 | |
| goto W | +1 | +1 | +5 | |
| window clean | +3 | −5 | +5 | |
| goto K | +1 | +1 | +5 | |
| return cloth | +1 | +1 | +1 | |
| get mop | +1 | +1 | +1 | |
| goto F | +3 | +1 | +5 | |
| floor clean | +1 | | −10 | |
| goto K | +1 | +1 | +5 | |
| return mop | +1 | +1 | +1 | |
| collect | +1 | +1 | +1 | |
| washup | +3 | +1 | +1 | |
| putaway | +1 | +1 | +1 | +1 |

**Figure 9.3**  Consequences of each robot activity in terms of the state variables B = battery, W = window, F = floor, C = clutter. Consequences are expressed in units of notional debt.

in relation to these states; these are tabulated in figure 9.3 in terms of notional debt. For example, the activity **washup** increases battery debt by 3 units, window costs by 1 unit, and floor costs by 1 unit. In terms of consequences this means that the activity of washing one dish uses 3 (out of 100) units of battery charge and increases the floor dirt by 1 unit. The window dirt also increases by 1 unit during the time it takes to do this activity.

A minimal description of the state of the system may not require all these state variables. As we will see below, it is parsimonious to make use of only those state variables that are required for a description of the consequences of the behavior. In order to illustrate this point, let us look at **washup**, the most complex of the activities. As we see from figure 9.2, **washup** is made up of a cycle of three subactivities: **collect**, **wash**, and **putaway**. The consequences of these subactivities, in terms of their effects on the three state

| Activity | Battery | Window | Floor |
|----------|---------|--------|-------|
| collect | +1 | +1 | +1 |
| washup | +3 | +1 | +1 |
| putaway | +1 | +1 | +1 |
| | | | |
| sum | +5 | +3 | +3 |

**Figure 9.4** Consequences of washup subactivities in terms of notional debt.

variables not directly concerned with washup, are tabulated in figure 9.4. As the subactivities occur in a sequence, their consequences can be portrayed as a vector in a **BWF** space, as shown in figure 9.5. Here it can be seen that the main effect of the number of dishes in circulation is to increase the length of the vector.

We should now consider the consequences of not washing the dishes. The main consequence of allowing clutter to increase, apart from the annoyance to those living in the house, is that a long-term debt is incurred. This debt arises from the assumption that the washing up will have to be done sometime. The nature and magnitude of the debt can be seen in figure 9.6. For a maximum clutter of 5 dishes, the debt would be $B = 25$, $W = 15$, and $F = 15$ (see figure 9.3). We can now calculate what it would cost to repay this debt.

Note that to remove 15 units of W would require $B = 26$, and would leave a residue of $W = 2$ and $F = 13$. To remove 15 units of F, plus $F = 13$ from window cleaning, would require $B = 13$ and would leave a residue of $W = 6$ and $F = 6$. In all, a maximum clutter would incur a debt of $B = 25 + 26 + 13 = 64$, $W = 6$, $F = 6$.

Thus we see that each activity has both direct and indirect consequences. The direct consequences arise from the impact of the activity on the environment (e.g., certain activities dirty the floor), from time it takes to perform the activity (the windows get dirtier with time), and from the effect of the activity on the internal state (e.g., fuel is consumed). The indirect consequences stem from the debt incurred by the activity. The debt arises because the direct consequences of an activity stimulate other activities. In order for the system to remain stable (see below) the debt must, to some extent, be repaid. One of the most important debts for the robot is that incurred by sleep.

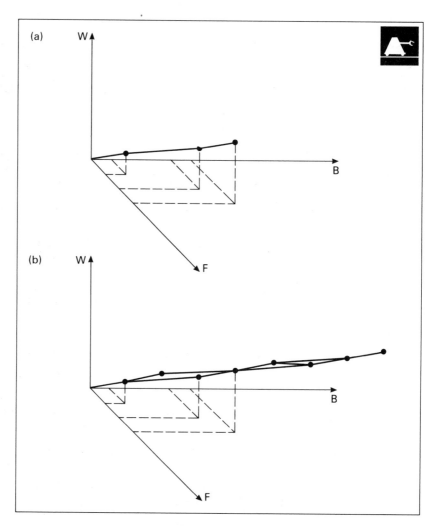

**Figure 9.5** Debt arising from washup expressed as consequences in BWF space. (a) trajectory arising from single collect-wash-putaway cycle. (b) Alternative trajectories (arising from the fact that subactivities may be repeated) possible as a result of multiple washup cycles.

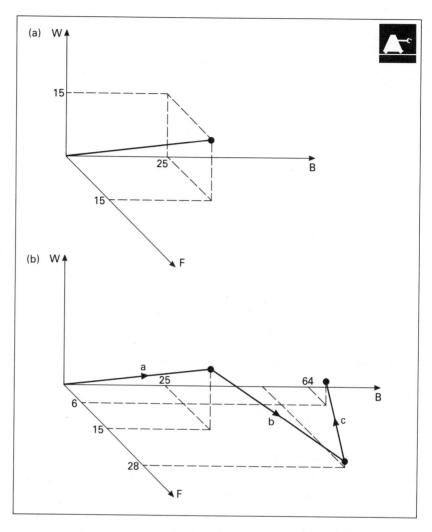

**Figure 9.6** Debt arising from not doing washup. (a) Initial debt arising from a maximum clutter of five dishes. (b) Further debts incurred during repayment of the initial debt, where a is the initial debt vector, b is the vector resulting from window cleaning, and c is the vector resulting from floor cleaning. Calculations based on figure 9.3.

| | Initial debt | B=O | W=40 | F=0 |
|---|---|---|---|---|
| STEP | ACTIVITY | | | |
| 1 | goto K | 2 | 41 | 5 |
| 2 | get cloth | 3 | 42 | 6 |
| 3 | goto W | 4 | 43 | 11 |
| 4–12 | window clean | 31 | 0 | 11 |
| 13 | goto K | 32 | 1 | 16 |
| 14 | return cloth | 33 | 2 | 17 |
| 15 | get mop | 34 | 3 | 18 |
| 16 | goto F | 35 | 4 | 23 |
| 17–18 | floor clean | 41 | 4 | 3 |
| 19 | goto K | 42 | 5 | 8 |
| 20 | return mop | 43 | 6 | 9 |
| | | | | |

**Figure 9.7**  Cumulative debt incurred during cleanup after robot recharges its batteries.

The robot must sleep to recharge its batteries. Let us assume that we start with $F = 0$, $W = 0$, and $B = 100$. That is, the whole battery needs recharging. This will take 20 sleep steps, each reducing the debt (i.e., increasing the voltage) by 5 units (see figure 9.3). Each step increases the window dirt by 2 units, so that after 20 steps $W = 40$. In other words, while the robot is sleeping it reduces its battery debt to 0, but during this time the windows get dirtier, increasing the window debt to 40.

Let us now assume that, after sleeping, the robot sets about reducing the debt. The steps required are tabulated in figure 9.7. After 20 steps, the robot has cleaned the windows and cleaned the floor, ending with a residual debt of $B = 43$, $W = 6$, and $F = 9$. Many of these activities are routinely incurred in cleaning the windows (e.g., fetching and returning implements) and in clearing up the floor dirt engendered in the course of this activity. Thus, much of the debt incurred by sleep is fixed and bears little relation to the time spent sleeping. This can be seen from figure 9.8, where the battery debt incurred in the activity of cleaning up after a period of sleep is plotted against the number of battery-recharging steps (a measure of sleep duration).

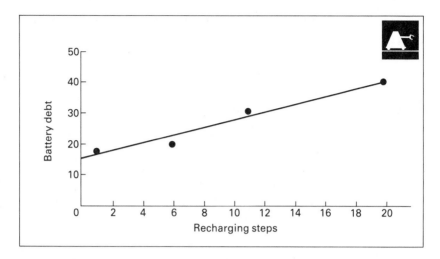

**Figure 9.8**    Battery debt incurred in cleaning up after a period of sleep, plotted as a function of the number of battery-recharging steps (a measure of sleep duration).

## 9.2   Stability

A fundamental notion of any system that has physical embodiment is *stability*. In general, a system is stable if, for a bounded input, the output is bounded. In terms of the state-space representation (see chapter 6), a system is stable if, for a bounded input, the state vector of the system is bounded. Systems with state vector **x**, which may be reduced to the form

$$\frac{d\mathbf{x}}{dt} = f(\mathbf{x}),$$

are suitable for the application of Liapunov's direct method of stability analysis. Since the systems in which we are interested can be reduced to this general form, the Liaponov method is the most appropriate general approach to stability.

The Russian mathematician Liapunov developed two methods of stability analysis. The first of these methods involved an approximation and considered stability only in the vicinity of the origin of the state space. The second (or *direct*) method, which appeared in Liapunov's doctoral thesis in 1892 and was published much later (Liapunov 1907), did not have these restrictions. It provided the necessary and sufficient conditions for the asymptotic stability of linear systems and sufficient conditions for the asymptotic stability of nonlinear systems. Until recently, the main difficulty encountered in applying Liapunov's direct method was that no means were available for generating the correct Liapunov function for solving a given stability problem. Many of these difficulties have now been overcome, and there is now an extensive literature that allows the designer to apply Liapunov's direct method in a systematic way (Bell 1969; Riggs 1970; Rouche et al. 1977; see Barnett and Cameron 1985 for a general introduction).

A system displaced from an equilibrium state may return to that state, or to some other equilibrium state, after a transient period. In such cases the system is said to be *asymptotically stable*. An alternative is that the disturbed system may enter a limit cycle, continually oscillating around a closed trajectory. Such a system is *globally stable* if it periodically returns to a particular state.

How can these stability ideas be applied to the design of our housekeeping robot? Let us assume that it is unacceptable for the robot to discharge it battery completely. To violate this obligatory criterion is the equivalent of death. This means that there is a lethal limit on one of the major state variables, as illustrated in figure 9.9.

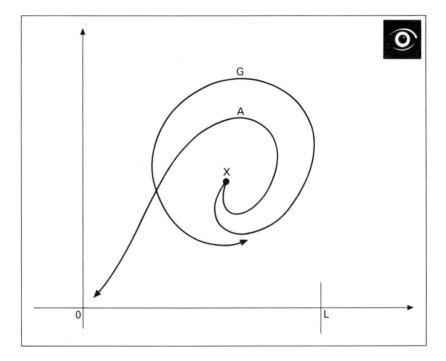

**Figure 9.9** Globally stable (G) and asymptotically stable (A) trajectories. L marks a lethal boundary.

Let us also assume that, since the robot is designed to clean floors, wash dishes, and so on, it is unacceptable for the robot to allow the kitchen to become dirtier and dirtier over time. The customer will not expect the robot to keep the kitchen perfectly clean, but the customer will expect some kind of asymptotic stability, in which the trajectory tends toward the origin, as shown in figure 9.9. On this basis we can say that, in terms of the rate of change of state, there is a hard and fast obligatory criterion. Of course, the extent to which a given robot in a given situation can cope with this stability criterion will depend, to some extent, on the demands of the environment. There may be some kitchens in which dirt accumulates so fast that the housekeeping robot can never keep up. An equivalent situation exists in animal behavior: an animal must be able to adapt to the physiological exigencies imposed by the environment (Sibly and McFarland 1974).

In general terms, the state of a system stays within a particular region as a result of various interacting processes, the consequences of which can be represented as vectors in an "adaptation space" such as that shown in figure 9.10. In this space vectors representing processes that tend to change the state of the system can often be combined into a single resultant vector, called the *drift*

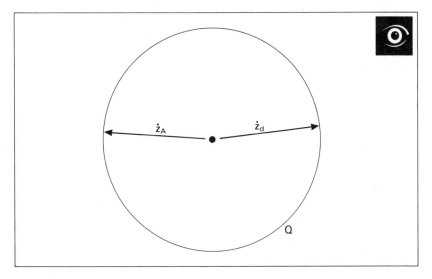

**Figure 9.10** Adaptation space Q defined in terms of limiting velocity vectors. A rate of drift $\dot{z}_d$ is opposed by a rate of adaptation $\dot{z}_A$. When $\dot{z}_d$ is greater than the limit set by Q, then adaptation is no longer adequate and the animal will die in the near future. (After Sibly and McFarland 1974.)

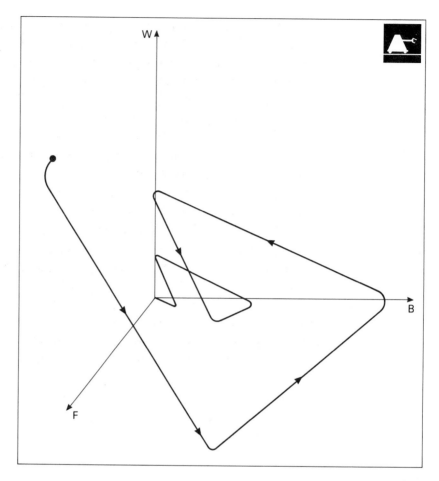

**Figure 9.11** Asymptotically stable debt trajectory resulting from reduction of a high initial debt.

vector, representing the rate of change of state due to these processes. The drift vector is opposed by an *adaptation* vector, which represents the combined effect of the various processes designed to counteract the drift. If the drift becomes so strong that the adaptation processes are unable to restrain it, then the system becomes unstable (see the Adaptation Theorem of Sibly and McFarland 1974).

It is the *rates* of drift and adaptation that are important. Figure 9.11 shows how our housekeeping robot could reduce an initial debt of W = 100 and F = 60 (based on the data provided in figure 9.3). (We are assuming here that the robot completes each activity before moving to another. In reality a MAD robot can decide to switch activities at any time, but we have not yet specified the necessary decision-making processes.) This is an example of

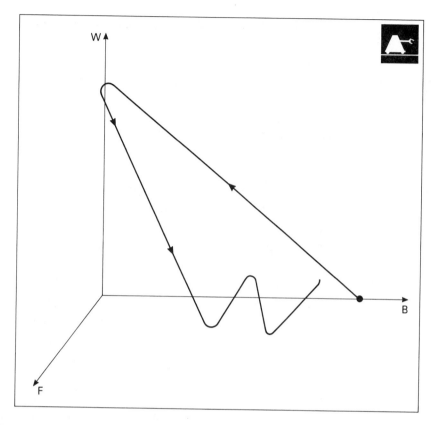

**Figure 9.12** Globally stable trajectory resulting from low initial debt but high drift.

asymptotic stability, the trajectory homing in toward the origin. However, the situation may not be so stable if the rates of drift are much higher (i.e., if the consequences of behavior are more severe). Suppose, for example, that window dirt accumulated much more quickly than is specified in figure 9.3. At some point the robot would be unable to keep up with the situation. In figure 9.12, for example, we can see the trajectory that would result if window dirt accumulated at double the rate pertaining in figure 9.3. Here the trajectory is not asymptotically stable, because it comes back almost to its starting point. It may be globally stable (figure 9.9), repeating the same cycle over and over, but it is probably on the verge of being unstable.

For our robot the consequences of activities are fixed, but this will not be the case in real life. In designing the goal function we need to have some idea of the range of variation in the consequences of the behavior. Our robot is stable if the situation is as depicted in figure 9.3, but it is probably unstable if the rate of accumulation of window dirt is doubled. How likely is this in a real-life situation? The answer to this type of question lies in the environmental circumstances in which the decision-maker is to operate. In the case of animals it lies in the nature of the ecological niche. In the case of a robot, only knowledge about actual customers or knowledge gained from market research can provide the answer. In designing the goal function, we can play it safe and use a very conservative estimate. For example, if we know (or assume) that the variation in the rate of window-dirt accumulation is normally distributed with a mean value of $dW/dt = 1.0$, and we know that the system is unstable if $dW/dt > 2.0$, then we can calculate the probability of exceeding this value. There are various methods for doing this type of calculation (see Bunn 1982, Houston and McFarland 1976, and chapter 4 above).

So far we have determined that the housekeeping robot will become unstable if $B > 100$ and $dW/dt > 2.0$. What about the other consequences of behavior? Obviously we can apply similar thinking to the rates associated with floor dirt (F) and clutter (C). There must also be values of these variables at which the robot becomes unstable because it is unable to keep up with the accumulating work. However, clutter will have little effect on stability, because the debt incurred is limited by the fact that there are only five dishes in all.

## 9.3   Customers' Requirements

In the current scenario, we are designing a housekeeping robot which is to be marketed by one or more robot retailing companies. These companies, our customers, decide whether or not a particular product is likely to sell well in a particular market. The equivalent situation in nature is the selective pressures that are characteristic of a particular ecological niche. Effectively, these pressures "decide" what design criteria are relevant in the prevailing environment (see chapter 5). Similarly, customers will buy our robot only if it satisfies certain design criteria.

In other words, in designing a housekeeping robot we must first determine the minimal acceptance criteria relevant to the goal function (in this chapter we are interested only in the robot's goal function). We assume that the robot has to find a niche in the market, and that it can do this only if certain basic criteria are met. What are these criteria?

So far, we have assumed only the most parsimonious obligatory criteria—That is, those criteria which we can be sure every customer will accept. Basically, we have assumed that every customer will want the robot to be, at least, asymptotically stable (see above). At this later stage of the design process we can take account of customers' whims by imposing facultative criteria.

Let us suppose that, to the customer, clean dishes are more important than clean floors or windows. The customer wants to be able to enter the kitchen, at any time, and find some clean dishes in the cupboard. Because there are only five dishes in all, it is clear that the robot must give high priority to washing dishes.

As we saw above, dish washing has little direct relevance to stability. The amount of clutter that can be created is limited by the fact that there are only five dishes. Thus, on stability criteria alone, washing dishes would have low priority. We are now postulating that it will have high priority for other reasons.

The situation here is similar to that of an animal. Factors directly relevant to survival, such as physiological regulation and predator avoidance, have high priority. These are effectively the stability criteria. But another factor, which has little relevance to survival, nevertheless has high priority, and that is reproduction. To maximize its lifetime reproductive success, an animal should adopt a life-history strategy that maximizes a joint function of individual survival and reproductive potential (Freeman and McFarland 1982; McNamara and Houston 1986; Sibly 1989). An animal must survive to reproduce, but there is little point in struggling to survive when the reproductive potential is zero. Similarly, a robot must be stable to carry out those tasks that the customer requires, but there is little point in attempting to maintain stability at the expense of those tasks.

We saw in figure 9.5 that the consequences of washing dishes can be represented in a **BWF** space. The main effect of the number of dishes in circulation is to increase the length of the vector **D**. The main effect of allowing clutter to increase is that a debt in incurred, amounting to a maximum of $B = 64$, $W = 6$, $F = 6$ (see above). The customer, however, is concerned less with the debt than with the lack of dishes in the cupboard. As can be seen from figure 9.11, if the system is asymptotically stable the debt is soon cleared away. The customer simply attaches utility to the number of dishes in the cupboard, as shown in figure 9.13. This does not mean that the customer is indifferent to the window and floor dirt.

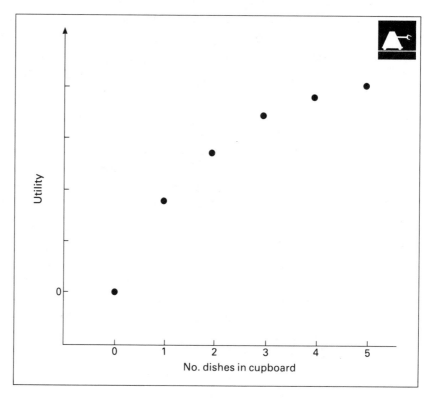

**Figure 9.13**  The robot's owner attaches utility to the number of dishes in the cupboard.

We would expect some tradeoff among these variables, and we discuss this in the next section.

## 9.4  Designing the Goal Function

The goal function is a design feature of an animal or a robot. The design of an animal is genetically based, the product of natural selection. The design of a man-made robot is based on human engineering, but the design principles are similar to those of nature.

So far, we have seen that the integrity of our housekeeping robot depends on its behavioral stability and on the degree to which its behavior satisfies the customers' requirements. As far as stability is concerned, we have identified three main variables: the battery level, B; the rate of change of window dirt accumulation, $dW/dt$; and the rate of change of floor dirt, $dF/dt$. As far as customers' requirements are concerned, we have identified just one variable: the number of dishes in the cupboard, P. For our present purposes we will assume that these are all the variables that we need to consider. We call these the *components* of the goal function. This completes the first stage in designing the goal function.

The next step is to determine how notional costs (see chapter 4) are to be associated with each component of the goal function. In chapter 3 we saw that, at the level of the individual, energy (or money) is spent in such a way that utility is maximized, and that there is a fairly obvious parallel between notional cost and utility (figure 3.2).

An animal in a particular state runs a specifiable risk of incurring real costs. It is obviously more risky to be near a lethal boundary (i.e., in purgatory) that to be far from it, but can we be more precise? Let us consider the fuel supply of our housekeeping robot. We already know that the level $B = 0$ is lethal, and that $B = 100$ is the maximum possible battery level. We can assume that the robot has some sort of sensor for monitoring the battery level, but this is not perfectly accurate. In figure 4.15 we assumed that the probability $P$ of the state $x$ moving to a new position along the state axis is given by a normal distribution. The area $A$ represents the probability of crossing the lethal boundary $B$. This area increases as the square of the distance $Ox$, as shown in figure 4.16. In other words, the risk of crossing the boundary B increases as the square of the battery deficit.

Similar arguments apply to the rate of change of state. There is a boundary (the Q boundary of Sibly and McFarland 1974; see figure 9.10) beyond which the rate of drift is simply too great for the robot's coping mechanisms. Beyond this boundary the robot is unstable. The arguments concerning the risk of crossing this boundary may be similar to those outlined above, or they may be more along the lines discussed in chapter 3.

As we saw in chapter 4, we must distinguish among three aspects of the cost: the cost of being in a particular state, the cost of performing an activity, and the cost of changing between activities. The notional cost of being in a particular state is a function of each state variable. Where there are lethal limits to a state variable, we can often expect the notional cost to be quadratic, although this will not always be the case (see chapter 4).

As a general rule, the cost of performing an activity increases as the square of the rate of performing the activity (see chapter 4). The two main reasons for this are (1) that faster behavior consumes proportionately more energy and (2) that, whenever a robot (or an animal) has a hard-wired preoccupation, its behavior in other respects will be repeatedly interrupted. Thus, if an animal is preoccupied with vigilance with respect to predators, its other behavior will be repeatedly interrupted by scanning for danger. Certain types of robots, while having no predators, are likely to have some hardwired preoccupations (see chapter 4), and these provide a basis for supposing that their behavior will be frequently punctuated by these preoccupations. In other words, such robots are (by interleaving) performing two activities concurrently. The tradeoff among concurrent interleaved activities is likely to result in quadratic costs (see chapter 4). We can expect similar considerations to apply to notional costs.

Our third consideration is the cost of changing from one activity to another. When an animal changes from one activity to another, it often has to pay for the change in terms of energy or time, as explained in chapter 4. The notional cost of changing is simply the individual's estimate, be it explicit or implicit, of the real cost of changing.

We have looked at various components of the goal function, including aspects of the notional cost of being in a particular state, the notional cost of performing a particular activity, and the notional cost of changing between activities. We now come to the problem of combining these components.

If the total cost C(x) can be represented as the sum of the cost associated with each x in x, then C(x) is said to be *separable*. Separability is approximately equivalent to probabilistic independence of the various factors (Sibly and McFarland 1976). This means that the notional risk associated with the value of one variable is independent of the values of other variables. The separability implies that the risk due to one component is independent of the risk due to another.

In the case of our housekeeping robot, there are four components of the goal function: the battery level (B), the number of dishes in the cupboard (P), the rate of change of window dirt $(dW/dt)$, and the rate of change of floor dirt $(dF/dt)$. In our specific version of the robot, outlined above, we can more or less ignore the last two of these, because the levels of W and F are so low that stability is never in question. Thus, we can illustrate the problem of separability by considering only B and P.

The question we have to ask is the following: Is the probability of running out of fuel independent of the risk of having an empty cupboard? The probability of running out of fuel (more correctly, of having to recharge the battery), within a given period of time, depends on the type of activity undertaken by the robot. Some activities use up more fuel than others. The robot is never idle (except when sleeping), so it is always expending energy. Collecting and washing dishes is no more expensive in terms of power than the average activity (figure 9.3), so the probability of running out of fuel due to these activities is no greater than normal.

The risk of having an empty cupboard depends on the degree of use of the dishes and the availability of time for collecting and washing dishes. The rate of dish use is (strictly) outside the robot's control and therefore independent of the robot's activities. The availability of time for collecting and washing dishes is influenced only by the prior requirement to recharge the batteries. In other words, if its battery has enough charge, the robot is free to collect and wash dishes. So we come to the question of whether the robot is more likely to have to recharge its battery during washing activities than during other activities. Apart from sleeping, the robot spends its time dealing with the dishes, the floor, and the windows. If the time available is equally divided among the three, then the robot is not more likely to have to recharge its batteries during washing activities. The data in figure 9.3 indicate that this is roughly the case.

There would appear to be no clear case for arguing that the risk of running out of fuel is dependent upon washing activities, or vice versa, so we can assume that the notional costs associated with battery level B and cupboard contents P are separable. In other words, the total cost is

$$C(\mathbf{x}) = C(B) + C(P). \tag{9.1}$$

We now need to look at the form of these functions. We argued above that the risk of running out of fuel was proportional to the square of the deficit i.e.,

$$C(B) = Ab^2, \tag{9.2}$$

where $b = 100 - B$ and A is a constant of proportionality.

Figure 9.13 shows the utility that the customer attaches to the cupboard contents P. The utility is equivalent to the notional cost of not having dishes in the cupboard, as illustrated in figure 9.14. This function approximates

$$C(P) = Kp^2, \tag{9.3}$$

where $p = 5 - P$ and K is a constant of proportionality.

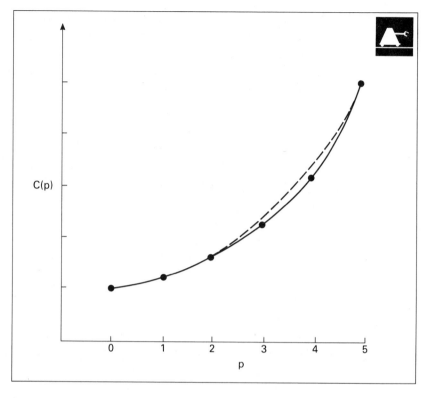

**Figure 9.14** The cost C(p) of not having dishes in the cupboard as a function of cupboard emptiness p. The dashed line is the square of p.

Equation 9.1 now becomes

$$C(\mathbf{x}) = Ab^2 + Kp^2. \tag{9.4}$$

We now have to consider the significance of the constants A and K. Equation 9.4 is a specific example of the more general equation

$$C(\mathbf{x}) = x_1^2/Q_1 + x_2^2/Q_2 = x_3^2/Q_3, \tag{9.5}$$

where the weighting parameter Q is the *resilience* (see chapter 3) of the variable x (see McFarland and Houston 1981, p. 112). These parameters represent fixed and immutable properties of the individual, unmodifiable by learning (McFarland 1978) except preprogrammed learning (McFarland and Houston 1981, pp. 170–172).

In the case of equation 9.4, the relative values of A and K simply determine the weights given to the two components of the goal function. When the time available for the relevant activities (sleep and washing) is constrained, these weights determine the amounts of time that should be devoted to each. In assigning values to A

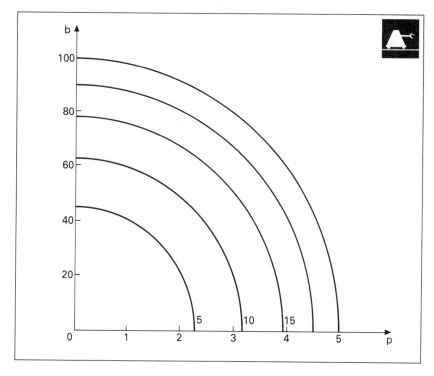

**Figure 9.15** Cost isoclines in the bp space. b is fuel deficit and p is cupboard emptiness.

and K we must take account of the fact that b and p are measured in different units. If we let A = 0.05 and K = 1.0, then equation 9.4 becomes

$$C(\mathbf{x}) = 0.05b^2 + 1.0p^2. \tag{9.6}$$

We can now map notional-cost isoclines onto the bp state space, as shown in figure 9.15. In other words, we can now see what notional cost is associated with any state that the robot might arrive at. This completes our design of the goal function.

In chapter 10 we will consider how these notional costs influence the behaviour of the individual.

**Points to Remember**

- The question of how a robot should deploy its behavioral options in time is not simply a matter of optimal time allocation. Stability, reliability, and customer appeal also have to be considered.
- A system displaced from a equilibrium state may return to that state, or to some other equilibrium state, after a transient period.

In such cases the system is said to be *asymptotically stable*. An alternative is that the disturbed system may enter a limit cycle, continually oscillating around a closed trajectory. Such a system is *globally stable* if it periodically returns to a particular state.

- In designing the goal function, we need to have some idea of the range of variation in the consequences of the behavior. Will the system be stable when the consequences fall within a certain range? The answer to this type of question lies with the environmental circumstances in which the decision-maker is to operate. In the case of animals, it lies with the nature of the ecological niche. In the case of robots, it is the customers requirements that matter.

- The customers (robot retailing companies) decide whether or not a particular robot is likely to sell well in a particular market. In nature, the selective pressures are the characteristics of a particular ecological niche. Effectively, these factors "decide" what design criteria are relevant in the prevailing environment.

- The *obligatory criteria* are the criteria which we can be sure every customer will accept. We can assume that every customer will want the robot to be, at least, asymptotically stable. The robot designer must also take account of customers' whims, which provide *facultative criteria*. All the criteria enter the design operation as components of the goal function, thus completing the first stage in designing the goal function.

- The next design step is to determine how notional costs are to be associated with each component of the goal function, and whether or not the components are separable.

- Separability is approximately equivalent to probabilistic independence of the various factors. This means that the notional risk associated with the value of one variable is independent of the values of other variables. The separability implies that the risk due to one component is independent of the risk due to another.

- There are many different ways in which the information inherent in the goal function may, or may not, be used by the decision-making mechanisms of the individual.

In chapter 1 we contrasted the traditional approach to control of the body with an alternative "parallel" approach. The traditional approach is to consider input, control, and output as separate functions. It involves a division into many subsystems, each of which is essential for even the most simple behavior. The essential subsystems are those providing perception, memory, planning, decision-making, effector control, etc. This results in a serial input-output architecture. The alternative approach, due largely to Brooks (1986), involves a number of task-accomplishing procedures acting in parallel. Of course, an entirely parallel architecture is not practicable. Such an architecture would result in a colony of agents, each with a different function. In most animal species, there is a single muscular system that is used for many different types of behavior. In the control of the motor system, it is inevitable that there will be convergence of control in the final common path (see chapter 2). Even Brooks' robot "insect" (1989) requires some such device to coordinate the semi-autonomous behavior of the legs.

If a robot is to be tailored to a particular niche, then the question of what kind of architecture is relevant in robot design is largely a question of how the goal function is to be implemented.

## 10.1    Implementation of Goal Functions

In the case of our housekeeping robot, we concluded in chapter 9 that there are four main components of the goal function: the battery level B, the number of dishes in the cupboard (P), the rate of change of window dirt $(dW/dt)$, and the rate of change of floor dirt $(dF/dt)$. In our specific version of the goal function (equation 9.4) we more or less ignored the last two of these, because the levels of W and F are so low that stability is never in question. Let us suppose for our present purposes that the risks of instability associated with these variables are $D(dw/dt)$ and $F(df/dt)$, respectively. If we assume that these risks are separable, equation 9.4 now becomes

$$C(\mathbf{x}) = Ab + Kp + D(dw/dt) + F(df/dt), \tag{10.1}$$

where $b = 100 - B$, $p = 5 - P$, and A, K, D, and F are constants of proportionality. The significance of the constants A, K, D, and F is that they are the resilience parameters, representing fixed and immutable properties of the individual robot or animal (see chapter 9).

This goal-function formulation is incomplete, because it takes no account of the notional costs of performing the activities themselves. Sibly and McFarland (1976) suggested that in animals the cost often increases as the square of the rate of performing the activity, and similar considerations may apply to robots (see chapter 4). In autonomous robots, tradeoff between concurrent interleaved activities is also likely to result in quadratic costs. Let us suppose, for our present purposes, that the housekeeping robot's activities (washup, windowclean, floorclean, sleep) can vary in their rate of performance (this is an extension of the model outlined in chapter 9), and that separable quadratic notional costs are associated with this variation. In accordance with conventional practice (McFarland and Houston 1981), we designate all states as x and all activity rates as u. The goal function outlined in equation 10.1 would then be modified as follows:

$$C(\mathbf{x}) = Ax_b{}^2 + Kx_p{}^2 + Dx_w{}^2 + Fx_f{}^2 + Eu_e{}^2 + Hu_h{}^2 + Nu_n{}^2 + Ru_r{}^2, \tag{10.2}$$

where the x's are the states mentioned in equation 10.1 and where $u_e = $ sleep rate, $u_h = $ washup rate, $u_n = $ windowclean rate, $u_r = $ floorclean rate, and E, H, N and R are scaling parameters.

How do these notional costs influence the behavior of the individual? There are many different ways in which the information inherent in the goal function may, or may not, be used by the desicion-making mechanisms of the individual. It may be that the notional costs are estimated by the individual in a cognitive manner; it may be that they simply monitored by the individual; it may be that the individual receives no information about the notional costs, but merely behaves (through the use of decision rules) as if the costs were relevant. These are all alternative ways of implementing the design that is specified by formulating a particular goal function.

First we must look at the fundamental design of our housekeeping robot. The robot is designed to perform window-cleaning, floor-cleaning, and dish-washing tasks. In addition, it must recharge its

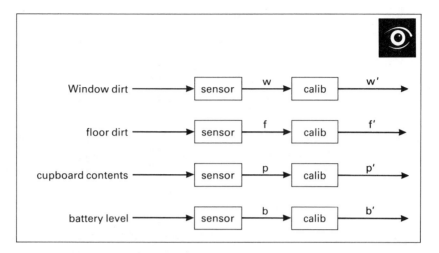

**Figure 10.1**  Calibration of sensors in household robot.

batteries. To perform these tasks, the robot must receive information about the state of the windows $(x_w)$, the floor $(x_f)$, the cupboard contents $(x_p)$, and the battery $(x_B)$. Let us assume that the robot has sensors specially designed to detect the values of these variables, as illustrated in figure 10.1. These sensors will vary in complexity. In the cast of the battery level only a simple sensor is required; however, for cupboard contents the robot requires a sensor that can discriminate dishes from other objects and can count the number of dishes in the cupboard.

The outputs of the sensors cannot drive behavior directly. They must first be calibrated in terms of their relative importance to the robot. The calibration transforms each sensor's output into a motivational variable, on the basis of which decisions can be made. When we come to the question of how the sensor outputs are to be calibrated, there are two basic design strategies that we should think about:

• The *procedural strategy* is the strategy normally assumed to apply to primitive (noncognitive) animals or automata (see chapter 6). According to this strategy, the calibrations should be designed to reflect the ecological circumstances, as outlined by Houston and McFarland (1976). The calibrated motivational variables then directly reflect the "importances" of the various sensory inputs, in terms of survival value or fitness. The animal or automaton can then act on this information in accordance with fairly simple procedures (see below).

- The *cognitive strategy* is more anthropocentric in inspiration. According to this strategy, the calibrations should be designed to reflect the "facts" represented by the sensory outputs. Some sensors will, by their very nature, distort the incoming information. Such distortions can sometimes be compensated by suitable calibration. The aim of the design is to present an accurate picture of the world that is monitored by the sensors. The calibrated variables then provide a body of knowledge that is "declarative" (see chapter 6), in the sense that it can be used for a number of purposes and is not tied to any particular procedure. The manipulation of such declarative knowledge is essentially a cognitive exercise.

The two strategies outlined here represent extremes, and it is perfectly possible to imagine a design that combines them. For our present purposes, however, we proceed beyond the calibration stage to inquire how the goal function might be incorporated into such designs.

There is a spectrum of possibilities. At the extreme "procedural" end of the spectrum is the possibility that the design incorporates no information about the goal function, but that the behaviour-control system is put together in such a way that the animal or robot behaves as if it were guided by the relevant notional costs. Such a system would be analogous to a physical system in which the behavior conformed with some extremal principle.

Another possibility, illustrated in figure 10.2a, is that the sensor outputs are weighted by elements of the goal function. The motivational variables (w', f', p', b') would then represent the relative importances of the sensory inputs, and could be used directly in rules of procedure leading to a behavioral outcome. The most obvious rule of procedure is that the strongest motivational tendency wins in a competition for behavioral expression. The behavioral outcome would then reflect the most important (in terms of the goal function) of the alternatives. This design has the merit of being simple and straightforward, but it has a number of disadvantages.

At the "cognitive" end of the spectrum is the possibility, illustrated in figure 10.2b, that the sensor outputs are calibrated purely in terms of the stimulus properties, thus providing a representation of the state of affairs monitored by the sensors. An advantage of this design is that the state representation so achieved could be used for a number of purposes. It is a form of declarative knowl-

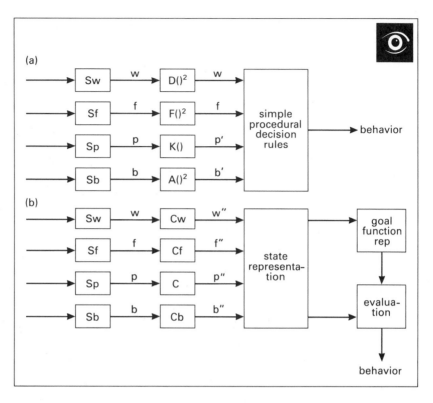

**Figure 10.2** Procedural (a) and nonprocedural (b) ways of calibrating sensory information in accordance with a specified goal function.

edge. To achieve a behavioral outcome that also took the goal function into account, it would be necessary to evaluate the state in relation to the goal function. This would require a separate representation of the goal function. A disadvantage of this approach is that it is more complicated than the procedural device (figure 10.2a) and would require a larger brain.

Before proceeding to look at examples of the various strategies, it may be useful to note their essential differences. In the procedural design, there is no explicit representation of the goal function, but it may be functionally represented in the calibration of the sensor outputs. This type of representation is sometimes called a *tacit representation*. In the cognitive design, on the other hand, the goal function is explicitly represented, like a table of values that can be consulted from time to time.

In the procedural design, there is no evaluation process apart from that embodied in the rules of procedure. In the cognitive design, on the other hand, there is an explicit evaluation process that works out the best (in terms of the goal function) behavioral outcome in relation to the prevailing state. This process will generally be a cognitive process, because the information it utilizes is represented in a declarative form and can be used for a number of purposes.

### 10.2 Implicit Goal Functions

The use of optimality principles in accounting for animal behavior can be seen as analogous to the use of extremal principles in physics (see chapter 7). A stone thrown through the air obeys a "least action" law, minimizing a particular function of kinetic and potential energy. The stone behaves as if seeking an optimal trajectory, although its behavior is in fact determined by forces acting in accordance with Newton's laws of motion. Similarly, an animal may behave as if seeking an optimal trajectory through the state space (Sibly and McFarland 1976; McFarland and Houston 1981), but such an account says little about the mechanisms involved. Optimality principles are, in effect, functional explanations that describe how the animal ougtht to behave in order to attain some objective. For a causal explanation, the equivalent of physical forces must be established. These will presumably take the form of a set of rules of thumb governing behavior, or of some equivalent cognitive mechanism.

It is possible for the rules governing behavior to conform to some extremal or optimality principle without there being any obvious sign of this in our formulation of the control system. For example, Sibly and McFarland (1976) used Pontryagin's Maximum Principle to calculate the optimal behavior for a hungry and thirsty dove in situations varying in food and water availability. Postulating an objective function similar to that of equation 10.2, they suggested that the dove uses two fairly simple rules of thumb:

- When only food or only water is available, it should be taken at such a rate that the deficit is reduced exponentially. Empirical support for this rule is reviewed in McCleery 1977.
- When food and water are both available, the choice between food and water at each point in the meal should be made according to whether the product of the deficit, the availability, and the limiting attempt rate is greater for food or for water. This amounts

to the following rule: Eat if (hunger × incentive value of food) > (thirst × incentive value of water); otherwise drink. Experimental support for this rule is provided in Sibly 1975.

These rules can be incorporated into a simple model that makes no explicit reference to the goal function but which nevertheless produces behavior that conforms with the type of goal function given in equation 10.2. In terms of our housekeeper example, let us consider a simplified version of this equation:

$$C(\mathbf{x}) = Ax_b^2 + Kx_p^2 + Eu_e^2 + Hu_h^2. \tag{10.3}$$

The symbols here have the same meanings as in equation 10.2, except that p is unrestricted (i.e., there are more than five dishes in the cupboard). This is a two-dimensional quadratic cost function, the same as that used in Sibly and McFarland 1976.

To minimize cost, the housekeeping robot can employ the following rule:

If $Ax_bEu_e > Kx_pHu_h$ perform activity $u_e$, else perform activity $u_h$.

This simple rule is the equivalent of that suggested above for feeding and drinking in doves.

The effect of applying this rule can be seen in figure 10.3., where it is compared with a simple rule. In this example, we start with the following values:

$A = K = E = H = 1$,

$x_b = 10$,

$x_p = 11$,

$u_e = 1$,

$u_h = 2$.

We can see that the simple rule (rule A) results in higher cumulative cost than the optimized rule (rule B). The performance attained by rule B is very close to optimal, given the constraint imposed by the orthogonal consequences of $x_b$ and $x_p$. Note that this is achieved without any explicit representation of the goal function's being represented by equation 10.3. Although the hunger and thirst must be internally calibrated, they can be proportional to the physiological state (i.e., the components of the goal function are not embedded in the calibration).

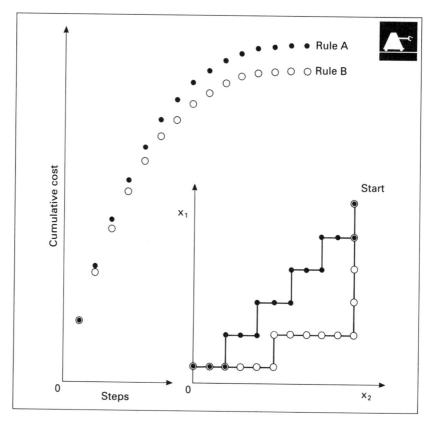

**Figure 10.3**  The cumulative cost of following rules (larger graph) and the changes of state that result (smaller graph). Rule A is a simple rule and rule B is an optimized rule.

## 10.3  Embedded Goal Functions

In animals, stimuli are monitored by sensors and are calibrated to produce cues. If we could measure them, we would expect to find that these cues were related to the survival values associated with the relevant states and stimuli. For example, Houston and McFarland (1976) consider the plight of the desert lizard *Aporosaura anchietae*, which forages on the surface of sand dunes. The probability of death from thermal stress can be represented as a function of temperature, as shown in figure 10.4a. The probability of death from predation is also likely to be a function of temperature (figure 10.4b), because the lizards are less mobile at lower temperatures. Taking these two aspects of survival into account, we might expect the calibration of thermosensitivity to be somewhat like that illustrated in figure 10.4c. In other words, the motivational variable that results from the calibration can be thought of as the part of the tendency to be active on the dune surface that is due to

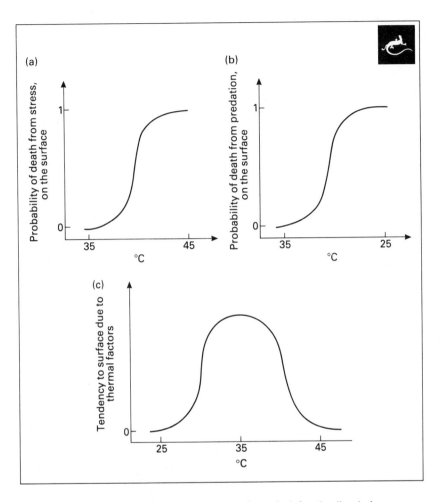

**Figure 10.4**  Hypothetical functions relating temperature and survival for the lizard *Aporosaura*. Graphs a and b plot cululative probability functions; graph c plots a calibration function derived from graphs a and b. (After Houston and McFarland 1976.)

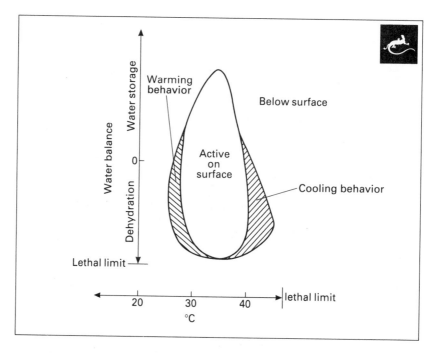

**Figure 10.5** Two-dimensional representation of the physiological states at which *Aporosaura* might be expected to be below the surface of the sand, or above the surface and involved in warming or cooling behavior, or actively foraging. Boundary lines indicate transitions between types of behavior. (After Houston and McFarland 1976.)

thermal factors. This variable is calibrated in such a way that it reflects the risk (due to thermal factors) of being on the dune surface. (Other factors affecting the tendency to forage on the surface, notably hunger and thirst, are discussed in Houston and McFarland 1976.)

If we restrict ourselves to considering the thermal and hydration factors affecting the lizard, we can construct a "survival space" within which the animal can be safely active on the surface of the dunes. An example is illustrated in figure 10.5. On the basis of the calibrations illustrated in figure 10.4, and of a similar calibration for hydration factors, Houston and McFarland (1976) constructed alternative models that would produce different possible survival spaces depending on the assumptions incorporated into the models. In particular they pointed out that, in addition to appropriate calibration of sensory information, there also has to be some appropriate combination rule relating the information from different modalities. For example, the tendency to be active on the surface due to hydration factors. Different combination rules give different results, as illustrated in figure 10.6. The main point made

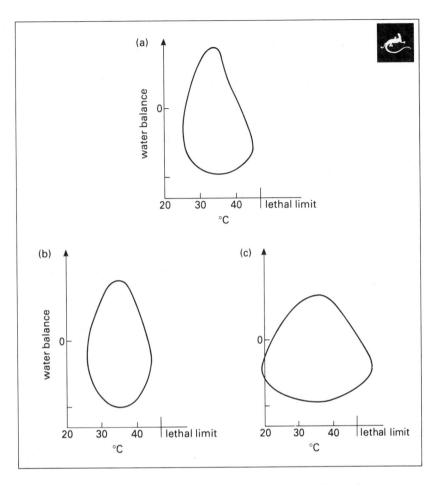

**Figure 10.6** Two-dimensional representation of the physiological states at which *Aporosaura* might be expected to be above or below the sand. (a) Boundary lines transposed directly from figure 10.5. (b) Boundary line based on an additive combination rule. (c) Boundary line based on a multiplicative combination rule. (After Houston and McFarland 1976.)

by Houston and McFarland (1976) is that the optimal combination rule is not independent of the calibration functions, so that in the design of an animal (or a robot) calibration and combination have to be taken together in a holistic optimization exercise. Houston and McFarland suggest the conjoint measurement approach of Krantz and Tversky, (1971) as a means of approaching this problem. Another approach that tackles both the scaling of the variables and their combination rules is the "functional measurement" approach of Anderson (1978).

In relation to robot architecture, the problem with the calibration approach is that it cannot be conducted in isolation from the combination rules or their equivalents. The performance of the robot (or animal) as a whole must fulfil certain criteria, and not all the responsibility for this can be placed on the calibration of sensory input.

In relation to our lizard example, the problem is to find an architecture that will ensure that the lizard will not incur undue risks of predation in venturing onto the dune surface to find food and water. Effectively this means that a lizard should not expose itself when its muscles are not sufficiently warmed up to enable it to run with sufficient speed to dive into loose sand and bury itself (Louw and Holm 1972). An architecture involving a simple permissive temperature threshold will not be adequate, because the risk of predation is counterbalanced by risks of starvation. Normally, the animal has little time to forage for food, because the temperatures are too high in the middle of the day and too cold at night (figure 10.7). As usual, the architecture must permit compromise and tradeoff among conflicting requirements.

## 10.4   The Planning Approach

Planning is an aspect of problem solving—that is, of deciding what to do in a given situation. In our view, plans are mental tools that may or may not be used in accomplishing tasks (see chapter 8). Our view is not the currently fashionable view, however. In general, the planning model in cognitive science treats a plan as a sequence of actions designed to accomplish some preconceived end. It is envisaged that the agent's problem is to find a path from some initial state to a desired goal state, given certain conditions along the way. (See Newell and Simon 1972 for the seminal formulation of this view, and Suchman 1987 for a critique.)

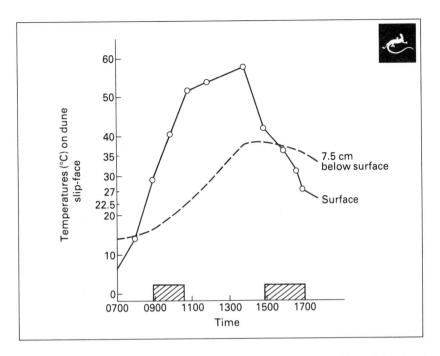

**Figure 10.7** Typical temperature conditions on the dune slip-face, the microhabitat of the lizard *Aporosaura*. Hatched blocks indicate the periods for which the lizard is above the surface of the sand. (After Louw and Holm 1972.)

A basic problem in robotics is planning movements to solve some prespecified task and then controlling the robot as it executes the commands necessary to achieve those movements. In this context, planning involves deciding on a course of action before acting. The robot is designed with some problem-solving system that can formulate a plan to achieve some stated goal, given some initial situation. The plan is a representation of a course of action for achieving the goal. Various ways of formulating plans have been suggested. The General Problem Solver (GPS) of Newell, Shaw, and Simon (1960) reasoned in terms of *means-end-analysis*, in which the goal is approached in a series of steps. Each step is initiated by calculating the difference between what has been achieved so far and the goal. On the basis of the characteristics of this difference, operations that are likely to reduce the difference are considered. Suitable operations are identified on a mainly heuristic basis. Useful introductory examples of this type of planning are provided by Fu et al. (1987). Another vehicle for planning is formal logic, especially since it became possible to construct logical proofs mechanically (Chang and Lee 1973). Simple examples are discussed by Fu et al. (1987) and by Janlert (1987).

The formulation of plans, or representations of possible courses of action, is not without its computational difficulties. These have been admirably reviewed by Janlert (1987) (see also chapter 5 above). We have no argument with the definition of a plan, but we disagree with the traditional views of how plans should be transformed into behavior. As we noted in chapter 7, goal-directed formulations are deficient because they violate the tradeoff principle. Thus, means-end-analysis is acceptable as a way of formulating a plan, but as a recipe for behavior it is primitive and restricted in its applicability. In a rational system, good design should be based on evaluation of options in terms of broad relevant criteria, such as those provided by a goal function. This approach in no way excludes planning, and it may be helpful here to discuss a simple example.

Now let us return to our simplified housekeeping robot. On the basis of equation 10.3, we can consider an architecture such as that outlined in Figure 10.2b. The general procedure is illustrated in figure 10.8. On the basis of the current state, the cost of performing the alternative activities sleep and washup is calculated. In this example there are only two alternative activities, but in more realistic examples there will be many alternatives. Calculating the cost of performing all possible activities (often called the *breadth-of-search* problem) can be computationally difficult.

As we saw in chapter 6, each calculation can be done for one, two, three, ... steps into the future. For example, the consequences (in terms of cost) of choosing a particular activity can be calculated along the lines indicated in figure 10.9. On the basis of the current state, the costs of options A and B (i.e., the cost of the consequences of performing the activity) are calculated and the results stored. The estimate of the state is then updated. In other words, answers are provided to the questions of what the state would be if activity A (or B) were performed. On the basis of these estimates we enter a second round, or stage, of calculation, but this time the amount of computation is doubled. In fact, for an exhaustive search in which the consequences of choosing every option are calculated, the amount of computation required doubles at every round. Clearly *depth of search* can present computational problems.

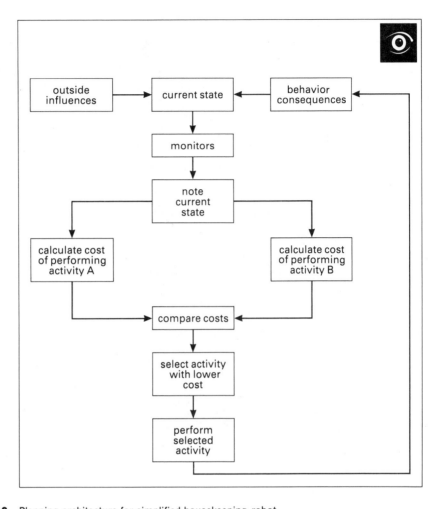

**Figure 10.8** Planning architecture for simplified housekeeping robot.

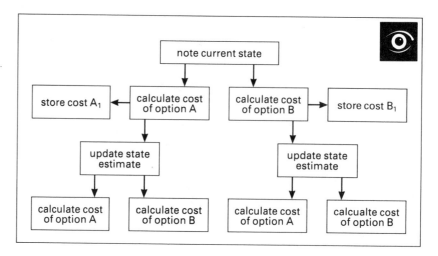

**Figure 10.9** Calculating the costs of successive options.

Let us base our cost calculation on equation 10.3 and use the same initial values as in figure 10.3. We calculate the cost of an option by the following procedure:

Activities $u_e$ and $u_h$ cannot be performed simultaneously; therefore,

Option A: $C = x_b{}^2 + x_p{}^2 + u_h{}^2$

Option B: $C = x_b{}^2 + x_p{}^2 + u_h{}^2$.

The consequences of choosing option A are

$$C(A) = (x_b - u_e)^2 + x_p{}^2 + u_e{}^2.$$

The consequences of choosing option B are

$$C(B) = x_b{}^2 + (x_p{}^2 - u_h{}^2) + u_h{}^2.$$

Using the values from figure 10.3, we get

$$C(A) = (10 - 1)^2 + 11^2 + 1^2 = 203,$$

$$C(B) = 10^2 + (11 - 2)^2 + 2^2 = 185.$$

So option B would be the better option.

In the case of two-stage planning, we update the state estimates, so that in the next round we get

$$C(AA) = (9 - 1)^2 + 11^2 + 1^2 = 186,$$

$$C(AB) = 9^2 + (11 - 2)^2 + 2^2 = 166,$$

$C(BA) = (10 - 1)^2 + 9^2 + 1^2 = 163,$

$C(BB) = 10^2 + (9 - 2)^2 + 2^2 = 153.$

This leads us to the decision trees portrayed in figure 10.10, which show a three-stage search of the consequences of choosing option A and option B. The numbers show the costs involved in each choice. Overall, the search shows that initially option B is a better choice than option A, because at no point in the search does option A result in lower cost than B (see figure 10.10a). However, once the choice has been made and one bout of activity B has been performed, a new search is called for (figure 10.10b). This search shows that option B is still the better choice.

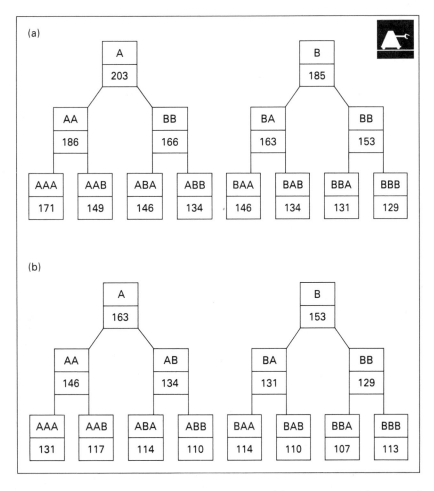

**Figure 10.10** Cost calculations used in example. (a) Initial search. (b) Search after performance of option B.

In this simple example, both the breadth and the depth of search are restricted—the breadth because there are only two options to choose between and the depth because we are merely exploring the possibilities here.

The autonomous agent evaluates the expected consequences of its own behavior (see chapter 6). To do this it must be able to refer to a set of evaluative criteria in the form of some kind of representation of the goal function. We do not mean to imply that all forms of expectation require planning. Indeed, psychologists have known for years how to model expectation implicitly, and this approach has found its way into AI modeling (see, e.g., Sutton 1991). The point is that the autonomous agent evaluates alternatives that are based on (sometimes implicitly) expected consequences.

As we saw in the above example (figure 10.10), in choosing among alternative possible activities the autonomous agent takes into account the total (instantaneous) cost (or utility) of the alternatives and chooses the smallest (or the largest). To the extent that some kind of declarative representation of the goal function is necessarily involved in this type of process, some cognition is involved. This does not mean that the whole of the evaluative process is a cognitive one. It is possible to imagine that some aspects of the goal function, especially those that the alternative candidates have in common, exert their influence in a contingent hard-wired manner.

### Points to Remember

- If a robot is to be tailored to a particular niche, then the question of what kind of architecture is relevant in robot design is largely a question of how the goal function is to be implemented.
- There are many different ways in which the information inherent in the goal function may, or may not, be made use of by the decision-making mechanisms of the individual.
- When we come to the question of how the sensor outputs are to be calibrated, there are two basic design strategies that we should think about. We can call these the *procedural* strategy and the *cognitive* strategy.
- According to the procedural strategy, the sensor calibrations directly reflect the "importances" of the various sensory inputs, in terms

of survival value or market fitness. The agent can then act on this information in accordance with fairly simple procedures.

- According to the cognitive strategy, the sensor calibrations reflect the "facts" as represented by the sensory outputs. The aim of the design is to present an accurate picture of the world that is monitored by the sensors. The calibrated variables then provide a body of knowledge that is "declarative" in the sense that it can be used for a number of purposes, rather than being tied to any particular procedure. The manipulation of such declarative knowledge is essentially a cognitive exercise.

- In procedural design, there is no explicit representation of the goal function, but it may be functionally represented in the calibration of the sensor outputs. In the cognitive design, on the other hand, the goal function is explicitly represented much like a table of values that can be consulted from time to time.

- Planning involves deciding on a course of action before acting, searching among possible actions, and evaluating these actions in relation to a representation of the goal function.

- In any complex animal there is likely to be a mixture of autonomous and automaton-like behavioral control. The type of control that an animal has over a particular behavior can sometimes be determined by goal-revaluation procedures.

Throughout its development, an animal may acquire new elements for its behavioral repertoire through changes in its motivational structure, in its behavior-control mechanisms, in its decision rules, and so forth. Some such changes may be genetically predetermined, but others are acquired through experience. Learning is a part of development that is contingent on the experiencing of environmental events.

When an animal learns to respond to environmental events in a new way, its behavioral repertoire undergoes permanent alternation. Learning is an irreversible process; although an animal may extinguish or forget some learned behavior, it can never revert to its previous state. Any such change in the animal's makeup is bound to alter its biological fitness. Because the learning processes have themselves long been subject to natural selection, we would expect learning to bring about beneficial changes on average. Learning is a part of adaptation, but this does not always mean that learning is always adaptive (McFarland 1991a).

Learning in animals takes many forms, varying with the lifestyle and the selective pressures characteristic of each particular species. Changes in the environment that are predictable from an evolutionary point of view are often handled by preprogrammed forms of learning. For example, imprinting is evolutionarily preprogrammed in the sense that it does not require feedback of information about the values of alternative courses of action. An imprinting animal learns willy-nilly the features of the parent, sibling, or habitat presented to it (McFarland and Houston 1981). In situations in which the animal is able to predict its future learning progress, it effectively has a choice between learning to exploit a new situation and remaining with a known and mastered situation. Thus, it is not always in an animal's interests to learn new things (McFarland and Houston 1981; Tovish 1982). In situations in which an animal is not able to predict its future learning progress, its task is complicated by the need to gain information. The optimal solution to this type of problem generally involves sampling as well as exploitation of resources (Houston et al. 1982). There appears to be an evolutionary tradeoff between the adaptive pressure to evolve learning and the ease of learning during a given lifespan (Todd and Miller 1991). Nevertheless, learning is widespread in the animal kingdom, especially among vertebrates, despite the great variety of lifestyles. It has been argued (Dickinson 1980) that there are certain universal features of the world, such as causality, that nearly all species will benefit from learning about. It therefore follows that there will be some universal laws of learning, and it is these that animal psychologists seek to discover. In this chapter we will concentrate on these aspects of learning.

## 11.1  Animal Learning

What follows is a basic outline of those aspects of animal learning that have some relevance to robotics.

### Classical Conditioning

The Russian physiologist Ivan Pavlov is generally credited with the discovery of conditioned reflexes. Pavlov was working on digestive processes. After investigating the secretion mechanisms of various digestive glands, he came to the conclusion that they were controlled exclusively by nervous mechanisms. For this work he was awarded the Nobel Prize in 1904. Pavlov noticed that salivation could be induced by the sight of food, or by other stimuli that normally preceded feeding. This led him to the discovery of the conditioned reflex.

In a typical experiment, Pavlov showed that if the presentation of food to a dog was repeatedly accompanied by the sound of a bell, then the dog would come to respond to the bell as if it were food. In his original conditioning experiments (figure 11.1), Pavlov restrained a hungry dog in a harness and presented small portions of food at regular intervals. When he signaled the delivery of food by preceding it with an external stimulus, such as a bell, the behavior of the dog toward the stimulus gradually changed. The animal began by orienting toward the bell, licking its lips, and salivating. When Pavlov recorded the salivation systematically by placing a small tube in the salivary duct, he found that the amount of saliva

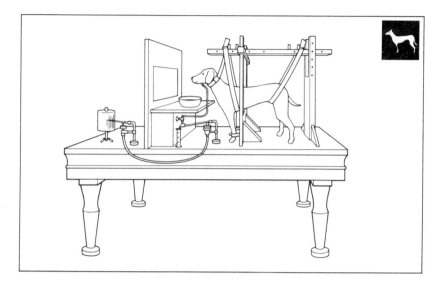

**Figure 11.1**  Pavlov's arrangement for the study of salivery conditioning.

collected increased as the animal experienced more pairings between the sound of the bell and the presentation of food. It appeared that the dog had learned to associate the bell with the food.

Pavlov referred to the bell as the *conditional stimulus* (CS) and to the food as the *unconditional stimulus* (UCS). Salivation in response to presentation of food was called the *unconditional response* (UCR); salivation in response to the bell was called the *conditional response* (CR).

Although Pavlov originally used the Russian equivalents of *conditional* and *unconditional*, his terminology was mistranslated at an early stage, and the terms *conditioned reflex, conditioned response, unconditioned response*, and *unconditioned reflex* became established in the English-language literature. However, it is modern practice to return to Pavlov's original terminology. During the process of conditioning, the presentation of the UCS (food) after the CS (bell) is said to reinforce the conditional reflex of salivation to the CS. The UCS, therefore, is regarded as a *reinforcer*.

A reinforcer is characterized less by its intrinsic properties as a stimulus than by its motivational significance to the animal. Thus, food acts as a positive reinforcer only if the dog is hungry, and an air puff to the eye acts as a negative reinforcer only if it is noxious or unpleasant for the animal. In many cases the reinforcer is innate in the sense that its motivational significance and its ability to support conditioning are integral to the animal's normal makeup. However, this does not have to be the case, and Pavlov showed that a CS could act as a reinforcer. For example, if a bell is established as a CS by the normal conditioning procedure, it will reliably elicit a CR (such as salivation). If a second CS (such as a light) then is paired repeatedly with the bell, in the absence of food, the animal will come to give the CR in response to the light alone, even though food never has been associated directly with the light. This procedure is known as *second-order conditioning*.

Pavlovian, or classical, conditioning is very widespread in the animal kingdom. It pervades every aspect of life in higher animals, including humans. Pavlov demonstrated that conditioning could occur in monkeys and in mice, and claims have been made for a wide variety of invertebrate animals. In evaluating such claims, however, we must take care to distinguish true classical conditioning from other forms of learning and quasi-learning.

## Acquisition

We can measure the acquisition of a conditional reflex in various ways. Pavlov used the amount of saliva collected during presentation of the CS, for example. In the case of eyelid conditioning, the probability of occurrence of the response is measured.

Pavlov held the view that the pairing of a CS and a UCS leads to the formation of an association between them. The CS becomes a substitute for the UCS and becomes capable of eliciting the responses normally elicited by the UCS. This is usually called the *stimulus-substitution theory*. An alternative theory maintains that CRs occur because they are followed by rewards. In other words the CR is reinforced by its consequences. This is usually called the *stimulus-response theory*.

The two theories differ in two main empirical respects. First, on the basis of the stimulus-substitution theory we would expect the CR to be very similar to the UCR, whereas it should be somewhat different according to stimulus-response theory. Second, Pavlov maintained that the association occurs between the CS and the UCS, which itself constitutes a reinforcing state of affairs. The stimulus-response theory maintains that learning depends on reinforcing consequences of the CR.

## Extinction

We have seen that presentation of a UCS increases the strength of a CR. Pavlov discovered that withholding such reinforcement led to the gradual disappearance of the CR. The process by which learned behavior patterns cease to be performed when they are no longer appropriate is called *extinction*.

In a classical-conditioning experiment, the dog learns that the bell (CS) signals the presentation of food. Salivation (CR) is therefore an appropriate response to make in anticipation of the availability of food. If food no longer is made available, then the dog should no longer treat the bell as a signal for food. This is precisely what happens; omission of food results in a decline in the salivary response to the CS. The behavior of the animal then appears to be the same as it was before conditioning.

If, after extinction, the CS again is paired with the reinforcer, the CR reappears much more rapidly than it did during the original conditioning. This suggests that the process of extinction does not abolish the original learning but that it somehow suppresses it. Further evidence for this conclusion comes from the phenomenon of *spontaneous recovery*, by which a response that has been extinguished recovers its strength with rest. For example, Pavlov (1927) reported an experiment in which the number of drops of saliva secreted to the CS was reduced from ten to three in a series of seven extinction trials. The latency (time delay) of the response also increased from 3 to 13 seconds. After a rest period of 23 minutes, the salivation on the first trial with the CS alone amounted to six drops, with a latency of 5 seconds.

Pavlov argued that the decline in the CR observed during extinction must be due to an accumulation of internal inhibition. He showed that if an extraneous novel stimulus was presented at the same time as the CS in a conditioned trial, the CR was disrupted. According to Pavlov (1927), "The appearance of any new stimulus immediately invokes the investigatory reflex and the animal fixes all its appropriate receptor organs upon the source of disturbance. . . . The investigatory reflex is excited and the conditioned reflex is in consequence inhibited." This phenomenon is called *external inhibition*. If the extraneous stimulus is presented during the course of extinction, the CR increases in strength on that trial. This *Pavlovian disinhibition* provides further evidence of the inhibitory nature of extinction. Unlike external inhibition, it is not

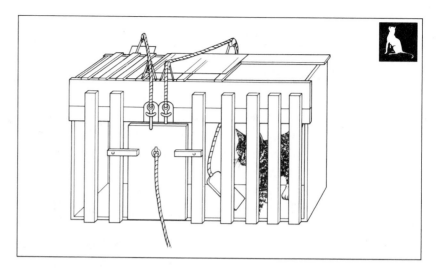

**Figure 11.2**  A cat in one of Thorndike's puzzle boxes.

due to competition between reflexes; rather, it is thought to be caused by an increase in arousal. It is a widespread phenomenon, and it can be shown to occur when a CR is declining for any reason—including habituation.

### Instrumental Learning

The principles of *instrumental conditioning* were discovered and developed in the United States. Edward Thorndike carried out a series of experiments in which cats were required to press a latch or pull a string to open a door and escape from a box to obtain food outside. The boxes were constructed with vertical slats so that the food was visible to the cat (figure 11.2). A hungry cat, when first placed in the box, shows a number of activities, including reaching through the slats toward the food and scratching at objects within the box. Eventually the cat accidentally hits the release mechanism and escapes from the box. On subsequent trials, the cat's activity progressively becomes concentrated in the region of the release mechanism, and other activities gradually cease. Eventually the cat is able to perform the correct behavior as soon as it is placed in the box.

Thorndike (1898) designated this type of learning "trial, error, and accidental success." It is nowadays called *instrumental learning*, the correct response being instrumental in providing access to the reward. This type of learning had been known to circus trainers for centuries, but Thorndike was the first to study it systematically and to develop a coherent theory of learning based on observations.

To explain the change in behavior observed during learning experiments, Thorndike (1913) proposed his *law of effect*. This stated that a response followed by a rewarding or a satisfying state of affairs would increase in probability of occurrence, whereas a response followed by an aversive or annoying consequence would decrease in probability of occurrence. Thus, he attributed the success of instrumental learning to the fact that learned behavior can be modified directly by its consequences. Thorndike (1911) assumed that a reinforcer increases the probability of the response upon which it is contingent because it strengthens the learned connection between the response and the prevailing stimulus situation. This became known as the "stimulus-response theory of learning," and versions of this theory were predominant for many years. Most present-day psychologists, while recognizing the validity of the law of effect as an empirical statement, doubt that behavior is modified by its consequences in the direct way that Thorndike and his followers supposed.

### Associative Learning

To investigate the hypothesis that animals possess mechanisms for detecting and learning about causal relationships, we must specify the nature of such relationships. There are basically two types of causal relationships, and there is little doubt that animals can learn about both (Dickinson 1980). An event (the *cause*) can cause another event to happen (the *effect*) or not to happen (a *noneffect*). The first event need not be an immediate cause of the effect or noneffect, but it may be an identifiable link in a chain of cause and effect. Indeed, the event noticed by the animal may not be part of the causal chain; it may merely be a sign that the causal event has occurred. It is the apparent cause that is important to the animal.

From the animal's viewpoint, there are always a variety of possible causes of an event, apart from that provided by the experimenter. The importance of such background, or contextual, cues has been demonstrated in experiments (see, e.g., Mackintosh 1976) in which the presence of a second stimulus decreased the amount by which a primary stimulus was associated with a shock even though there was perfect correlation between the primary stimulus and the shock. This phenomenon is called *overshadowing*. The degree of overshadowing depends on the relative salience of the overshadowed and overshadowing stimuli.

Animals will learn to associate two events only if they are accompanied initially by an unexpected or surprising occurrence (Mackintosh 1974). In a normal conditioning experiment, the surprise is provided by the reinforcer. Thus, if a stimulus is paired with a shock, and if neither the stimulus nor the contextual cues initially predict its occurrence, the shock will be surprising. However, if the animal already has experienced shock in the presence of stimulus A, then, if both A and B are correlated with shock, the presence of A will block learning about B. This phenomenon, first discovered by Kamin (1969), is known as *blocking*. Generally, the more surprising the reinforcer, the more the animal learns.

In the natural environment, certain types of causes are more likely to produce certain effects than other types of causes. For example, if a cat jumps into an apple tree at the same time a dog barks and then an apple falls to the ground, we are more likely to think that the cat was responsible than that the dog's bark caused the apple to fall. Both the cat's jumping and the dog's barking bear the same temporal relationship to the fall of the apple, but other aspects of these events lead us to assume that the cat was the cause of the apple's falling, Similarly, we can show that animals are more likely to form associations among certain types of stimuli than among others. For example, rats readily associate taste with subsequent illness but do not easily learn to associate a tone or light with illness (Domjan and Wilson 1972). Rats also learn to associate two events when they are in the same sensory modality (Rescorla and Furrow 1977) and when they are in the same spatial location (Testa 1975; Rescorla and Cunningham 1979).

## Summary

Animals can learn to associate two events if the relationship between them conforms to what we normally call a causal relationship. Thus, animals can learn that one event (the cause) predicts another event (the effect), or that one event predicts that another event (a noneffect) will not occur. They also can learn that certain stimuli predict no consequences in a given situation, or that a class of stimuli (including the animal's own behavior) is causally irrelevant. The conditions under which these type of associative learning occur are those that we would expect on the hypothesis that animals are designed to acquire knowledge about the causal relationships in their environment. Thus, an animal must be able to distinguish potential causes from contextual cues. For this to occur, there must be some surprising occurrence that draws the animal's attention to particular events, or the events must be (innately) relevant to particular consequences. If these conditions are not fulfilled, contextual cues may overshadow potential causal events, or learning may be blocked by prior association with a now-irrelevant cue. Thus, the conditions under which associative learning occurs are consistent with our commonsense views about the nature of causality.

## 11.2  Hebbian Learning

In his 1949 book *The Organization of Behavior*, Donald Hebb introduced various hypotheses about the neural substrate of learning and memory, including what is now known as the *Hebb synapse*. According to Hebb (1949, p. 62), "When an axon of cell A is near enough to excite cell B or repeatedly or persistently takes part in firing it, some growth process or metabolic change takes place in one or both cells such that A's efficiency, as one of the cells firing B, is increased." This statement can be translated into a precise quantitative expression:

$$\Delta T_{BA} = F(V_A, V_B). \tag{11.1}$$

This equation states that the change in synaptic strength between neuron A, with average firing rate $V_A$, and neuron B, with average firing rate $V_B$, is some joint function of the presynaptic and postsynaptic firing rates. The most straightforward particular form of this function is the simple product

$$\Delta T_{BA} = k V_A V_B, \tag{11.2}$$

where k is a small numerical constant. This emphasizes the current instantaneous firing rate, and might be appropriate for simple associative learning. For classical conditioning some modification is required, because the precise timing of the relationships between the presynaptic and postsynaptic signals is important. There are various schemes for implementing such requirements (Sejnowski and Tesauro 1989).

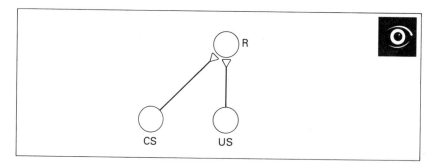

**Figure 11.3** Hebbian classical conditioning. The unconditional stimulus (US) elicits a response in the postsynaptic cell (R). Temporal coincidence of the response and the conditional stimulus (CS) strengthens the synapse between CS and R.

The Hebb rule can be used to form associations between one stimulus and another. Where such associations are static, the neural circuit functions as an associated memory (Longuet-Higgins 1968; Anderson 1970). Dynamic associations enable the network to learn to predict that one stimulus pattern will be followed at a later time by another, as in classical conditioning. A simple neural model of the classical conditioning process is illustrated in figure 11.3. There is a strong unmodifiable synapse from US to R, which ensures that the US automatically evokes the response. There is a modifiable synapse from CS to R, which in the naive animal is initially weak.

In classical conditioning the temporal order of stimuli is important. If the US appears before the CS, then no learning occurs. Therefore, equation 11.2 must be modified, because as it stands learning will occur regardless of the order in which the neurons come to be activated. Moreover, when the CS neuron alone became capable of eliciting R, equation 11.2 would cause the synapse to continue to be strengthened upon presentation of the CS alone. In classical conditioning in animals, presentation of the CS alone causes extinction of R.

The literal Hebb rule must be modified to produced appropriate conditioning phenomena (Tesauro 1986). A popular (e.g. Klopf 1982; Sutton and Barto 1981) way to do this is as follows:

$$\Delta T_{BA} = k\overline{V}_A\dot{V}_B, \tag{11.3}$$

where $\overline{V}_A$ represents the stimulus trace of $V_A$ (the weighted average of $V_A$ over previous times), and $\dot{V}_B$ is the time derivative of $V_B$. The stimulus trace ensures that conditioning occurs only forward, and not backward, while the use of the time derivative of the post-synaptic firing rate ensures that extinction will occur in the absence of the US. Many variants of equation 11.3 take account of other conditioning phenomena, such as second-order conditioning and blocking. For example, Klopf (1989) proposes a "drive-reinforcement" model of neuronal function, which is implemented within a single complex neuron. Halperin (1991) outlines a mini-network with similar capabilities. These models make some attempt to incorporate the motivational element of reinforcement, and are able to reproduce many of the aspects of conditioning discovered by experimental psychologists.

## 11.3 Neural Networks

A neural network consists of a large number of interconnected artificial "neurons." These may be simple signal-transmitting devices or more complex attempts to mimic real neurons. The performance of a neural network depends on (1) the properties of the individual neurons, (2) the architecture that specifies which neurons are connected to which and of what type the connections are (e.g., excitatory or inhibitory), and (3) the rules governing changes of strength in those connections that are variable.

Connectionism is neurally inspired modeling (Arbib 1987) using the above properties of neural nets. It should be distinguished from neural modeling, which is an attempt to model the neural activity of real brains. Connectionist models are of many types (see Arbib 1987 for a review), and some are capable of learning.

The three main types of learning employed in connectionism are *self-organizing* learning, *supervised* learning, and *reinforcement* learning. A self-organizing system changes its properties on the basis of a single uniform learning rule, no matter what the task (Arbib 1987). Examples include Hopfield nets (Hopfield 1982; Hopfield and Tank 1986) and Boltzmann machines (Hinton et al. 1984). In supervised learning, the system is "trained" to behave in the desired manner by the judicious administration of reinforcement at appropriate stages in the learning process. Examples are the "perceptrons" of Rosenblatt (1962) and Minsky and Papert (1969). In reinforcement learning, the agent continually receives sensory feedback from the consequences of its own behavior and, in addition, receives a (usually scalar) reinforcement signal. Thus, reinforcement learning is learning by trial and error from performance feedback. The reinforcer evaluates the consequences of the behavior generated by the agent, but does not indicate "correct" behavior.

Sutton (1991) reviews the major steps in the development of reinforcement learning in the 1980s. These steps are illustrated by the four architectures shown in figure 11.4. All reinforcement learning involves the learning of a mapping from the state (in a given situation) to an appropriate activity. This mapping, called a *policy*, specifies what the agent will do in the given situation at each stage of learning. If the role of the reinforcement is simply to modify the policy, then we have a policy-only architecture, as illustrated in Figure 11.4a. Activities correlated with high reward have their probability of being repeated increased, while those correlated with low reward have their probability decreased. Examples of such algorithms for policy-only architectures are to be found in Barto and Sutton 1981 and in Barto and Anandan 1985. This type of learning is similar to the S-R learning proposed by Thorndyke (1911, 1913) for animals.

Reinforcement-comparison architectures (figure 11.4b) adjust the reinforcement baseline in relation to the state. This is done by making a prediction of the reinforcement (based on the state) and measuring the difference between the predicted and actual rewards. This prediction error is used to update the policy. Examples may be found in Barto, Sutton, and Brouwer 1981 and in Williams 1986. Reinforcement-comparison architectures do not enable the agent to optimize reinforcement in the long term. Suppose, for example, that high immediate reward so depletes the environment that only low reward can be obtained in the future. Such delayed effects of behavior are not taken into account. A possible remedy is the adaptive heuristic critic (AHC) architecture (figure 11.4c).

Instead of predicting immediate reward, the AHC architecture predicts *return*, a measure of long-term cumulative reward (Barto et al. 1983; Barto et al. 1989). The return is formulated in terms of expected value, and is subject to a discount rate. A further innovation, called *Q-learning* (Watkins 1989), is to make predicted return a function of behavior as well as of state.

Q-learning, illustrated in figure 11.4d, predicts two kinds of return for the current state: the predicted return for the activity with the highest predicted return and the predicted return for the activity actually selected. These two predictions are combined in an

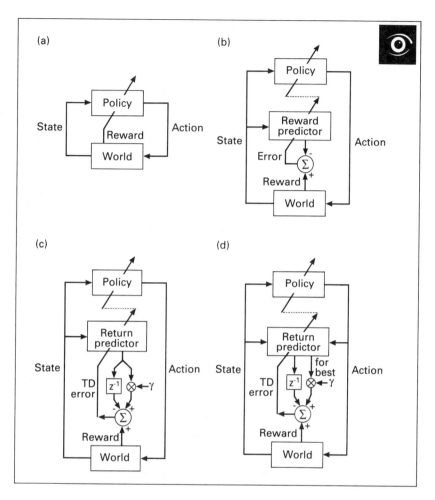

**Figure 11.4** Reinforcement learning architectures. (a) Policy only. (b) Reinforcement comparison. (c) Adaptive heuristic critic. (d) Q-learning. (After Sutton 1991.)

AHC architecture. The Q-learning architecture sets up a situation in which information is made available about the best outcome and the outcome to be expected from performing a particular activity. What is to be done with such information is an important question.

Reinforcement learning architectures are effective at trial-and-error learning, but they are not capable of planning or other cognitive activities (Sutton 1991). Modern animal learning theorists consider that some form of cognitive activity is involved even in classical conditioning, and have evidence to support this view. One possible approach is to incorporate some kind of "world model" into a robot's learning architecture. This approach is similar to the attempts by Gallistel (1990) and others to account for classical conditioning in animals in terms of internal "representations" of the world.

Dyna architectures are reinforcement learning architectures extended to include an internal world model. The model is used for a direct replacement for the world in a reinforcement architecture, such as those illustrated in Figure 11.4. Reinforcement learning continues in the usual way, but learning steps are also run using the model in place of the world—in other words, using predicted outcomes rather than real ones. For each real experience with the world, many hypothetical experiences generated with the world model can also be processed. The cumulative effect of these hypothetical experiences is that the policy approaches the optimal policy given the current world model. A form of planning has thus been achieved (Sutton 1991).

Combinations of Dyna architectures and Q-learning have proved fairly successful in simulated robot navigation tasks (Sutton 1991). As we will see in the next chapter, the study of self-improving reactive agents shows that internal world models may be a useful aid to robot learning, but not necessarily an essential one.

## 11.4 Computational Approaches to Learning

Much effort within the field of artificial intelligence has gone into machine learning, which is primarily concerned with computational theories of systems that learn. Introductions to this topic, which is largely beyond the scope of this book, can be found in Tiles et al. 1990 and Winograd and Flores 1986. Typical of the approach is the development of SOAR.

SOAR is an intelligent architecture based on concepts derived from the work of Newell and Simon (1972) on human problem solving. SOAR, initially promoted by Laird, Newell, and Rosenbloom (1987) as the embodiment of a unified theory of cognition, is capable of a variety of types of learning (Steier et al. 1987). In particular, it can perform both symbolic-level learning and knowledge-level learning. This distinction, originally made by Dietterich (1986), is based on whether or not the knowledge level, measured in a suitable manner (Newell 1981), increases with learning. A system that improves its computational performance without increasing the amount of knowledge it contains performs at the symbol level of learning. If facts are added that are not implied by the existing knowledge, then knowledge-level learning is attained. Rosenbloom et al. (1987) showed how SOAR can expand its knowledge level to incorporate new information about objects. This was accomplished with "chunking" (Rosenbloom et al. 1988), a symbol-level learning mechanism, as the only learning mechanism. One new mechanism was added to SOAR for this work: the ability to generate new long-term symbols to serve as the names of objects.

It may well be that advances in machine learning will lead to the development of intelligent computer-based systems. These will not, however, exhibit intelligent behavior. As we saw in chapter 1, intelligent behavior requires a body. Although it may be possible to incorporate some aspects of machine learning into robots, the size of the "brain" required is likely to be very large and to involve high capital costs. A relatively simple robot with high capital costs gives poor value for money. Such a system is inevitably poorly adapted (McFarland 1991a). To be capable of intelligent behavior of the type we discussed in chapter 1, the robot must be well adapted. Therefore, developments in machine learning, while interesting and important in themselves, do not represent the way forward for present-day intelligent robots. When robots become more sophisticated, in the sense that their ecological niche is more complicated, then we can expect that value for money will be gained through knowledge-level learning.

## 11.5 Emergent Properties of Learning

Theories of learning sometimes turn out to have unexpected effects, so we should not be surprised to discover emergent properties in simple learning systems designed for robots. An example

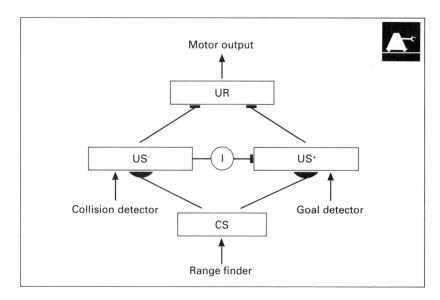

**Figure 11.5**  Connections between the neural fields of the neural net controlling the behavior of a simulated mobile robot. (After Verschure et al. 1991.)

is provided in the interesting study by Verschure et al. (1991) of distributed adaptive control. Starting with a neural model of a basic classical conditioning mechanism, these authors developed a strongly situated system for robot control. When simulated, this system exhibited emergent anticipatory behaviour.

The system is equipped with a Hebb-type learning mechanism that allows it to combine sensory inputs (CSs) with reflex responses (URs) which are triggered by a set of USs. The US-UR relationship is pretuned (in the authors' terminology, it has a *predefined value system*), and the agent is motivated to keep moving until it touches a target with its front end, or snout.

This basic design is translated into a number of neural fields, as illustrated in figure 11.5. Information from the environment is provided by a range finder, which projects sensory input to the CS field. This field is connected to two US fields by modifiable weights (initially set at 0), shown as large synapses in figure 11.5. The US fields have opposite signs. One (−ve) receives information from a collision detector; the other (+ve) receives information from a goal detector, which locates the direction of the target.

Both US fields are connected to a UR field in which the motor responses are stored. In essence, these responses are turn left, turn right, retract, and advance. Substantial activity in the −ve US field gives rise to avoidance behavior. After a collision, the robot will re-tract and turn through a predefined angle opposite to the direction of the collision. (In the simulations, a standard avoidance angle of 9° was used.) The +ve US field is capable of locating the target, categorizing its position into an inner area (within 5° of straight ahead) and an outer area (beyond 5°). Location of the target within the inner area causes a 1° turn toward it; location in the outer area causes a 9° turn. Thus, the robot turns slowly if it is already nearly headed toward the target, and quickly if something is in its outer field of view. In this way the robot is able to approach objects.

The UR field consists of a number of *command neurons* (Kupfer-mann and Weiss 1978), which code specified motor responses. Whenever a specific command neuron is activated, a specific motor response is automatically executed. The connections between the US fields and the UR field are prewired and not modifiable. They are indicated by small synapses in figure 11.5. In addition, there is a specific inhibitory relationship between the −ve and +ve US fields. Activity in the −ve US field inhibits the output of the =ve US field. This prevents the robot from bumping into things if it is currently involved in approach behavior. In other words, approach behavior can be temporarily overruled by avoidance behavior.

The model robot was tested using the ASSIM simulation pro-gram (Krose and Dondorp 1989). With this simulator the robot architecture can be detailed, with all connections and sensor trans-fer functions specified mathematically. The mobile robot can be positioned in a predefined environment and its behavior studied. This was done in two stages: First the architecture relating to avoidance behavior was tested on its own (the +ve US field and the inhibitory relation being omitted). Second, simulations with the complete architecture were performed.

The arena for the first experiment was a rectangular space with five identical obstacles, located at the center and near the four cor-ners. The first 500 steps are shown in figure 11.6a. After colliding with the central obstacle, the robot turns left and makes a number of collisions with other obstacles. Figure 11.6b shows the robot's trajectory between steps 900 and 1000. The robot has successfully learned to avoid the obstacles, and no collisions are now evident. The relative roles of the collision detector and the range finder over the first 1000 trials are illustrated in figure 11.7. During the first 100 steps, 29 avoidance movements are initiated as results of physical collisions and 8 are initiated by the range finder. There-

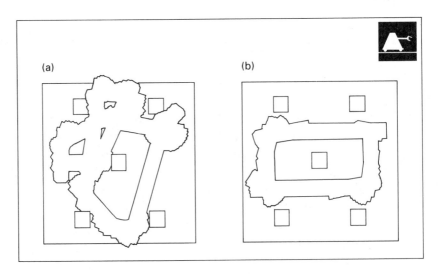

**Figure 11.6** Outlines of paths traced by simulated mobile robot (a) during first 500 trials (note collisions with square obstacles) and (b) during trials 900–1000 (note lack of collisions) of a learning session. (After Verschure et al. 1991.)

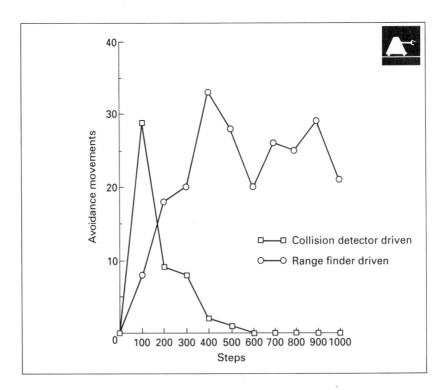

**Figure 11.7** Relative roles of collision detector and range finder during 1000 learning trials. (After Verschure et al. 1991.)

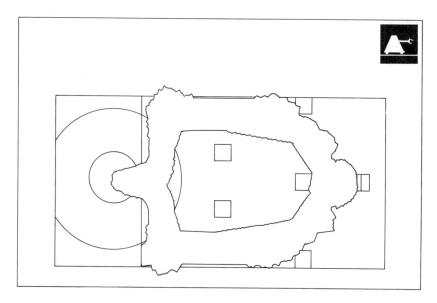

**Figure 11.8**  Outline of paths traced by simulated mobile robot learning to reach a target (inner circle). (After Verschure et al. 1991.)

after, the initial avoidance reflex (UR) resulting from physical collision (US) is supplanted by the conditional reflex (CR) initiated through learned association with data from the range finder (CS). Thus, the rise in avoidance movements initiated by the range finder is effectively a learning curve.

The arena for the second experiment was a rectangular space containing a number of obstacles and having a doorway at one end. Beyond the doorway is a target which is attractive to the robot within the range shown by the circle in figure 11.8. If the robot approaches the target, it stops moving as it enters the inner circle. Figure 11.8 shows superimposed paths taken by the robot over 20 runs. During the first run the robot collided 23 times and took 139 steps to reach the target. The fact that no collisions took place after the eleventh run showed that the robot had successfully learned to avoid obstacles and reach the target.

This robot develops associations between specific sensory inputs and responses, which associations are driven by learning criteria provided by a predefined value system (see below). For example, during the trajectory illustrated in figure 11.6a, every collision establishes a sense-act reflex. This reflex is the basis for conditioning, in that it provides the associative mechanisms with a criterion (reinforcement) that guides the coupling of more sophisticated sensors (the range finders) to the relevant environmental features (the proximity of objects). In other words, learning to anticipate collisions takes place because certain range-finder data become associated with the consequences of collisions. As the robot gains experience over time, it slowly shifts from collision-driven behavior to range-finder-driven behavior (figure 11.7) and thus starts anticipating obstacles. This anticipatory behavior is emergent, because there is no component of the system designed to do anticipation *per se*. Steels et al. (in press) have demonstrated that these principles can be incorporated into the design of a real mobile robot that learns to avoid obstacles after about twenty collisions.

It is interesting to note that the early animal learning theorists also understood this property of simple conditioning mechanisms. Hull (1931) proposed a number of intermediate mechanisms derived from the basic laws of conditioning. In particular, in repeating a sequence of activities leading to a goal, as in a rat running through a maze, there are always stimuli that have become conditioned to the goal as a result of previous trials. In Hull's system these give rise to fractional antedating goal responses which are reinforced because they are followed by rewarding consequences. Subsequently, as explained by Mackintosh (1974), such theories became incorporated into incentive theory (incentive being anticipation of reinforcement). Thus, an animal psychologist should not be surprised to find emergent anticipatory responses in robot behavior, but should be impressed to see it demonstrated in such a simple system.

## 11.6  The Predefined Value System and the Goal Function

The simulated agent described by Verschure et al. (1991) is equipped with a predefined value system which is expressed in specific US-UR combinations, in the tuning of command neurons, and in specific properties of sensors and effectors.

The associations formed between specific sensory inputs and responses are driven by learning criteria provided by the predefined value system, which is a kind of "teacher" guiding the learning process. In a sense the learning is supervised by the value system in interaction with the environment (Verschure et al. 1991).

The predefined value system is, in effect, an implicit (or partially embedded) goal function. As we saw in chapter 10, there are various possibilities. At the extreme "procedural" end of the spectrum is the possibility that the design incorporates no direct information about the goal function, but that the behavior-control system is put together in such a way that the animal or robot behaves as if it were guided by the relevant notional costs. Such a system would be analogous to a physical system in which the behavior conforms with some extremal principle. Another possibility is that the sensor outputs are weighted by elements of the goal function. The relative importance of the sensory inputs can then be used directly in rules of procedure leading to a behavioral outcome. The general point is that some type of representation—implicit or explicit—of the relative importances of sensory inputs, and of the notional costs of the primary state variables, is an inevitable feature of the well-designed agent.

Learning requires feedback about success and failure, and this feedback must be based on an immutable set of values (see McFarland and Houston 1981 for a discussion). In other words, learning has to operate in relation to the goal function. Thus, the improvement in performance that results from learning is an improvement in relation to the goal function. Now, the goal function may or may not be a good representation of the cost function that is characteristic of the robot's ecological niche. In animals it can never be a perfect representation, because of evolutionary lag, genetic diversity, and ecological competition. In robots the same logic holds (see chapter 4). This means that learning is not always adaptive. Learning in robots is adaptive only insofar as the goal function resembles the cost function (McFarland 1991a).

Thus, in order for learning to be adaptive (i.e., of advantage), the (predefined) value system must reflect the cost function that is characteristic of the ecological niche. The more the set of values, or goal function, resembles the cost function, the better adapted the agent will be. Note that it is not possible for the agent to learn to modify the goal function to make it more like the cost function. Since learning is itself dependent upon the goal function to provide reinforcement value, it cannot itself modify the value system. This is why the value system must be a predefined one.

The goal function can influence learning in a number of different ways. In an automaton, where the goal function is entirely implicit, simple types of learning are possible, as we have seen from the above robot example. In animals, where we can expect some aspects of the goal function to be embedded (see chapter 10), learning is likely to be complicated by instinctive bias (Hinde and Stevenson-Hinde 1973; McFarland 1985).

In chapter 10 we saw how a planning architecture embodies an explicit goal-function representation, whereas an automaton has no such representation. The planner is therefore in a position to learn as a result of cognition (manipulation of declarative knowledge), whereas the automaton can only engage in learning to alter system parameters. Cognitive learning requires some access to a representation of the goal function, because trial and error implies an experiment on the part of the agent, the results of which have to be evaluated. The results can be evaluated only by reference to an immutable set of values (goal function), which must be explicitly represented and available for consultation by the planning mechanism. In this way the agent can gain declarative knowledge—knowledge that the consequences of a particular activity are likely to be such-and-such. As we will see below, experiments by Dickinson and others on reward devaluation suggest that some animals do have such knowledge.

## Points to Remember

- Learning is a part of development that is contingent on the experience of environmental events. When an animal learns to respond to environmental events in a new way, its behavioral repertoire undergoes permanent alteration.
- Learning in animals takes many forms, depending on the lifestyle and the selective pressures characteristic of each particular species. Changes in the environment that are predictable from an evolutionary point of view are often handled by preprogrammed forms of learning.
- A reinforcer is characterized less by its intrinsic properties as a stimulus than by its motivational significance to the animal.
- The process by which learned behavior patterns cease to be performed when they are no longer appropriate is called *extinction*.
- The importance of background, or contextual, cues has been demonstrated in experiments in which the presence of a second stimulus decreased the amount by which a primary stimulus is associated with reinforcement. This phenomenon is called *overshadowing*.
- If an animal has already experienced reinforcement in the presence of stimulus A, then, if both A and B are correlated with reinforce-

ment, the presence of A will block learning about B. This phenomenon is known as *blocking*.

- According to Hebb (1949), "When an axon of cell A is near enough to excite cell B or repeatedly or persistently takes part in firing it, some growth process or metabolic change takes place in one or both cells such that A's efficiency, as one of the cells firing B, is increased."

- A neural network consists of a large number of interconnected artificial "neurons." These may be simple signal-transmitting devices or more complex attempts to mimic real neurons.

- Connectionism is neurally inspired modeling using the properties of neural nets. It should be distinguished from neural modeling, which is an attempt to model the neural activity of real brains.

- Reinforcement learning architectures are effective at trial-and-error learning. Apart from Dyna architectures, they are not capable of planning or other cognitive activity.

- A system that improves its computational performance without increasing the amount of knowledge it contains performs at the *symbol level* of learning. If facts are added that are not implied by the existing knowledge, then the *knowledge level* of learning is attained.

- A robot that develops associations between specific sensory inputs and responses which are driven by learning criteria provided by a predefined value system can develop anticipatory behavior as an emergent property:

- The value system is expressed in specific US-UR combinations, in the tuning of command neurons, and in specific properties of sensors and effectors. It is, in effect, an implicit (or partially embedded) goal function.

- Learning requires feedback about success and failure, and this feedback must be based on an immutable set of values. Thus, learning has to operate in relation to the goal function.

- For learning to be adaptive (i.e., of advantage), the (predefined) value system must reflect the cost function that is characteristic of the ecological niche. The more the set of values, or goal function, resembles the cost function, the better adapted the agent will be.

- It is not possible for the agent to learn to modify the goal function to make it more like the cost function. Since learning is itself dependent upon the goal function to provide reinforcement value, it cannot itself modify the value system. This is why the value system must be predefined.

In this book we have identified, though not equated, intelligent behavior with adaptiveness. In other words, intelligent behaviour can be understood only on the basis of competition among agents, whether they be animals, robots, or humans. In real life, animals compete for scarce resources. Humans compete with other animals for these same resources. Robots will compete with each other in the market; they will also compete with humans for jobs.

Intelligent behavior is not the product of a particular mechanism for generating behavior. Although intelligence is often equated with cognitive ability, cognitive mechanisms may be inferior to automatic hard-wired mechanisms in certain ecological circumstances.

The principles for understanding intelligent behavior of living systems and intelligent behavior of robots are the same. The design of these systems must be holistic, permitting emergent functionality (including morphology, automatic behavior, and cognition). The design process implies tradeoffs among these and other features of the system. Tradeoff (or optimality) principles cannot be ignored.

The capability for intelligent behavior can be introduced into the design of robots in a number of ways: Well-designed morphology and automatic behavior can produce intelligent behavior if the environmental conditions can be anticipated during the design phase. Where this is not possible, cognitive (planning and reasoning) processes can be employed to respond intelligently to unpredictable environmental changes.

Cognition requires judgement (i.e., evaluation) of the likely consequences of future behavior. Such evaluation implies a degree of motivational autonomy. Therefore, planning systems must be designed to take proper account of motivational autonomy.

An automaton capable of complex intelligent behavior would need a very large brain, because all responses to possible states of the world would have to be preprogrammed. This problem can be alleviated by implementing a partial automaton plus some cognitive capabilities, as mentioned above. Note that these cognitive abilities require judgement criteria (part of the goal function) to be built in (or compiled).

Communication capabilities are designed according to the same principles as other features of the intelligent, autonomous system. One consequence is that the categories appropriate for encoding information for communication are not likely to be the same ones as for internal control of behavior. In particular, behavior control cannot be goal-directed, although this can be a useful way of representing behavior for the purpose of communication.

The above summary of our conclusions has implications for artificial intelligence, economics, ethology, and psychology. Experts in these fields will, no doubt, disagree with many of our conclusions. Our main concern is that such disagreement should not be due to misunderstanding. In an attempt to circumvent this possibility, we append the following summary.

### 12.1 Summary of Major Issues Affecting Other Disciplines

*Intelligence* In defining intelligent behavior, what matters is the behavioral outcome, not the nature of the mechanism by which the outcome is achieved. In particular, intelligent behavior does not necessarily involve cognition. Therefore, we must distinguish between cognition (a possible means to an end) and intelligence, (an assessment of performance in terms of some functional criteria).

*Rationality* Rational thought does not necessarily guarantee rational behavior. Theories of rational action are commonly used in the disciplines of economics, statistics, and cognitive science. These theories have nothing to say about the psychological processes that generate rational action. They merely state what would be rational under certain circumstances. Animals behave rationally in the sense that their behavior is transitive and obeys microeconomic laws. Their behavior shows rationality of process and may in some cases also include rationality of content.

*Economics* Economic principles apply not only to humans but to all animal species, because all animals have to allocate scarce means among competing ends. A freely mobile robot is in a similar situation to an animal, in that its state is influenced both by environmental conditions and by the robot's own behavior. In addition, the robot has to earn its place in the world.

*Cost functions* An animal or a robot in a particular state runs a risk of incurring real costs (decrements in fitness or marketability). The cost of being in a particular state is a function of each state variable. These costs can be combined into a single cost function dealing with real risks and real costs and benefits. Therefore, the cost function is shaped largely by environmental forces: market forces in the case of machines and the forces of natural selection in the case of animals.

*Design* Although the mechanism by which a machine is designed differs from the design mechanism pertaining in the animal kingdom, the principles remain the same. The principle of optimal design simply asserts that a system (whether animate or inanimate) that is capable of modification in successive versions will tend to evolve toward an optimal configuration with respect to the selective pressures (or market forces) acting on the successive versions. Both design and behavior involve decisions. A decision of a person, an animal, or a robot is simply the process by which the decision variables are changed. This process can occur as part as a design operation or as part of behavior.

*Tasks and tools* The procedures that an operator uses to execute tasks are functions of the task (the state changes to be achieved) and of the tools used. There are many kinds of tools. Plans are mental tools that can be employed in particular tasks in a manner analogous to physical tools.

*Autonomy* Most robots are automata, in the sense that their behavior is entirely state-dependent. Some may be autonomous agents, which are self-controlling in the sense that they have some kind of motivation. This self-control makes them relatively uncontrollable by outside agents. The essence of autonomous behavior is motivational evaluation, which involves the assignment of utility to behavioral alternatives. Once the utilities have been assigned, then a decision can be made.

*Action theory* Basically, action theories are goal-directed theories, because they envisage a mental state of affairs that is related to the goal (i.e., some form of knowing about the likely consequences) that is instrumental in guiding the behavior. Action theories are incompatible with the view that behavior-control mechanisms are designed in accordance with tradeoff principles. They are flawed, because the notion of (rational) choice among alternative courses of action is basically incompatible with the notion of sticking to a course of action once it has been chosen.

*Marketability* The question of how a robot should deploy its behavioral options in time is not simply a matter of optimal time allocation; questions of stability, reliability, and customer appeal also have to be considered. The obligatory criteria are those criteria which we can be sure every customer will accept. We can assume that every customer will want the robot to be, at least, asymptotically stable. The designer of a robot must also take account of customers' whims, which provide facultative criteria. All the criteria enter the design operation as components of the goal function, thus completing the first stage in designing the goal function. If a robot is to be tailored to a particular niche, then the question of what kind of architecture is relevant in robot design is largely a question of how the goal function is to be implemented. There are many different ways in which the information inherent in the goal function may, or may not, be used by the decision-making mechanisms of the individual.

*Learning* Learning requires feedback about success and failure, and this feedback must be based on an immutable set of values. Thus, learning has to operate in relation to the goal function. For learning to be adaptive (i.e., of advantage), the (predefined) value system must reflect the cost function that is characteristic of the ecological niche. The more the set of values, or goal function, resembles the cost function, the better adapted the agent will be. It is not possible for the agent to learn to modify the goal function to make it more like the cost function. Since learning is itself dependent upon the goal function to provide reinforcement value, it cannot itself modify the value system.

*Holism* Our approach to robot design is holistic, relying on ecology-based design and on some emergent functionality. Without becoming mystical, we can say that the design of animal behavior is clearly holistic in the sense that it is a complex mixture of genetically based design and individual adaptation and learning. So complex is this design that it may be argued that to use animals as a model for designing robots is a waste of time and effort. We do not subscribe to this view, but we do recognize that it is this aspect of robot design that presents the greatest challenge.

So far, our approach has some room for planning and other forms of cognition, but much less than is the case with classical AI. We recognize that a planner is in a position to learn as a result of cognition (manipulation of declarative knowledge), whereas an automaton can engage in learning only to alter the parameters of its system. We maintain (below) that an intentional (or goal-directed) account of an animal's action is warranted only if it can be shown that the action meets two behavioral criteria: the belief criterion and the desire criterion. Although there is evidence that, in some animals, some form of knowledge-based integration can occur between an activity and its consequences, there is no good evidence for intentional behavior.

## 12.2 Lessons for Ethology

In this book we have drawn heavily on ethological knowledge and methodology. We believe that ethology has an important contribution to make to the development of artificial intelligence. At the same time, our approach has exposed some shortcomings of ethology. The most important of these is that ethological models are never grounded. In the course of a modeling exercise, the ethologist often states that the animal performs various activities without specifying how these activities are to be carried out. In robotics the designer is forced to consider the actual consequences of behavior that result from interaction with the real world. The ethologist is not able to do this; consequently, ethological models, though often elegent, tend to lack realism.

One area of ethology where lack of groundedness presents a serious obstacle to progress is animal cognition. Following Griffin (1976, 1981), a number of ethologists (see Griffin 1984; Mitchel and Thompson 1986; Whiten and Byrne 1987) have attributed cognitive or intentional states to animals on the basis of passive observation of their behavior under free-living conditions. Others (see, e.g., Kummer et al. 1990; McFarland 1991b) have been more skeptical. Heyes and Dickinson (1990) point out that such observation, however careful, can be misleading, and that the attribution of intentionality to animals should be based on specific behavioral criteria that cannot be applied through passive behavioral observation in an uncontrolled environment. They set out to specify the behavioral criteria that must be met if an action is to warrant an intentional account.

Heyes and Dickinson (1990) argue that an intentional account of an animal's action is warranted only if it can be shown that the action meets two behavioral criteria: the belief criterion and the desire criterion. "Assessing the belief criterion requires that performance of the action is investigated in an environment that differs from the target context only in the content of the instrumental belief that it will support. If action is acquired in a context that will not support the appropriate belief, an intentional account is unwarranted." (Heyes and Dickinson 1990, p. 101) The second criterion is that "it must be demonstrated that the performance of the action adjusts appropriately to manipulations designed to alter the desire for the outcome. Furthermore, the desire criterion requires that the adjustment is demonstrated to depend upon training contingencies that support the appropriate instrumental belief. Applying these two criteria has revealed that the simple instrumental act of lever pressing performed by rats in the laboratory can support an intentional account." (ibid.) It is not our purpose to enter into detailed discussion of these important claims, but it is of interest to see how the views of Dickinson and his co-workers marry with our own.

In any complex animal there is likely to be a mixture of autonomous and automaton-like behavioral control. Dickinson (1985) claims that the type of control that an animal has over a particular behavior can be determined by a goal revaluation procedure. If the animal's behavior changes appropriately after an alteration in the value of reward, without further experience of the instrumental relationship, the behavior should be regarded as a "purposive" action. On the other hand, if the behavior remains insensitive to changes in the value of reward, the behavior should be regarded as a habit, controlled in a procedural manner. By using this assay, Dickinson (1985) finds that simple food-rewarded activity is sensitive to reward devaluation in rats after limited training but not after extended training. The development of automaton-like behavior with extended training appears to depend, not on the amount of training *per se*, but rather on the fact that the overtrained animal no longer experiences a correlation between variations in performance and variations in the associated consequences. In agreement with this idea, limited exposure to an instrumental relationship that arranges a low correlation between performance and reward also favors the development of automaton-like behavior. Thus, the same activity can be either "purposive" or habit-like, depending upon the type of training it has received.

A number of problems are raised by Dickinson's (1985) portrayal of rather extreme versions of the two different possibilities and by the fact that he uses the same words we use but with different meanings. Dickinson contrasts "responses" and "actions." The former are elicited by stimuli, and (by implication) the animal gains no feedback about the consequences of the response. The latter is "controlled at the time of performance by the animal's knowledge about the consequences of this activity," and this behavior is "truly purposeful and goal-directed" (p. 67). In our terminology, Dickinson's "responses" are *automaton-like* (that is, performed in a procedural manner), although Dickinson calls them autonomous (meaning autonomous of the current value of the reward). Dickinson's "actions," in our terminology, involve planning and are therefore autonomous. By "truly purposeful and goal-directed," Dickinson means reward-directed, not goal-directed in our sense (see chapter 7).

The efficacy of goal-revaluation (Dickinson's term), or reward revaluation (our term), is best illustrated by a discussion of particular experiments. In one crucial experiment, Adams and Dickinson (1981) trained hungry rats to press a lever for one of two types of food (sugar or chow), while they received the other on a schedule designed to ensure that lever pressing and food presentation were uncorrelated. Thus, for sugar the rewards were contingent on lever pressing, while for chow they were noncontingent. In another group of rats, the roles of sugar and chow were reversed. The experimenters then devalued the contingent foods for one group of rats (A) while maintaining the value of the noncontingent foods. For another group (B), the noncontingent foods were devalued and the value of the contingent foods was maintained. Food was devalued by allowing the rats to have access to the food in the absence of the lever, and injecting them with lithium chloride soon after they ate the food. (Lithium chloride makes rats mildly ill and induces an aversion to the food with which it is associated.) Both groups were given an extinction test in the lever-pressing situation. The result was that the contingent (A) group pressed at a lower rate in the extinction test than the noncontingent (B) group. To test whether the aversion procedure had been differentially successful, reacquisition tests were then given. These showed that both the contingent foods in group A and the noncontingent foods in group B had lost their capacity to act as rewards. In other words, the food is devalued in both cases, but the noncontingent group is relatively insensitive to this because of lack of knowledge of the relation between the behavior and the reinforcer. The implication is that the contingent group has such knowledge (in a declarative form) and makes use of it.

Although instrumental responses appear to be purposeful in being directed at the goal of achieving a certain state of affairs, this does not necessarily mean that a goal-directed mechanism (see chapter 7) is involved. For a discussion of this issue see McFarland 1989b. What matters for our present purposes is that some form of knowledge-based integration should occur between an activity and its consequences. The evidence that such integration can occur in rats is convincing. Moreover, it appears that extended practice of an instrumental act produces a transition of control from the declarative to the procedural form, thereby setting up a habit (or schema) that is performed automatically without reference to its consequences (Dickinson 1980, 1985).

Moreover, noncontingent exposure to a reinforcer can be sufficient to bring about motivational control of instrumental performance (Dickinson and Dawson 1988, 1989). In other words, it appears that, provided the animal knows *that* the reinforcer is relevant to its motivational state (as a result of prior experience that is independent of the instrumental behavior it is now required to perform), it will perform a particular action that is instrumental in obtaining the reinforcement.

This type of evidence suggests that cognitive learning (learning that involves manipulation of some declarative representation) can occur in some animals. Such learning requires some kind of planning architecture that embodies an explicit representation of the goal function. An automaton has no such representation of the goal function and can engage only in noncognitive forms of learning. The relationships between motivation and learning that are elucidated by the experiments of Dickinson and his co-workers are those that we would expect on the basis that the animals concerned are autonomous agents.

An important aspect of the above discussion is that progress in understanding animal cognition has been made by experimental psychologists, not by ethologists. The psychologists have at their disposal a powerful experimental tool, namely the learning experiment as a frame of reference, which enables them to explore the issues involved in cognition in a way that is not open to ethologists. The problem for the ethologist is that for every cognitive account of an animal's behavior there is always an equally valid behaviorist account. Ethologists cannot resolve this dilemma, because their models are not grounded. They cannot specify what would happen under the two different theories, because they have no way of putting the theories to empirical test.

## 12.3  The Future—Emergent Functionality?

The concept of emergent functionality has become an important design approach in robotics, both at the practical (Brooks, 1989) and at the theoretical (Steels 1991) level. The functionality of a machine usually arises directly from particular components, or systems of components, each of which is designed with a particular function in mind. Emergent functionality arises by virtue of interaction among components not themselves designed with the particular function in mind. Thus, emergent functionality can arise through serendipity.

Theories of emergent functionality imply some desirable outcome that is achieved, not by direct control, but as a result of holistic properties anticipated on the basis of lower-level, or at least different, design criteria. In this respect emergent functionality is similar to what evolutionary biologists call *preadaptation*.

Preadaptation arises in evolution because the function of a characteristic can change more rapidly than its structure. For example, parrots tend to have strong bills, evolved for breaking into hard fruits and nuts. The kea (*Nestor notabilis*) is a New Zealand parrot that rips through the skin of sheep with its sharp beak to feed on fat. It has a beak much like those of other parrots, and before the arrival of sheep in New Zealand it fed on plants. The parrot-type beak preadapts the bird to feed on flesh, provided this becomes available in a form that is accessible to the parrot. Unlike hawks, parrots do not have the mechanisms required for catching live prey.

The term *preadaptation* does not mean evolving structures in anticipation of future need (Bock 1959), but implies that the animal is ready to exploit certain situations should they occur. Thus, fishes did not evolve lungs so that they could someday invade the

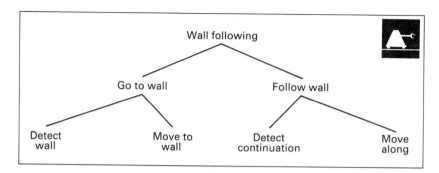

**Figure 12.1**  Hierarchical decomposition of wall following. (After Steels 1991.)

land, but those fishes that possessed lungs to help them cope with drought conditions were preadapted to live on land.

The similarity between the concepts of emergent functionality and preadaptation arises from the equivalence between a desired design outcome and an evolutionary selective pressure (see chapter 5). A desirable outcome that is achieved as a result of emergent functionality is equivalent to a desirable outcome (in terms of reproductive success) that is achieved by the preadapted animal once it encounters the new favorable environmental situation. It is the selective pressures created by this new situation that favor the preadapted animal.

Steels (1991) contrasts "hierarchical systems" in which there is a direct relationship between structure and function against systems with emergent functionality. The components of a hierarchical system are distinct in the sense that their functionality can be tested independently from the other components. Moreover, this functionality is a recognizable subfunction of the global functionality of the system. For example, in building a wall-following robot along hierarchical principles, the global functionality would be decomposed into different subfunctions, as illustrated in figure 12.1. The components function independently of each other, and can be constructed and put together in a modular fashion. Each subfunction is either directly realized by a particular component or further decomposed. Thus, "detect wall" may be decomposed into "read sensors" and "interpret sensors to see whether it is a wall."

Hierarchical systems have certain advantages and disadvantages (Steels 1991). Their modularity is an aid to design, fault diagnosis, and repair. On the other hand, hierarchical systems are not fault tolerant. As soon as a component breaks down, the whole system fails. There is a critical dependence on prior analysis by the designer, and interaction with the environment is inevitably delegated to certain components of the system. These two factors imply prior categorization of the environmental situations that may be encountered. Such prior categorization is difficult when a system has to cope with the richness of the real world, and this difficulty tends to lead to a lack of robustness. A robust system keeps functioning in situations that bring it temporarily out of balance; for example, a wall-following robot should continue to function when pushed against a wall.

Systems with emergent functionality have certain advantages which can be illustrated by the example of the wall-following robot. An emergent-functionality approach to wall following has been developed by Rodney Brooks and his students at MIT. In contrast with the hierarchical approach (figure 12.1), the components of a wall-following robot of this type (such as the one realized by Mataric [1990]) have direct contact with the environment through sensors and effectors. The components directly implement behaviors, such as stroll (move forward until an obstacle in encountered, then stop and back up), avoid (turn right or left when there is an obstacle in front of the robot), and align (turn by a small angle when the distance to the object behind is less than the distance in front). There is no additional control structure to combine these components. They are all simultaneously active, and this is possible because the conditions triggering them are mutually exclusive (Steels 1991). Figure 12.2 shows routes taken by a robot of this type in an untidy room. These routes show that consistent boundary tracking does emerge from the combination of the three behaviors. If the robot is pushed toward the wall, it will reestablish its distance.

Systems with emergent functionality are strongly *situated* (see chapter 8) in the sense of being embedded in the environment in which they operate (Steels 1991). This is due to the fact that each component has a direct interaction with the environment, and it allows direct and quick reaction to changes in the environment. Thus, the wall-following robot will immediately react to changes in wall position. New behaviors can be added much more easily in situated systems than in hierarchical systems, and tend to have high fault tolerance. In general, hierarchical systems perform well when the environment in which they operate is unchanging and

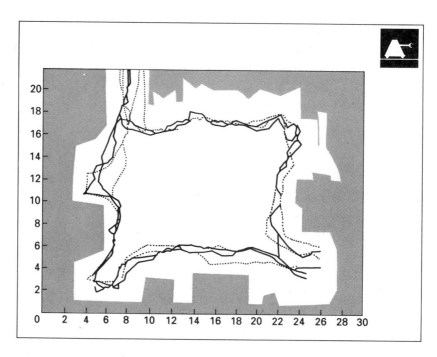

**Figure 12.2**  Boundaries traced by mobile robot in real-world environment. (After Steels 1991.)

can be specified in advance. When there is a lot of dependence on the environment, and when it is difficult for the designer to foresee all circumstances in advance, systems with emergent functionality are better. A number of such systems have been described by Brooks (1991) and by Steels (1991).

In outlining a formal structure for systems with emergent functionality, Steels (1991) suggests that they require three properties: (1) Systems with emergent functionality are dynamical systems. (2) An emergent property is a particular devolution of a variable which is not directly controlled and which is asymptotically stable. (3) The functions describing the devolution of the emergent property have at least two interacting components. In these respects the concept of emergent functionality is remarkable similar to those of passive control (Milsum 1966) and goal-seeking systems (see chapter 7).

Finally, what is the main problem in designing robots to be like animals? In our view, the main problem is to find that mixture of built-in implicit knowhow and acquired (explicit?) knowhow that will enable the robot to attain maximum adaptation to its niche.

**Points to Remember**

- The ethological approach has much to offer artificial intelligence, but it suffers from lack of groundedness—particularly in the field of animal cognition.
- An intentional account of an animal action is warranted only if it can be shown that the action meets two behavioral criteria: the belief criterion and the desire criterion.
- There is evidence that, in some animals, some form of knowledge-based integration can occur between an activity and its consequences. Moreover, it appears that extended practice of an instrumental act produces a transition of control from the declarative to the procedural form of behavior control.
- Emergent functionality arises by virtue of interaction among components not themselves designed with the particular function in mind.
- Theories of emergent functionality imply some desirable outcome that is achieved, not by direct control, but as a result of holistic properties anticipated on the basis of lower-level design criteria.
- Systems with emergent functionality are strongly situated in the sense of being embedded in the environment in which they operate. This is due to the fact that each component has a direct interaction with the environment, and it allows direct and quick reaction to changes in the environment.
- A formal structure for systems with emergent functionality requires three properties: (1) Systems with emergent functionality are dynamical systems. (2) An emergent property is a particular devolution of a variable which is not directly controlled and which is asymptotically stable. (3) The functions describing the devolution of the emergent property have at least two interacting components.

# Bibliography

Ach, N. 1910. *Über den Willensakt und das Temperament: Eine experimentelle Untersuchung*. Quelle und Meyer.

Adams, C. D., and Dickinson, A. 1981. Instrumental responding following reinforcer devaluation. *Quarterly Journal of Experimental Psychology* 33B: 109–112.

Alcock, J. 1989. *Animal Behavior*, fourth edition. Sinauer.

Alexander, R. 1982. *Optima for Animals*. Edward Arnold.

Allen, J. 1984. Towards a general theory of action and time. *Artificial Intelligence* 23: 123–154.

Allison, J. 1979. Demand economics and experimental psychology. *Behavioral Science* 24: 403–415.

Allison, J. 1983. *Behavioral Economics*. Praeger.

Anderson, J. R. 1976. *Language, memory, and thought*. Erlbaum.

Anderson, J. R. 1983a. *The Architecture of Cognition*. Harvard University Press.

Anderson, J. R. 1983b. Methodologies for studying human knowledge. *Behavioral and Brain Sciences* 10: 467–505.

Arbib, M. A. 1966. Automata theory and control theory—a rapprochement. *Automatica* 3: 161–189.

Arbib, M. A. 1969. Automata theory. In *Topics in Mathematical System Theory*, ed. R. Kalman et al. McGraw-Hill.

Arbib, M. A. 1973. Automata theory in the context of theoretical neurophysiology. In *Foundations of Mathematical Biology*, ed. R. Rosen.

Arbib, M. A. 1987. *Brains, Machines, and Mathematics*, second edition. Springer-Verlag.

Arbib, M. A., and Zeigler, H. P. 1969. On the relevance of abstract algebra to control theory. *Automatica* 5: 589–606.

Baerends, G. P., Brouwer, R., and Waterbolk, H. 1955. Ethological studies of *Lebistes reticulatus* (Peters). 1. An analysis of the male courtship pattern. *Behavior* 8: 249–334.

Baerends, G. P., and Kruijt, J. P. 1973. Stimulus selection. In *Constraints on Learning: Limitations and Predispositions*, ed. R. A. Hinde and J. Stevenson-Hinde. Academic Press.

Barnett, S., and Cameron, R. 1985. *Introduction to Mathematical Control Theory*, second edition. Clarendon.

Baron, J. 1988. *Thinking and Deciding*. Cambridge University Press.

Bartlett, F. C. 1932. *Remembering*. Cambridge University Press.

Barto, A. G., and Anandan, P. 1985. Pattern recognizing stochastic learning automata. *IEEE Transactions on Systems, Man, and Cybernetics* 15: 360–375.

Barto, A. G., and Sutton, R. S. 1981. Landmark learning: An illustration of associative search. *Biological Cybernetics* 42: 1–8.

Barto, A. G., Sutton, R. S., and Brouwer, P. S. 1981. Associative search network: A reinforcement learning associative memory. *Biological Cybernetics* 40: 201–211.

Barto, A. G., Sutton, R. S., and Anderson, C. W. 1983. Neuronlike elements that can solve difficult learning control problems. *IEEE Transactions on Systems, Man, and Cybernetics* 13: 834–846.

Barto, A. G., Sutton, R. S., and Watkins, C. J. C. H. 1989. Learning and Sequential Decision Making. Technical Report 89–95, Dept. of Computer and Information Science, University of Massachusetts, Amherst.

Bell, D. 1969. Liapunov's direct method in non-linear control systems analysis. In *Modern Control Theory and Computing*, ed. D. Bell and A. Griffin. McGraw-Hill.

Bernoulli, D. 1738. Specimen theoriae novae de mensura sortis. *Commentarii academiae scientiarum imperialis Petropolitanae* 5: 175–192.

Bock, W. J. 1959. Preadaptation and multiple evolutionary pathways. *Evolution* 13: 194–211.

Boden, M. 1987. *Artificial Intelligence and Natural Man*, second edition. MIT Press.

Bösser, T. 1986. Modeling of skilled behavior and learning. In Proceedings of the IEEE International Conference on Systems, Man, and Cybernetics.

Bösser, T. 1989. Evaluation of new workplaces by modeling and simulation of operator procedures. In *New Developments in Job Analysis*, ed. K. Landau and W. Rohmert. Taylor and Francis.

Bösser, T., and Melchior, E. M. 1990. Cognitive modeling, rapid prototyping and user centered design with the SANE toolkit. In *Esprit 90 Conference Proceedings*. Kluwer.

Brand, M. 1970. *The Nature of Human Action*. Scott, Foresman.

Brand, M. 1984. *Intending and Acting*. MIT Press.

Brooks, R. 1986. A robust layered control system for a mobile robot. *IEEE Journal of Robotics and Automation* RA-2, April: 14–23.

Brooks, R. 1989. A robot that walks: Emergent behavior from a carefully evolved network. *Neural Computation* 1: 253–262.

Brooks, R. 1991. Challenges for complete creature architectures. In *From Animals to Animats*, ed. J. Meyer and S. Wilson. MIT Press.

Bryant, P. E., and Trabasso, T. 1971. Transitive inferences and memory in young children. *Nature* 232: 456–458.

Bunn, D. 1982. *Analysis for Optimal Decisions*. Wiley.

Cain, A. J. 1964. The perfection of animals. In *Viewpoints in Biology*, ed. J. D. Carthy and C. L. Duddington. Butterworths.

Chalmers, M., and McGonigle, B. O. 1983. Metamemorial strategies during problem solving by nine year olds. Paper presented at annual meeting of Developmental Section of BPS.

Chang, C. L., and Lee, R. C. T. 1973. *Symbolic Logic and Mechanical Theorem Proving*. Academic Press.

Cherry, C. 1957. *On Human Communication*. MIT Press.

Clark, H. H. 1969. Linguistic processes in deductive reasoning. *Psychological Review* 76: 387–404.

Cohen, J. 1966. *Human Robots in Myth and Science*. Allen and Unwin.

Cohn, D. 1954. Optimal systems. I. The vascular system. *Bulletin of Mathematical Biophysics* 16: 59–74.

Cohn, D. 1955. Optimal systems. II. The vascular system. *Bulletin of Mathematical Biophysics* 17: 219–227.

Cooper, L. A. 1982. Internal representation. In *Animal Mind—Human Mind*, ed. D. R. Griffin. Springer-Verlag.

Cooper, L. A., and Shepard, R. N. 1973. The time required to prepare for a rotated stimulus. *Memory and Cognition* 1: 246–250.

Cooper, W. S. 1987. Decision theory as a branch of evolutionary theory: A biological derivation of the savage axioms. *Psychological Review* 94: 395–411.

Corning, W. J., Dyal, J. A., and Lahue, R. 1976. Intelligence: An invertebrate perspective. In *Evolution, Brain, and Behavior: Persistent Problems*, ed. R. B. Masterson et al. Erlbaum.

Curio, E. 1975. The functional organization of anti-predator behavior in the Pied Flycatcher: A study of avian visual perception. *Animal Behavior* 23: 1–115.

Darwin, C. 1871. *The Descent of Man and Selection in Relation to Sex*. John Murray.

Dawkins, D., and Krebs, J. 1979. Arms races between and within species. *Proceedings of the Royal Society* B 205: 489–511.

Dawkins, R. 1986. *The Blind Watchmaker*. Longmans.

Dawkins, M. 1983. Battery hens name their price: Consumer demand theory and the measurement of ethological "needs." *Animal Behavior* 31: 1195–1205.

Davidson, D. 1963. Actions, reasons and causes. *Journal of Philosophy* 60: 685–700.

Davidson, D. 1978. Intention. In *Philosophy of History and Action*, ed. Y. Yoval. Reidel.

Delius, J. D., and Vollrath, F. W. 1973. Rotation compensation reflexes independent of the labyrinth: Neurosensory correlates in pigeons. *Journal of Comparative Physiology* 83: 123–134.

Dennett, D. C. 1978. *Brainstorms*. Bradford Books.

Dennett, D. C. 1983. Intentional systems in cognitive ethology: The "Panglossian paradigm" defended. *Behavioral and Brain Sciences* 6: 343–390.

Dennett, D. C. 1984. *Elbow Room*. Oxford University Press.

Dennett, D. C. 1987. *The Intentional Stance*. MIT Press.

de Soto, C. B., London, M., and Handel, S. 1965. Social reasoning and spatial paralogic. *Journal of Personality and Social Psychology* 2: 513–521.

de Waal, F. 1982. *Chimpanzee Politics: Power and Sex among Apes*. Harper and Row.

de Waal, F. 1986. Deception in the natural communication of chimpanzees. In *Deception*, ed. R. W. Mitchell and N. S. Thompson. SUNY Press.

Dickinson, A. 1980. *Contemporary Animal Learning Theory*. Cambridge University Press.

Dickinson, A. 1985. Actions and habits: The development of behavioral autonomy. *Philosophical Transactions of the Royal Society* B 308: 67–78.

Dickinson, A., and Dawson, G. R. 1988. Motivational control of instrumental performance: The role of prior experience of the reinforcer. *Quarterly Journal of Experimental Psychology* 40B: 113–134.

Dickinson, A., and Dawson, G. R. 1989. Incentive learning and the motivational control of instrumental performance. *Quarterly Journal of Experimental Psychology* 41B: 99–112.

Dietterich, T. G. 1986. Learning at the knowledge level. *Machine Learning* 1: 287–315.

Domjan, M., and Wilson, N. E. 1972. Contribution of ingestive behaviors to taste-aversion learning in the rat. *Journal of Comparative Physiology and Psychology* 80: 403–412.

Drent, R. H. 1970. Functional aspects of incubation in the herring gull. In *Title of Book*, ed. G. P. Baerends and R. H. Drent.

Edgeworth, F. Y. 1881. *Mathematical Psychics*. Kegan Paul.

Edwards, W. 1954. The theory of decision making. *Psychological Bulletin* 51, no. 4: 380–417.

Edwards, W. 1961. Behavioral decision theory, *Annual Review of Psychology* 12: 473–498.

Elio, R. 1986. The representation of similar well-learned cognitive procedures. *Cognitive Science* 10: 41–73.

Feynman, R. P., Leighton, R. B., and Sands, M. 1963. *The Feynman Lectures on Physics*. Addison-Wesley.

Fikes, R., and Nilsson, N. 1971. STRIPS: A new approach to the application of theorem proving to problem solving. *Artificial Intelligence* 2: 189–205.

Fitts, P. M. 1964. Perceptual-motor skill learning. In *Categories of Human Learning*, ed. A. Melton. Academic Press.

Foos, P. W. 1980. Constructing cognitive maps from sentences. *Journal of Experimental Psychology, Human Learning and Memory* 6: 25–38.

Freeman, S., and McFarland, D. 1982. The Darwinian objective function and adaptive behavior. In *Functional Ontogeny*, ed. D. McFarland. Pitman.

Fu, K. S., Gonzalez, R. C., and Lee, C. S. G. 1987. *Robotics*. McGraw-Hill.

Gallistel, C. R. 1990. *The Organization of Learning*. MIT Press.

Gladwin, T. 1970. *East Is a Bird: Navigation and Logic on Pulawa Atoll*. Harvard University Press.

Goldman, A. 1970. *A Theory of Human Action*. Prentice-Hall.

Goldman, A. 1976. The volitional theory revisited. In *Action Theory*, ed. M. Brand and W. Watson. Reidel.

Gould, J. L. 1980. The case for magnetic-field sensitivity in birds and bees (such as it is). *American Scientist* 68: 256–267.

Gould, J. L. 1981. Language. In *The Oxford Companion to Animal Behavior*, ed. D. J. McFarland. Oxford University Press.

Griffin, D. R. 1976, 1981. *The Question of Animal Awareness.* Rockefeller University Press.

Griffin, D. R. 1984. *Animal Thinking.* Harvard University Press.

Hacker, W. 1982. Objective and subjective organization of work activities. In *The Analysis of Action*, ed. M. von Cranach and R. Harre. Cambridge University Press.

Hall, E. L., and Hall, B. C. 1985. *Robotics.* Holt-Saunders.

Halliday, T. R., and Slater, P. J. B., eds. 1983. *Animal Behavior. 1. Causes and Effects.* Blackwell.

Halperin, J. R. P. 1991. Machine motivation. In *From Animals to Animats*, ed. J. Meyer and S. Wilson. MIT Press.

Hebb, D. O. 1949. *The Organization of Behavior.* Wiley.

Heckhausen, H., and Kuhl, J. 1985. From wishes to action: The dead ends and short cuts on the long way to action. In *Goal Directed Behavior*, ed. M. Frese and J. Sabini. Erlbaum.

Heiligenberg, W. 1976. The interaction of stimulus patterns controlling aggressiveness in the cichlid fish *Haplochromis burtoni. Animal Behavior* 24: 452–458.

Heiligenberg, W., Kramer, U., and Schulz, V. 1972. The angular orientation of the black eye-bar in *Haplochromis burtoni* (Cichlidae: Pisces) and its relevance to aggressivity. *Z. vergl. Physiol.* 76: 168–176.

Heim, A. W. 1987. Intelligence: Its assessment. In *The Oxford Companion to the Mind*, ed. R. Gregory. Oxford University Press.

Heiserman, D. 1981. *How to Design and Build Your Own Custom Robot.* Tab Books.

Heller, R., and Milinski, M. 1979. Optimal foraging of sticklebacks on swarming prey. *Animal Behavior* 27: 1127–1141.

Herrnstein, R. J., Loveland, D. H., and Cable, C. 1976. Natural concepts in pigeons. *Journal of Experimental Psychology*, and *Animal Behavior* and *Processes* 2: 285–302.

Heyes, C., and Dickinson, A. 1990. The intentionality of animal action. *Mind and Language* 5: 87–104.

Hicks, J. R., and Allen, R. G. D. 1934. A re-consideration of the theory of value. *Econometrica* 14: 52–76, 196–219.

Hinde, R. A., and Stevenson-Hinde, J., eds. 1973. *Constraints on Learning.* Academic Press.

Hinton, G. E., Sejnowski, T. J., and Ackley, D. H. 1984. A learning Boltzman machine. *Cognitive Science* 9: 147–169.

Hodos, W. 1982. Some perspectives on the evolution of intelligence and the brain. In *Animal Mind—Human Mind*, ed. D. R. Griffin. Springer-Verlag.

Hollard, V. D., and Delius, J. D. 1983. Rotational invariance in visual pattern recognition by pigeons and humans. *Science* 218: 804–806.

Hopfield, J. 1982. Neural networks and physical systems with emergent collective computational properties. *Proc. Nat. Acad. Sci.* 79: 2554–2558.

Hopfield, J., and Tank, D. W. 1986. Computing with neural circuits: A model. *Science* 233: 625–632.

Houston, A., Kacelnik, A., and McNamara, J. 1982. Some learning rules for acquiring information. In *Functional Ontogeny*, ed. D. McFarland. Pitman.

Houston, A., and McFarland, D. 1976. On the measurement of motivational variables. *Animal Behavior* 24: 459–475.

Houston, A., and McFarland, D. 1980. Behavioural resilience and its relation to demand functions. In *Limits to Action: The Allocation of Individual Behavior*, ed. J. E. R. Staddon. Academic Press.

Houston, A., and McNamara, J. M. 1988. A framework for the functional analysis of behavior. *Behavioral and Brain Sciences* 11: 117–154.

Howard, I. P. 1982. *Human Visual Orientation.* Wiley.

Howard, I. P., and Templeton, W. B. 1966. *Human Spatial Orientation.* Wiley.

Hull, C. L. 1931. Goal attraction and directing ideas conceived as habit phenomena. *Psychol. Rev.* 38: 487–506.

Huntingford, F. 1984. *The Study of Animal Behavior.* Chapman & Hall.

Huttenlocher, J. 1968. Constructing spatial images: A strategy in reasoning. *Psychol. Rev.* 75: 550–560.

Inhelder, B., and Piaget, J. 1964. The early growth of logic in the child. Routledge & Kegan Paul.

Irwin, C. 1985. Inuit navigation, empirical reasoning and survival. *Journal of Navigation* 38: 178–190.

Janlert, L. 1987. Modeling change—The frame problem. In *The Robot's Dilemma*, ed. Z. W. Pylyshyn. Ablex.

Jerison, H. J. 1973. *Evolution of the Brain and Intelligence.* Academic Press.

Johnson, W. E. 1913. The pure theory of utility curves. *Econ. J.* 23: 483–513.

Kaebling, L. P. 1987. An architecture for intelligent reactive systems. In *Reasoning about Actions and Plans*, ed. M. P. Georgeff and A. L. Lansky. Morgan Kaufmann.

Kalman, R. E. 1963. Mathematical description of linear dynamical systems. *J.S.I.A.M. Control.* series A, 1: 152–192.

Kalman, R. E., Falb, P. L., and Arbib, M. A. 1969. *Topics in Mathematical System Theory.* McGraw-Hill.

Kamin, L. J. 1969. Predictability, surprise, attention and conditioning. In *Punishment and Aversive Behavior*, ed, B. A. Campbell and R. M. Church. Appleton-Century-Crofts.

Klopf, A. H. 1982. *The Hedonistic Neuron: A Theory of Memory, Learning, and Intelligence.* Hemisphere.

Klopf, A. H. 1989. Classical conditioning phenomena predicted by a drive-reinforcement model of neuronal function. In *Neural Models of Plasticity*, ed. J. H. Byrne and W. O. Berry. Academic Press.

Kosslyn, S. M. 1981. The medium and the message in mental imagery: A theory. *Psychol. Rev.* 88: 46–66.

Koza, J. R. 1991. Evolution and co-evolution of computer programs to control independently acting agents. In *From Animals to Animats*, ed. J. Meyer and S. Wilson. MIT Press.

Krechevsky, I. 1932. Hypotheses in rats. *Psychological Review* 39: 516–532.

Krose, B. J. A., and Dondorp, E. 1989. A sensor simulation system for mobile robots. In *Intelligent Autonomous Systems 2*, ed. T. Kanade et al. Elsevier.

Kummer, H., Dasser, V., and Hoyningen-Huene, P. 1990. Exploring primate social cognition: Some critical remarks. *Behavior* 112: 84–98.

Kupfermann, I., and Weiss, K. R. 1978. The command neuron concept. *Behavioral and Brain Sciences* 1: 3–39.

Laird, J., Rosenbloom, P., and Newell, A. 1986. *Universal Subgoaling and Chunking.* Kluwer.

Laird, J. E., Newell, A., and Rosenbloom, P. S. 1987. Soar: An architecture for general intelligence. *Artificial Intelligence* 33: 1–64.

Larkin, S. 1981. Time and Energy in Decision-Making. D. Phil. thesis, University of Oxford.

Larkin, S., and McFarland, D. 1978. The cost of changing from one activity to another. *Animal Behavior* 26: 1237–1246.

Lea, S. E. G. 1978. The psychology and economics of demand. *Psychol. Bull.* 85: 441–466.

Lendrem, D. 1986. *Modelling in Behavioural Ecology.* Croom Helm.

Leong, C. Y. 1969. The quantitiative effect of releasers on the attack readiness of the fish *Haplochromis burtoni* (Cichlidae: Pisces). *Z. vergl. Physiol.* 65: 29–50.

Lewin, K. 1935. *A Dynamic Theory of Personality.* McGraw-Hill.

Lewis, D. 1972. *We the Navigators: The Ancient Art of Landfinding in the Pacific.* National University Press, Canberra.

Liapunov, A. M. 1907. Probleme general de la stabilite du movement. *Ann. Fac. Sci. Toulouse* 9: 203–474.

Lima, S. L., Valone, T. J., and Caraco, T. 1985. Foraging efficiency-predation risk trade-off in the grey squirrel. *Animal Behavior* 33: 155–165.

Lorenz, K., and Tinbergen, N. 1938. Taxis und Instinkthandlung in der Eirollbewegung der Graugans. *Z. Tierpsychol.* 2: 1–29.

Louw, G. N., and Holm, E. 1972. Physiological, morphological and behavioral adaptations of the ultrapsammophilous Namid Desert lizard *Aporosaura anchietae* (Bocage). *Madogua* 1: 67–85.

Mackay, D. M. 1972. Formal analysis of communicative processes. In *Non-Verbal Communication*, ed. R. A. Hinde. Cambridge University Press.

Mackintosh, N. J. 1974. *The Psychology of Animal Learning*. Academic Press.

Mackintosh, N. J. 1976. Overshadowing and stimulus intensity. *Animal Learning and Behavior* 4: 186–192.

Mackintosh, N. J. 1983. *Conditioning and Associative Learning*. Clarendon.

Macphail, E. M. 1982. *Brain and Intelligence in Vertebrates*. Clarendon.

Macphail, E. M. 1985. The null hypothesis. In *Animal Intelligence*, ed. L. Weiskrantz. Clarendon.

Maes, P. 1991. A bottom-up mechanism for behavior selection in an artificial creature. In *From Animals to* Animats, ed. J. Meyer and S. Wilson. MIT Press.

Mansfield, E. 1979. *Microeconomics: Theory and Applications*. Norton.

Marshall, A. 1890. *Principles of Economics* (eighth edition, 1948). Macmillan.

Mataric, M. J. 1990. A Distributed Model for Mobile Robot Environment-Learning and Navigation. Technical Report 1228, AI Lab, Massachusett, Institute of Technology.

May, K. O. 1954. Transitivity, utility, and aggregation in preference patterns. *Econometrica* 22: 1–13.

Maynard Smith, J. 1978. Optimisation theory in evolution. *Annual Review of Ecological Systems* 9: 31–56.

McCleery, R. 1977. On satiation curves. *Animal Behavior* 25: 1005–1015.

McCorduck. 1979. *Machines Who Think*. Freeman.

McCulloch, W., and Pitts, W. 1943. A logical calculus of the ideas immanent in nervous activity. *Bull. Math. Biophys.* 5: 115–133.

McFarland, D. 1971. *Feedback Mechanisms in Animal Behavior*. Academic Press.

McFarland, D. 1977. Decision-making in animals. *Nature* 269: 15–21.

McFarland, D. 1978. Optimality considerations in animal behaviour. In *Human Behavior and Adaptation*, ed. V. Reynolds and N. Blurton-Jones. Taylor and Francs.

McFarland, D. 1982. Introduction to functional analysis of behavior. In *Functional Ontogeny*, ed. D. McFarland. Pitman.

McFarland, D. 1983a. Functional analysis of competing homeostatic systems. In *Thermal Physiology*, ed. J. R. S. Hales. Raven.

McFarland, D. 1983b. Behavioral transitions: A reply to Roper and Crossland (1982); Time-sharing: a reply to Houston (1982). *Animal Behavior* 31: 305–308.

McFarland, D. 1985. *Animal Behavior*. Longman Scientific.

McFarland, D. 1989a. The teleological imperative. In *Goals, No Goals, and Own Goals*, ed. A. Montefiore and D. Noble. Unwin-Hyman.

McFarland, D. 1989b. *Problems of Animal Behavior*. Longmans.

McFarland, D. 1991a. What it means for robot behavior to be adaptive. In *From Animals to Animats*, ed. J. Meyer and S. Wilson. MIT Press.

McFarland, D. 1991b. Defining motivation and cognition in animals. *International Studies in the Philosophy of Science* 5: 153–170.

McFarland, D. 1992. Animals as cost-based robots. *International Studies in the Philosophy of Science* 6: 133–153.

McFarland, D. 1993. Rational behaviour of animals and machines. In press.

McFarland, D., and Houston, A. 1981. *Quantitative Ethology: The State-Space Approach*. Pitman.

McFarland, D., and Sibly, R. 1972. "Unitary drives" revisited. *Animal Behavior* 20: 548–563.

McFarland, D., and Sibly, R. 1975. The behavioral final common path. *Phil. Trans. R. Soc.* B 270: 265–293.

McFarland, D., and Wright, P. 1969. Water conservation by inhibition of food intake. *Physiology and Behavior* 4: 95–99.

McGonigle, B., and Chalmers, M. 1980. On the genesis of relational terms: A comparative study of monkeys and human children. *Antropologia Contemporanea* 3: 236.

McGonigle, B., and Chalmers, M. 1984. The selective impact of question form and input mode on the symbolic distance effect in children. *Journal of Experimental Child Psychology* 37: 525–554.

McGonigle, B., and Chalmers, M. 1986. Representations and strategies during inference. In *Reasoning and Discourse Processes*, ed. T. Myers et al. Academic Press.

McNamara, J. M., and Houston, A. I. 1986. The common currency of behavioral decisions. *American Naturalist* 127: 385–378.

Menzel, E. W., and Wyers, E. J. 1981. Cognitive aspects of foraging behavior. In *Foraging Behavior—Ecological, Ethological, and Psychological Approaches*, ed. A. C. Kamil and T. D. Sargent. Garland STMP Press.

Metz, J. A. J. 1977. State space models for animal behavior. *Annals of Systems Research* 6: 65–109.

Metz, H. 1981. *Mathematical Representations of the Dynamics of Animal Behavior.* Mathematisch Centrum, Amsterdam.

Milinski, M., and Heller, R. 1978. Influence of a predator on the optimal foraging behavior of sticklebacks (*Gasterosteus aculeatus* L.). *Nature* (Lond). 275: 642–644.

Miller, G. A., Galanter, E., and Pribram, K. H. 1960. *Plans and the Structure of Behavior.* Holt.

Milsum, J. H. 1966. *Biological Control Systems Analysis.* McGraw-Hill.

Milsum, J. H., and Roberge, F. A. 1973. Physiological regulation and control. In *Foundations of Mathematical Biology*, volume 3, ed. R. Rosen. Academic Press.

Minsky, M. L. 1975. A framework for representing knowledge. In *The Psychology of Computer Vision*, ed. P. H. Winston. McGraw-Hill.

Minsky, M. L., and Papert, S. 1969. *Perceptrons: An Introduction to computational Geometry.* MIT Press.

Mittelstaedt, M. 1964. Basic control patterns of orientational homeostasis. *Symp. Soc. Exp. Biol.* 18: 365–385.

Mitchel, R. W., and Thompson, N. S. 1986. *Deception.* SUNY Press.

Mogenson, G. J., and Calaresu, F. R. 1978. Food intake considered from the viewpoint of systems analysis. In *Hunger Models*, ed. D. A. Booth. Academic Press.

Montefiore, A., and Noble, D., eds. 1989. *Goals, No Goals, and Own Goals.* Unwin-Hyman.

Moore, E. F. 1956. Gedanken-experiments on sequential machines. In *Automata Studies*, ed. C. E. Shannon and J. McCarthy. Princeton University Press.

Morgan, C. L. 1894. *An Introduction to Comparative Psychology.* Scott.

Morris, R. L. 1987. PSI and human factors: The role of PSI in human-equipment interactions. *Current Trends in PSI Research* 1–27.

Moyer, R. S. 1973. Comparing objects in memory: Evidence suggesting an internal psychophysics. *Perception and Psychophysics* 13: 180–184.

Murray, C. D. 1926. The physiological principle of minimum work II. *Proc. Nat. Acad. Sci.* 12: 299–304.

Nagel, T. 1974. What is it like to be a bat? *Philosophical Reviews* 83: 435–450.

Neisser, U. 1976. *Cognition and Reality.* Freeman.

Neisser, U. 1979. The concept of intelligence. In *Human Intelligence: Perspectives on its theory and measurement*, ed. R. J. Sternberg and D. K. Detterman. Ablex.

Nelson, K. 1965. The temporal patterning of courtship behavior in the glandulocaudine fishes (Ostariophysi, Characidae). *Behavior* 24: 90–146.

Nerode, A. 1958. Linear automaton transformations. *Proc. Amer. Math. Soc.* 9: 541–544.

Newell, A. 1981. Reasoning, problem-solving, and decision processes: The problem-space as a fundamental category.

Newell, A., and Simon, H. 1963. GPS, a program that simulates human thought. In *Computers and Thought*, ed. E. A. Feigenbaum and J. Feldman. McGraw-Hill.

Newell, A., and Simon, H. 1972. *Human Problem Solving.* Prentice-Hall.

Nilsson, N. 1973. A hierarchical robot planning and execution system. In Technical Note 76, Artificial Intelligence Center, Stanford Research Institute, Menlo Park, California.

Noble, D. 1989. What do intentions do? In *Goals, No Goals, and Own Goals*, ed. A. Montefiore and D. Noble. Unwin-Hyman.

Northcutt, R. G. 1981. Evolution of the telencephalon in nonmammals. *Ann. Rev. Neurosci* 4: 301–350.

Pagel, M. D., and Harvey, P. H. 1988. The comparative method. *Q. Rev. Biol.*

Paivio, A. 1975. Perceptual comparisons through the mind's eye. *Memory and Cognition* 3: 635–647.

Papandreou, A. G. 1957. A test of a stochastic theory of choice. *University of California Publications in Economics* 16: 1–18.

Pareto, V. 1906. *Manuale di economica politica, con una introduzione ulla scienza sociale*. Societa Editrice Libraria, Milan.

Pavlov, I. P. 1927. *Conditioned Reflexes* Oxford University Press.

Peirce, C. S. 1931–35. Collected papers of Charles Peirce (six volumes), ed. Hartshorne and P. Weiss. Harvard University Press.

Petrusic, W. A., Varro, L., and Jamieson, D. G. 1978. Mental rotation validation of two spatial ability tests. *Psychol. Res.* 40: 139–148.

Pew, R. W. 1974. Human perceptual-motor performance. In *Human Information Processing: Tutorials in Performance and Cognition*, ed. B. H. Kantowitz. Erlbaum.

Posner, M. I. 1978. *Chronometric Explorations of Mind*. Erlbaum.

Potts, G. R., and Scholz, K. W. 1975. The internal representation of a three-term series problem. *Journal of Verbal Learning and Verbal Behavior* 14: 439–452.

Pylyshin, Z. W., ed. 1987. *The Robot's Dilemma: The Frame Problem in Artificial Intelligence*. Ablex.

Rachlin, H. 1989. *Economics and Behavioral Psychology*. In *Limits to Action*, ed. J. E. R. Staddon. Academic Press.

Rachlin, H. 1989. *Judgment, Decision, and Choice*. Freeman.

Rescorla, R. A., and Cunningham, C. L. 1979. Spatial contiguity facilitates Pavlovian second-order conditioning. *Journal of Experimental Psychology: Animal Behavior Processes* 5: 152–161.

Rescorla, R. A., and Furrow, D. R. 1977. Stimulus similarity as a determinant of Pavlovian conditioning. *Journal of Experimental Psychology: Animal Behavior Processes* 3: 203–215.

Riggs, D. S. 1970. *Control Theory and Physiological Feedback Mechanisms*. Williams & Wilkins.

Roeder, K. D. 1963. *Nerve Cells and Insect Behavior*. Harvard University Press.

Roeder, K. D. 1970. Episodes in insect brains. *American Scientist* 58: 378–389.

Rohwer, S., and Rohwer, F. C. 1978. Status signaling in Harris sparrows: Experimental deceptions achieved. *Animal Behavior* 26: 1012–1022.

Romanes, G. J. 1882. *Animal Intelligence*. Kegan Paul.

Rosen, R. 1967. *Optimality Principles in Biology*. Butterworths.

Rosen, R. 1970. *Dynamical System Theory in Biology*. Wiley.

Rosenblatt, F. 1962. *Principles of Neurodynamics*. Spartan.

Rosenbloom, P. S., Laird, J. E., and Newell, A. 1988. The chunking of skill and knowledge. In *Working Models of Human Perception*, ed. B. Elsendoorn and H. Bouma. Academic Press.

Rosenblueth, A., Wiener, W., and Bigelow, J. 1943. Behavior, purpose and teleology. *Philosophy of Science* 10: 18–24.

Rouche, N., Habets, P., and Laloy, M. 1977. *Stability Theory by Liapunov's Direct Method*. Springer-Verlag.

Rozin, P. 1976. The evolution of intelligence and access to the cognitive unconscious. *Progress in Psychobiology and Physiological Psychology* 6: 245–280.

Russel, B. 1921. *The analysis of Mind*. Macmillan.

Ryle, G. 1949. *The Concept of Mind*. Hutchinson.

Sacerdoti, E. 1977. *A Structure for Plans and Behavior*. Elsevier.

Samuelson, P. A. 1938. A note on the pure theory of consumer's behavior. *Econometrica* 5: 61–71, 353–354.

Samuelson, P. A. 1948. Consumption theory in terms of revealed preference. *Econometrica* 15: 243–253.

Savage, L. J. 1954. *The Foundations of Statistics*. Wiley.

Schank, R., and Abelson, R. 1977. *Scripts, Plans, Goals and Understanding*. Erlbaum.

Schmidt, R. A. 1975. A schema theory of discrete motor skill learning. *Psychological Review* 82: 225–260.

Searle, J. 1979. The intentionality of intention and action. *Inquiry* 22: 253–280.

Searle, J. 1981. Intentionality and method. *Journal of Philosophy* 78: 720–733.

Seitz, A. 1940. Die Paarbildung bei einigen Cichliden I. *Z. Tierpsychol.* 4: 40–84.

Sejnowski, T. J., and Tesauro, G. 1989. The Hebb rule for synaptic plasticity: Algorithms and implementations. In *Neural Models of Plasticity*, ed. J. H. Byrne and W. O. Berry. Academic Press.

Sellars, W. 1973. Action and events. *Nous* 7: 179–202.

Shepard, R. N., and Metzler, J. 1971. Mental rotation of three-dimensional objects. *Science* 171: 701–703.

Sibly, R. M. 1975. How incentive and deficit determine feeding tendency. *Animal Behavior* 23: 437–446.

Sibly, R. M. 1989. What evolution maximizes. *Functional Ecology* 3: 129–135.

Sibly, R. M., and Calow, P. 1986. *Physiological Ecology of Animals*. Blackwell.

Sibly, R. M., and McCleery, R. H. 1976. The dominance boundary method of determining motivational state. *Animal Behavior* 24: 108–124.

Sibly, R. M., and McCleery, R. H. 1985. Optimal decision rules for gulls. *Animal Behavior* 33: 449–465.

Sibly, R. M., and McFarland, D. J. 1974. A state-space approach to motivation. In *Motivational Control Systems Analysis*, ed. D. J. McFarland. Academic Press.

Sibly, R. M., and McFarland, D. J. 1976. On the fitness of behavior sequences. *American Naturalist* 110: 601–617.

Silver, M. 1985. "Purposive behavior" in psychology and philosophy: A history. In *Goal Directed Behavior*, ed. M. Frese and J. Sabini. Erlbanm.

Skutch, A. F. 1976. *Parent Birds and Their Young*. University of Texas Press.

Slutsky, E. E. 1915. Sulla teoria del bilancio del consumatore. *Giorale degli economisti* 51: 1–26.

Steels, L. 1991. Towards a theory of emergent functionality. In *From Animals to Animats*, ed. J. Meyer and S. Wilson. MIT Press.

Steier, D. M., Laird, J. E., Newell, A., Rosenbloom, P. S., Flynn, R., Golding, A., Polk, T. A., Shivers, O. G., Unruh, A., and Yost, G. R. 1987. Varieties of learning in Soar. In *Proceeding of the Fourth International Workshop on Machine Learning*, ed. P. Langley. Morgan Kaufman.

Stephens, D. W., and Krebs, J. R. 1986. *Foraging Theory*. Princeton University Press.

Suchman, L. 1987. *Plans and Situated Actions*. Cambridge University Press.

Sutton, R. S. 1991. Reinforcement learning architectures for animats. In *From Animals to Animats*, ed. J. Meyer and S. Wilson. MIT Press.

Sutton, R., and Barto, A. G. 1981. Toward a modern theory of adaptive networks: Expectation and prediction. *Psychol. Rev.* 88: 135–170.

Tansley, K. 1965. *Vision in Vertebrates*. Methuen.

Terrace, H. S. 1987. Chunking by a pigeon in a serial learning task. *Nature* 325: 149–151.

Tesauro, G. 1986. Simple neural models of classical conditioning. *Biological Cybernetics* 55: 187–200.

Testa, T. J. 1975. Effects of similarity of location and temporal intensity pattern of conditioned and unconditioned stimuli on acquisition of conditioned suppression in rats. *Journal of Experimental Psychology: Animal Behavior Processes* 1: 114–121.

Thomas, S. D. 1987. *The Last Navigator*. Holt.

Thorndike, E. L. 1898. Animal intelligence: An experimental study of the associative processes in animals. *Psychol. Rev. Monogr. Suppl.* 2, 8: 1, 16.

Thorndike, E. L. 1991. *Animal Intelligence*. Macmillan.

Thorndike, E. L. 1913. *The Psychology of Learning (Educational psychology II)*. Teachers College, New York.

Tiles, J. E., McKee, G. T., and Dean, G. C. 1990. *Evolving Knowledge in Natural Science and Artificial Intelligence*. Pitman.

Tinbergen, N. 1959. Comparative studies of the behavior of gulls (Laridae): A progress report. *Behavior* 15: 1–70.

Toates, F. M. 1986. *Motivational Systems*. Cambridge University Press.

Todd, P. M., and Miller, G. E. 1991. Exploring adaptive agency. II. Simulating the evolution of associative learning. In *From Animals to Animats*, ed. J. Meyer and S. Wilson. MIT Press.

Tolman, E. C. 1932. *Purposive Behavior in Animals and Men*. Appleton-Century-Crofts.

Tovish, A. 1982. Learning to improve the availability and accessibility of resources. In *Functional Ontogeny*, ed. D. McFarland. Pitman.

Trabasso, T., and Riley, C. A. 1975. On the construction and use of representations involving linear order. In *Information Processing and Cognition: The Loyola Symposium*, ed. R. L. Solso. Erlbaum.

Trivers, R. L. 1985. *Social Evoluton*. Benjamin/Cummings.

Tuddenham, R. D. 1963. The nature and measurement of intelligent. In *Psychology in the Making*, ed. L. Postman. Knopf.

Turing, A. M. 1936. On computable numbers with an application to the Entscheidungsproblem. *Proc. London Math. Soc.* 42: 230–265.

Turing, A. M. 1950. Computing machinery and intelligence. *Mind* 59: 433–460.

van Lawick-Goodall, J. 1970. Tool-using in primates and other vertebrates. In *Advances in the Study of Behavior*, ed. D. S. Lehrman et al. Academic Press.

Vershure, P. F. M. J., Krose, B. J. A., and Pfeifer, R. 1991. Distributed adaptive control: The self-organization of structured behavior. *Robotics and Autonomous Systems* 9: 181–196.

von Cranach, M. 1982. The psychological theory of goal-directed action: Basic issues. In *The Analysis of Action*, ed. M. von Cranach and R. Harre. Cambridge University Press.

von Cranach, M., and U. Kalbermatten. 1982. Ordinary interactive action: Theory, Methods, and Some Empirical Findings. In *The Analysis of Action*, ed. M. von Cranach and R. Harre. Cambridge University Press.

von Neumann, J., and Morgenstern, O. 1944. *Theory of Games and Economic Behavior*. Princeton University Press.

Walter, W. G. 1953. *The Living Brain*. Duckworth.

Warren, J. M. 1973. Learning in vertebrates. In *Comparative Psychology: A Modern Survey*, ed. D. A. Dewsbury and D. A. Rethlingshafer. McGraw-Hill.

Watkins, C. J. C. H. 1989. Learning with Delayed Rewards. Ph.D. dissertation. Cambridge University.

Watson, J. B. 1913. Psychology as the behaviorist views it. *Psychol. Rev.* 20: 158–177.

Weber, M. 1968. Basic sociological terms. In *Economy and Society*, ed. G. Roth and C. Wittich. Bedminster.

Weizenbaum, J. 1983. ELIZA: A computer program for the study of natural language communication between man and machine. *Communications of the ACM* 26?: 23–27. Reprinted from *Communications of the ACM* 29?: 36–45 (1966).

Whiten, A., and Byrne, R. W. 1987. Tactical deception in primates. *Behavioral and Brain Sciences* 11: 231–273.

Wiener, N. 1948. *Cybernetics*. Wiley.

Wiley, R. H. 1983. The evolution of communication: Information and manipulation. In *Animal Behaviour 2: Communication*, ed. T. R. Halliday and P. J. B. Slater. Blackwell.

Wilkes, K. 1991. *Of Mice and Men*.

Williams, R. J. 1986. Reinforcement Learning in Connectionist Networks: A Mathematical Analysis. Technical Report 8605, San Diego Institute for Cognitive Science.

Winograd, T., and Flores, F. 1986. Understanding computers and cognition.

Winterhalder, B. 1981. Foraging strategies in the boreal forest: An analysis of Cree hunting and gathering. In *Hunter-Gatherer Foraging Strategies*, ed. B. Winterhalder and E. Smith. University of Chicago Press.

Winterhalder, B. 1983. Opportunity-cost foraging models for stationary and mobile predators. *American Naturalist* 122: 73–84.

Wirtshaften, D., and Davis, J. D. 1977. Set points, settling points, and control of body weight. *Physiology and Behavior* 19: 75–78.

Wold, H. 1952. Ordinal preferences or cardinal utility? *Econometrica* 20: 661–665.

Woodfield, A. 1976. *Teleology*. Cambridge University Press.

Ydenberg, R. C., and Houston, A. I. 1986. Optimal trade-offs between competing behavioral demands in the great tit. *Animal Behavior* 34: 1041–1050.

Zach, R. 1979. Shell dropping: Decision making and optimal foraging in Northwestern crows. *Behavior* 68: 106–117.

# Index